THE PAGEANT

OF AMERICA

Independence Edition

VOLUME XIII

THE PAGEANT OF AMERICA

A PICTORIAL HISTORY OF THE UNITED STATES

RALPH HENRY GABRIEL
EDITOR

HENRY JONES FORD   HARRY MORGAN AYRES
ASSOCIATE EDITORS

OLIVER McKEE
ASSISTANT EDITOR

CHARLES M. ANDREWS	ALLEN JOHNSON
HERBERT E. BOLTON	WILLIAM BENNETT MUNRO
IRVING N. COUNTRYMAN	VICTOR H. PALTSITS
WILLIAM E. DODD	ARTHUR M. SCHLESINGER
DIXON RYAN FOX	NATHANIEL WRIGHT STEPHENSON

ADVISORY EDITORS

DAVID M. MATTESON
INDEXER

From a photograph in color

THE LINCOLN MEMORIAL, WASHINGTON, D. C.

THE PAGEANT OF AMERICA

THE
AMERICAN SPIRIT
IN ARCHITECTURE

BY

TALBOT FAULKNER HAMLIN

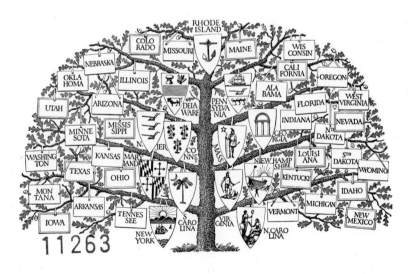

NEW HAVEN · YALE UNIVERSITY PRESS

TORONTO · GLASGOW, BROOK & CO.
LONDON HUMPHREY MILFORD
OXFORD UNIVERSITY PRESS

TABLE OF CONTENTS

TABLE OF CONTENTS

THE AMERICAN SPIRIT IN ARCHITECTURE

IT is difficult for twentieth-century Americans to realize how life was lived by the men and women who left Europe in the seventeenth century to dare the great adventure in the American wilderness. A few were of the gentry, many were the common folk of the commercial towns and many more came from the rural vills where their forefathers had been peasants for generations. All had seen the stone castles where lived lords and ladies in the splendor and luxury of the time. Some had dwelt in the town houses of wood or stone crowded close together inside protecting city walls. More were familiar with the rude habitations of the rural vills. There were the substantial dwellings of the yeomen with naked timbers showing through walls of brick or stucco, the whole surmounted by roofs of thatch or slate or even tile. Not far away were the cottages of the poorer folk, sometimes with wattle sides two or three feet high and thatched roofs sloping steeply from short ridgepoles. Here poultry and farm animals often shared the shelter with the family. Occasionally in the forests were rough, conical huts of boughs or thatch. The men and women who faced life in wild, seventeenth-century America brought memories of the old homes they had known in the communities they had left behind.

Inevitably the first white habitations in America were crude. Captain John Smith, whose strong hand guided the Virginia colony through some of its most trying days, wrote a description of the squalid beginnings of Jamestown: "In foule weather we shifted into an old rotten tent; for we had few better. . . . This was our Church, till we built a homely thing, like a barne, set upon Cratchets, covered with rafts, sedge, and earth, so was also the walls: the best part of our houses [were] of the like curiosity; but for the most part farre much worse workmanship, that could neither well defend wind nor raine." Such habitations were but little better than the bark dwellings of Powhatan and his people farther in the interior. In New England the Puritans of Massachusetts Bay Colony first sheltered themselves in dugouts or rough shelters, some of which were reported, in the year 1631, to have caught fire "in the roofs covered with thatch or boughs . . . in these poor Wigwames (they sing Psalms, pray, and praise their God) till they can provide them houses." Such habitations show how closely Englishmen approximated the culture of the Indians in starting their settlements on this distant American frontier. Yet the "Wigwames," like the houses that followed, embodied English rather than Indian ideas. Soon the early huts gave way to habitations with wooden walls of hewn timber. But the timbers seem to have been placed on end side by side, in vertical positions. About the village was the palisade, which, perhaps, had been borrowed from the Indian towns. On many of the dwellings were the thatched roofs so familiar in the English vills. Like their inherited system of husbandry, the English peasants brought to America the type of house which they had known at home. And for the gentry they began to build the more pretentious frame house that, in English counties, stood apart from the cottages of the village.

The early, trying years of settlement past, American communities along the Atlantic seaboard took on a more settled and comfortable aspect. The climate was good and the soil fertile. On the whole the families who came to New England and Pennsylvania, to

Virginia and the Carolinas, prospered. In seventeenth-century New England appeared the village of feudal England but without the feudal lord. The villagers were partners in an economic and a religious enterprise. They acquired an area of land in common and divided it into home lots and outlying fields. The village lots were large enough to give room for fruit trees and a garden near the dwelling. Such towns, though seeming to straggle along a single street, were laid out with care and forethought to meet the needs of the community. Near the center, as in England, was the church, and hard by, the parsonage, which sometimes also served as schoolhouse. Lanes were laid out leading to the distant fields to which in season the villagers daily went to work, as their English peasant forefathers had trudged from the vills to the arable fields. When the village had fully occupied its desirable adjoining land, it threw out offshoots, and in desirable bottoms a few miles farther in the interior, new church spires and clustering towns would rise. As the seventeenth century passed into the eighteenth, the village houses added lean-tos, measuring the increase in the prosperity of the householder and in the size of his family. The old common pasture in the midst became the "green," where sometimes stood the church and the low brown and gray stones of the churchyard. The turbulence of the frontier period was forgotten, and the repose of the ancient vills of England reappeared in the country towns of Massachusetts and Connecticut.

But the village of the independent husbandman was not limited to New England. Dutch towns under the influence of the Low Countries grew up in the Hudson valley. In Pennsylvania, Quaker towns, often with stone houses, dotted the rich flood plains of the Delaware River. After the opening of the eighteenth century, German villages appeared farther inland, bringing to the New World some flavor of the Fatherland. Some of them were groups of communal houses, built to conform to the practices of a religious sect. The Germans spread into the back-country as far south as the Carolinas.

With them went other newcomers, Scotch-Irish Presbyterians. The life of these folk, as far from the coast settlements as the frontier had then marched, still showed the roughness and crudeness that had marked the Virginia and New England settlements a hundred years before. Yet the dwelling on the Yadkin in western North Carolina to which Daniel Boone brought his bride did not resemble the earliest habitations of Jamestown or Plymouth. It was the log cabin that was to become the traditional habitation of every frontier until the treeless prairies were reached. Perhaps the cabin whose sides were built of logs laid horizontally was brought to America by the Swedes, who, in 1638, established New Sweden on the Delaware River. Such houses were the customary form of dwelling in their forested country. Perhaps it was the independent invention of American frontiersmen, an adjustment to the conditions of American forest and climate. Whatever its origin, the one-room structures with, perhaps, a rude loft overhead, made appropriate homes for the race who had sturdily set their hands to the task of clearing the forest.

About the cabin village of the frontier was the palisade, and at the corner of this a blockhouse, a square log structure, built after the manner of the cabin, but with a second story projecting on every side beyond the first. This projection was no English overhang, but a defence against the Indian, who, with increasing bitterness, watched the whites advancing into his country. Even if the log cabin is not, the blockhouse seems to be, the creation of the American frontier. From such forts where, perhaps, he had stored his pelts, a fur trader upon occasion made his way on a matter of business to the growing cities of the coast.

In the coast cities of eighteenth-century America he found quite a different atmosphere from that of either the small rural village or the wild frontier. Before the end of the seventeenth century the sea trade had sprung up and, in the eighteenth, had grown vastly in importance. It brought wealth and ready money to urban America. It created the merchant who hazarded his capital on distant ventures. In New England, New York and Pennsylvania, the wealthy merchant took his place as part of an emerging aristocracy. His enlarged outlook and increased fortune demanded expression in more sumptuous dwellings, while his aristocratic tendencies made him desire a more formal dignity than was to be found in the naked timbers and the unpretending lean-to of the house of the century before.

But eighteenth-century America produced a more striking aristocracy than that of the commercial coast city. From Maryland south to Georgia the planter appeared. His northern counterpart was the landlord of the great estate in the Hudson valley. In the latter half of the eighteenth century, this landed aristocracy reached its full development and gave to America a disproportionate number of the leaders of the Revolution and of the founders of the new nation. It was a provincial gentry, to be sure, held in no very high esteem by their English cousins. Yet there was culture and urbanity among them, and a vitality and strength which contrasted sharply with that of the somewhat similar Spanish landed aristocracy in Mexico.

It chanced that both these aristocracies flourished at a time when in England the architectural ideas that grew out of the Renaissance were reaching full fruition. In the seventeenth century two great masters, Inigo Jones and Sir Christopher Wren, brought the spirit of the Renaissance architecture to England. In the eighteenth century the group was larger, if less distinguished. The Renaissance was, in part, a return to the ideals and ideas of Greece and Rome. In England, the classic forms of Rome, when that city was the capital of the world, were used to express the artistic feeling of the time of Queen Anne and the first three Georges. Roman forms, modified by Italian and English influence, became the mode of the times, decorating the churches, the public buildings, and the homes of the gentry with porticos, columns and pilasters. The artists departed freely from the classical originals and adapted ancient forms to the needs of a different age and civilization. The resulting style, for want of a better name, has been called Georgian.

The dignity of the Georgian forms fitted well with the mood of the vigorous upper classes of English colonial America. Monumental mansions with porticos and columns arose along the Cooper, the Potomac and the Hudson Rivers, and in the commercial cities from Boston to Charleston. Churches and public buildings were erected under the influence of the classical forms which the Renaissance had brought to England. The leaders of America were reaping large returns from the exploitation of virgin soil or the prosecution of an ever expanding sea trade. Their position in society seemed secure and the future was bright. They had money to build good buildings, and their communities contained artisans whose skill approached that of the workers of the Old World. So was established in America the developed colonial style.

But, if the aristocrats of the English colonies built buildings of dignity and beauty, they never achieved the splendor of the work of their Spanish contemporaries in Mexico. Spanish America was dotted with public buildings, churches, monasteries, missions and stately mansions. In 1573, before Raleigh had undertaken his ill-fated Roanoke venture, the Spaniard cleared the site of the chief temple of the Aztecs and laid down the foundations of the cathedral of Mexico City. For two hundred and forty years the building progressed, while architects of many schools worked on it through the shifting styles of the passing centuries. But the final structure closely approximated the original concept. Thousands of Indian artisans and workmen found in this cathedral an opportunity to express the marked artistic instincts of their race. It remains the greatest of the material monuments left by the Spanish régime in North America. In estimating the architectural work of the English colonists it is well to bear in mind that of their Spanish contemporaries south of the border. If Georgian architecture is still a living force in the United States, so also are the forms used by the early Spaniards. But there have been moments in the history of both Mexico and the United States when it has seemed that the influence of the old masters had vanished.

In the northern nation the Revolution marked an architectural turning point of importance, not because the war brought a decline or change of taste but because the creation of a new nation presented Americans with a whole new set of intellectual problems. Obviously, the most important of these was the organization of an effective government, a task which was accomplished in the Constitution of 1787 and the administrations of President Washington. The appropriate housing of this government became at once a problem. The final solution was in harmony with a state of mind much in evidence after the War of Independence. Americans who had successfully defied the most powerful empire in the world, while they themselves were weakened by dangerous dissension at home, felt, with some justification, that their accomplishment was one of the greatest of history. When, eight years after the surrender of Cornwallis, they saw their late allies, the people of France, rise to overthrow the Bourbon monarchy, many Americans believed that the French Revolution was inspired by their own. It was easy to picture the United States as the torch bearer leading the oppressed peoples of the world towards liberty. America had thrown off the yoke of a king and established a republic. In days when the study of the classics was the core of education, men's minds inevitably ran back to that earlier republic which had produced Gracchus and Cicero. The heroes of the Revolution were compared to those of republican Rome; the disbanded officers of the army became the Order of the Cincinnati: the upper house of the national congress was called the Senate. Thoughtful leaders of the young nation turned naturally to Rome for the inspiration of the buildings that were to house the republican government which they had created. At the forefront of the movement was the gifted and versatile Thomas Jefferson.

During the first few decades of its national history the young republic, of so little consequence in the society of nations, dreamed, a little *naïvely*, of its Roman greatness, and deliberated its local problems in Roman halls. The aristocracy which had developed in the eighteenth century had not been unseated by the Revolution. But, although gentlemen naturally assumed the direction of the new government, their political power was becoming more and more unstable. In the North, as the nineteenth century progressed, the ideal of aristocracy steadily gave way before the insistent demands of a frontier-born democracy. In 1818 the people of Connecticut overthrew the power of the clergy and of the established Congregational Church. Two years later New York state, against the advice of some of its wisest sons, adopted full manhood suffrage. After another eight years, in 1828, Andrew Jackson, man of the people, was elevated to the high office of President in the first national triumph of the most important democratic movement up to that time. But, if the ideal of aristocracy was fading in the North, its influence grew even stronger with the passing decades in the South. To the final day of the Cotton Kingdom the planter maintained the aristocratic tradition. To the last he loved the quiet, stately house, set far from the highway at the end of a vista of noble trees. The South and the North went different ways, developing different civilizations, that of the planter clinging to the ideals of seventeenth- and eighteenth-century England, that of the North more in harmony with the England of John Stuart Mill and the abolition of political injustice. Such was the background for one of America's most striking architectural developments.

Latrobe had used Greek forms in America as early as the end of the eighteenth century. They dominated the structure built to house the second Bank of the United States, which Jackson later so fiercely attacked. In 1820, at the very time when the democratic tide in America was rising to full flood, Greece was seeking to throw off the yoke of the Turk. Rarely has any struggle for liberty so profoundly stirred the sympathy of Americans. The attention of the western world was turned to the people who lived in the midst of the ruins of the greatest of ancient civilizations. The more cultured leaders of the rising democracy of the New World, still under the influence of an education that was largely classical, looked past the nineteenth-century Greeks to their ancient forebears. If Rome had been a republic, Greece, in the heyday of her greatness, had been a democracy. If the architecture of republican Rome expressed the ideals of the aristocracy that shaped the early destinies of the American republic, the Greek temple symbolized the aspiration of thoughtful American democrats who dreamed of lifting their country to something of the glory that was Greece. So in the old America east of the Appalachians and in the new America of the Mississippi valley, in cities and in rambling country villages, the Greek temple became a courthouse, a church, and even a dwelling. The traveler along country roads passed many an isolated square white farmhouse, with huge pillars reaching up two stories. Perhaps the husbandman, who knew neither Greek nor Latin, felt vaguely that this austere house expressed his dignity as a citizen participating in the government of a great people.

But the middle two-thirds of the nineteenth century in America were not favorable for genuine architectural development. Except, perhaps, for political institutions, American culture was yet in its imitative stage. A series of "revivals" influenced the building of the country. The Greek Revival was the most popular, and after it came a Gothic and even an attempt at an Egyptian revival. To make up for a paucity of inspiration at home the building forms of other times and other civilizations were called upon. Great architecture is the work of a people whose life rests on a stable economic foundation, whose traditions run far into the past, and who have become conscious of the peculiarities of their culture. Nineteenth-century America was full of disruptive forces. The old slow-going culture of eighteenth-century America lingered only in the South. More than a century had passed while the frontier worked its way from Jamestown to the Appalachian Mountains, and from Manhattan Island to the upper waters of the Susquehanna. But, in the nineteenth century, the frontier swept with incredible swiftness across the continent. All America seemed on the move. Virginia and the Carolinas felt the change as their old plantations declined in productivity, their ancient mansions fell into disrepair, and the sons and daughters of the old families moved to the fresh cotton lands of Mississippi and Alabama. New Englanders, wearying of their struggle with a stony soil, left for the new country of Pennsylvania, Western New York, Ohio and beyond. Later the men of Tennessee, Alabama, and Mississippi went on to Texas and those of Ohio and Indiana, to Wisconsin, Iowa, Oregon and California. To increase the confusion, industrialism appeared in New England just prior to the War of 1812 and, before the Civil War, had spread slowly throughout the northeastern states. Many a community whose traditions went back to the seventeenth century was revolutionized in a decade by the advent of a factory. Yet in all this flux there was one field in which American builders rose to genius.

The sea trade, born of the seventeenth century, had continued into the nineteenth and had prospered. In the eighteen 'thirties, 'forties and 'fifties, the ship carpenters of the Atlantic coast created the American clipper ship, as beautiful and majestic a vessel as ever crossed the ocean. Like the ancient cathedrals of Europe, it was constructed by artisans who built their very lives into their work. Its beauty lay in the fact that the whole harmonious creation, its proportions, the curved bow, the rounded stern, the forest of rope-festooned masts and spars, was true to function. There was nothing false, nothing superfluous. The clippers were built to make swift voyages to China and return and, in their day, they led the merchant ships of the world. But industrialism, modifying the life on land, also revolutionized that of the sea. The steam-driven vessel usurped the ocean-carrying trade. The great clippers, the acme of the evolution of the sailing ship, passed away, their images lingering in the colored prints of the day and in the memories of old seamen.

The middle of the nineteenth century saw the culmination of the disruptive forces at work in American life. For four years two hostile sections, influenced by different ideals, fought to determine the question whether the South should become an independent nation. The passage of the Homestead Act, during the conflict, stimulated the westward movement of population after peace had come. Industrialism passed out of the phase of slow and tentative development and began to revolutionize American civilization. In the years from 1860 to 1880, the national life was confused as never before by powerful and conflicting forces. Over all hung the shadow of a moral decline, as the high idealism of 1861, which called the young men of the North and South to war, faded into a vindictive reconstruction of the conquered South and into a sordid corruption that reached high places in the national government. The architecture of these years reflects the shifting standards of the times. With a few notable exceptions, like the remodeling of the national capitol, architectural taste declined. The refined colonial forms, and the dignified buildings inspired by the art of Rome and Greece, gave place in general to ill-proportioned structures crowded with confused detail. The jig saws and turning lathes of a vigorous industrial expansion completed the architectural collapse.

Then began the slow process of re-establishing the builder's art. Rarely have men faced problems more difficult. Industrialism was creating out of the commercial cities of the early nineteenth century monster population centers that sprawled without plan beside harbors or at the meeting point of many railroads. Property values on certain streets reached prodigious heights. The sky-scraper rose in answer to the demand for the fullest possible utilization of the land, and to bring as many offices as possible close to the important business centers. But these new buildings were themselves the product of other factors with which the architect had to reckon, the advent of cheap and dependable steel, and new inventions like the elevator. Steel, reinforced concrete, and the swift development of engineering after the Civil War, made possible building feats beyond the dreams of earlier generations. The congestion of population in great cities and the complex life of an industrial age called for new types of structures. Mounting fortunes created a group who demanded palatial surroundings. Each succeeding decade saw material changes become more rather than less rapid. To these the architect must adjust himself, and besides them, to intellectual changes of almost equal importance.

By the opening of the twentieth century, the old classical tradition in American education had been largely modified. No longer was a knowledge of Greek or Latin the core of learning. Many an old college of the eighteenth and nineteenth centuries had grown into a university and, following the Morrill Act of 1862, new state universities had sprung into vigorous life. Women were given educational opportunities equal to those of men. Technical schools of engineering and agriculture attracted ever increasing thousands of students. Natural science, social science, history and English assumed positions of importance in the curricula of the colleges of liberal arts. These educational developments broadened the foundations of the growing intellectual life of America. Outside the colleges, museums of science and of art were being established or enlarged, where home-staying Americans could come in contact with the art life of western civilization as it unfolded from its primitive beginnings to their own day. As wealth increased and education became more general, more and more Americans made their way to Europe to study in the universities or the schools of art, or to travel amid the splendors of vanished ages. It fell to the lot of the architect to contribute materially to this cultural development.

Two Americans, both of the École des Beaux-Arts at Paris, led the way in the Renaissance which followed the mid-century architectural collapse. Richard M. Hunt brought back to America a sound appreciation of the principles of his art and, by precept and example, wielded a powerful influence over younger men. Henry H. Richardson chose Romanesque for Trinity Church at Boston, and believed that he had discovered the forms capable of being developed into a truly national style. But Romanesque with which Richardson produced such beautiful results proved too difficult for many of his imitators. The style passed, but not until many buildings of sturdy masonry had been reared which still stand as monuments to this first great effort toward better things. Richardson died in middle life in 1886. Seven years later the Columbian exposition at Chicago marked the beginning of a new phase of the Renaissance. Again Americans turned to classical forms. The beautiful buildings on the shore of Lake Michigan had an influence which amazed their designers. The half-forgotten forms of Rome and Greece became immediately and widely popular. The buildings of the age of industry took on a striking resemblance to those of the early years of the republic. Moreover the dignity and splendor of classical arches and columns were in harmony with the increasing importance of the nation which, with the defeat of Spain in 1898, passed to the status of a world power of the first rank.

But the use of the ancient forms was no mere revival. Intellectual America had passed beyond the stage of imitation. The new classicism was followed by eclecticism. Archæologists were fast reconstructing the civilizations of the ancient world. The schools of the new day had brought the architectural development of the world within the view of the student. So the builder of the early twentieth century, facing problems frequently without precedents, chose what seemed to him the best from the procession of styles that has marked the progress of the centuries. Perhaps classical forms have predominated, but Gothic, one of the greatest intellectual achievements of the Middle Ages, has found in America a friendly environment, and has sprung into new life in the western continent. Byzantine from Constantinople and forms from India, China and Japan may be seen reflected here and there in the streets of America.

A few forces must be reckoned with in estimating the future. The greater part of the vast natural resources of the United States still lie unexploited. Unless dragged down by a world *débâcle* from without or a revolution from within, it seems clear that, for a time, America must continue to increase in wealth. America's world position must inevitably be affected by the increase of her population and her growing economic strength. But industrial America has passed through the phase of crass materialism. The philanthropies, like the commerce of the United States, have become world-wide. Education has become almost a national religion, and buildings like the Princeton dormitories or the Yale quadrangles are the cathedrals of this modern faith. America stirs with an intellectual life that finds no counterpart in her earlier history. Her scholars are making contributions to the sum of human knowledge; her literary people are beginning to express the thoughts and emotions of a new civilization that has followed the factory, the machine and the giant corporation; her religious leaders are aiding in the great task of enriching an ancient faith by adjusting its doctrines to the knowledge of the new day. It remains for the future to disclose whether American builders, with unsurpassed material and intellectual resources at their command, will reach artistic heights commensurate with their opportunities.

RALPH H. GABRIEL

CHAPTER I

EARLY EUROPEAN BACKGROUNDS

OVER a hundred years passed between the first discovery of the American continent and the establishment on its eastern coast of permanent English settlements. Save for the Spanish in Florida and vain attempts of French Huguenots in North Carolina, it was not till 1607 that a successful and permanent village was founded — Jamestown in Virginia; and it was not until 1620 that the first New England colony was established. From that time on until very recently a double phase — southern and northern — has characterized American culture. Differences in climate made necessary differences in the agricultural foundation upon which the early settlements rested. Moreover, the northern colonies were built in a hilly region much of which had been covered in ancient times by continental glaciers. The villages and plantations of the South were in the beginning established upon a low, flat coastal plain. The southern and northern phases of American culture each spread slowly westward until in the nineteenth century two civilizations, in many ways quite distinct from one another, appeared within the United States. This growing divergence between the North and the South is one of the important factors in American architectural development.

From its earliest days the Virginia colony was characterized by the traditions of feudal England, under which it was founded. To it came adventurous younger sons, seeking in the new country not only wealth, but also a position that they could not win at home. Into it poured indentured servants, who, after they had worked out their time, became tenant farmers or small landholders: a growing body frequently in opposition to the owners of the great estates. To it was brought shipload after shipload of negro slaves to work the tobacco plantations. Thus by adventurer, indentured servant, small farmer, and slave there was developed a system of large estates lining the river banks of the colony, spreading north into Maryland and south into the Carolinas and Georgia — estates that were naturally as much like the great English estates as their owners could make them. And so eventually there grew up a native aristocracy, builders of great houses and parish churches, supporting a courtly and refined society, orthodox, conservative, elegant.

Much different were those who settled the forested shores of New England: intensely serious men and women seeking a place where they could own land and where they could worship in their own way. Canny, full of practical common sense, narrow and often intolerant, and yet full of a contradictory enthusiasm for the great English tradition of political liberty, they gave to the country they founded a character of independence and deep seriousness that is unmistakable. Mostly of humble birth themselves, there was at first among them no aristocracy save that of learning; the minister was the great man. They had no great plantations. New England farmers huddled together in compact villages and from these centers hewed an ever-widening circle out of the forest.

Between North and South was a middle area in which influences and peoples were strangely mixed. New Amsterdam guarded the mouth of the Hudson, a true Dutch trading center. The Dutch came to America not for religious freedom like the New Englanders, not primarily for the founding of a new feudal aristocracy (although such an aristocracy did inevitably develop later along the Hudson), but because, as wise business men, they saw the supreme need and enormous value of New Amsterdam for trade. The Dutch came to America to buy and sell.

Swedish traders came early to this central region, too, and later, the Germans; both, in their little settlements in Pennsylvania, Delaware and New Jersey, developed a culture that has contributed much to the richness of the American background. But it was another religious exodus from England that gave final form to the colony of Pennsylvania and eventually dominated the culture of much of the surrounding regions as well, for the influence of the Quakers under William Penn has never quite died out.

In New England the settlers found a country of rolling hills, rising in places into mountainous ruggedness, covered with thousands of miles of forest that furnished wonderful building materials — oak and white pine, spruce and birch. It was a rocky country, but the stone was hard to work, and lime for mortar was scarce. There was an abundance of clay for bricks, but what need of much brick building when timber was so plentiful?

In the South, along the coasts, the colonists found a country of sand; but inland the marshes spread up the rivers, and there was abundant timber. Clay for bricks was even more plentiful than in the North, and more important still, lime was easily obtainable. From an early period, therefore, masonry building was more common in the South than in the North.

These new colonists, South and North, were not settling an uninhabited country. The Indians they found were barbaric but not "savage." They had developed a certain sense of political organization in the tribe; they knew the value of intertribal alliances. They had a rude agriculture. They lived in villages, more or less permanent, with round-topped bark or hide houses. But the Indian tragedy began almost immediately; save in a few exceptional cases — Penn's treaty is the most important — they were driven by the ignorance, the fear, the hostility, the suspicion, and the greed of the settlers into permanent and futile enmity. Indian culture, therefore, had little effect upon the colonists, except in woodcraft, in which the settlers proved apt pupils of their enemies. In building, especially, no effect of Indian example is to be expected, for European needs were too far developed to be satisfied with the simple Indian dwellings.

So, in the new country, the settler sought solace from the terrible homesickness which must often have engulfed him, by building around himself, after the earliest wattled or palisadoed shacks, a new England or a new Holland, as like the country he had forever left behind as the materials he had to work with and the climate he must consider would allow. Thus the gabled overhanging houses of New England enshrine the memory of England's half-timbered picturesqueness, the great manors of the early South perpetuate in America the tradition of the Jacobean English "place," and the stepped gables of New Amsterdam were but simpler versions of the forms of Holland. For each settler wished to build a home; and home, to him, could mean only the environment of the land of his birth.

1   From a photograph

A VIEW ON CASTLE HILL, LINCOLN, ENGLAND

FROM towns like this, settlers came to the new country seeking often freedom for their worship in the North or gainful adventure in the South. In the foreground is a typical many gabled English town house of the sixteenth century, with high roofs, stuccoed walls, deep-shadowed overhangs. Beyond is a stately Georgian brick-fronted mansion of the eighteenth century. The memory of these forms was the most vital influence at work in the design of America's early buildings.

SHAKESPEARE'S BIRTHPLACE

THIS house is in more rural Stratford-on-Avon, in Warwickshire. Its form is characteristic of the lower, more rambling houses of the smaller villages; the half timbering of its walls is not developed here as a decorative motif, but is the simple expression of the actual structural timbers. Timbering of precisely this type is often found beneath the shingles or clapboards that almost universally wall our early houses.

2   From a photograph

3   From the *International Studio*, 1912, after a painting by Sydney R. Jones

HORLEY, OXFORDSHIRE

A TYPICAL village street from the Oxfordshire hill country shows in masonry many of the same cottage forms that in this country were reproduced in wood. Simple gables, massive chimneys, small windows in early American houses are direct heritages from the English forms.

THE WEST INDIA COMPANY'S HOUSE

IN the days when New York was a Dutch colony this was the Amsterdam home of the Dutch West India Company. The Dutch brought with them the traditions of red brick and white trim, of simple, large windows, of dormer (roof) windows, instead of the English gables, of gables decorated with scrolls and steps, parallel with the street, instead of leading directly to it, as was more usual in England.

4   From a Dutch print engraved in 1783

5   From a Dutch print engraved in 1783

COURT OF THE DUTCH WEST INDIA COMPANY'S HOUSE

THE court of the West India Company's house in Amsterdam, first occupied in 1674, reveals simplicity and a more marked Renaissance influence; but its roofs, its windows, and particularly its dormers show the same feeling that characterizes the early Dutch work in America.

EARLY JAMESTOWN, VIRGINIA

THERE are no authentic pictures of the first buildings erected by white men in the country; and none of the buildings are left. This picture of the Indian massacre near Jamestown, from Theodore de Bry's famous work on America, is the original of many "early views of Jamestown." Architecturally it shows general simplicity of type, the use of half-timber work in the town itself, and a fort whose outline is broken by the square church tower. But the whole must not be taken literally — it is at best no more than an imaginative reconstruction.

6   Detail from the engraving in Theodore de Bry, *Grands Voyages*, Part XIII, Frankfort, 1634

LOG HOUSE, EAST DOWNINGTOWN, PENNSYLVANIA

THIS log house in East Downingtown, Penn., built about 1710, is one of the earliest extant in America. In its simplicity of form, the smallness of its openings, the use of partially squared logs, it resembles the homes of countless of the early settlers, without distinction of locality.

LOG CABIN NEAR DARBY, PENN-SYLVANIA

ANOTHER early Pennsylvania log cabin stands

7   From a photograph by L. A. Sampson

near Darby, Penn. Put thatch on the roof instead of shingles, and wooden shutters — or at most, oiled paper — instead of glass windows, and you have a picture of a Pilgrim house. A glance at Chapter XI will show how the pioneers clung to a similar type of house, one generation building on its frontier what their forefathers had built on theirs. Some authorities believe that the early New England cabins had the walls built of vertical logs driven into the ground, like palisades, rather than laid horizontally.

8   © Rau Studios, Inc.

INDIAN HOUSES OF THE EAST COAST OF AMERICA

THE early immigrants found a country largely covered with dense forests, and inhabited by Indian tribes that had already achieved considerable progress in communal living. Early sketches and maps show many views of Indian villages, and prove one type of building almost universal among them — a wooden, curved-top framework, covered with hides or skins. Yet this type of Indian building, common as it was, and admirably suited to the materials at hand, exerted not the least influence upon the building of the European settlers. Their memories of the places they had left were too strong for that, their customs too different. They aimed to create at once in the new home a replica of the home they had left.

9   Indian Village in Virginia, from Theodore de Bry, *Grands Voyages*, Part I, 1590

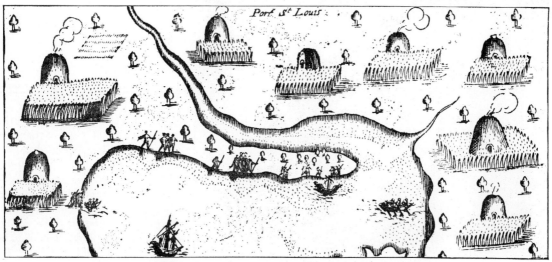

10   Map of Plymouth Harbor, from *Les Voyages du Steur de Champlain*, Paris, 1613

11   Courtesy of the Committee on Old Houses of the Connecticut Society of the Colonial Dames of America

THE NORTON HOUSE, GUILFORD, CONNECTICUT

THE Norton house at Guilford, Connecticut, was built in 1694; unfortunately it is no longer standing. Although later in date than many other existing houses, nevertheless in the simplicity of its timbering and its diminutive windows it is a perfect example of the earliest buildings.

Note its similarity on the one hand to the Downingtown log house; on the other to the cottage type (No. 3). It is one step further toward the reconstruction in New England of the loved atmosphere of the England that had been left behind.

12   From William Tudor, *Life of James Otis*, Boston, 1823

ALLYN HOUSE, PLYMOUTH, MASSACHUSETTS

THE Allyn house in Plymouth, shown in an old view of 1823, is typical of the larger framed houses which followed the first shelters. Its overhang, its central gable, its diamond-paned, leaded casement windows and the simple doorway all reveal the attempt to be, in the new country, as English as climate and materials would allow.

FIRST MORAVIAN SCHOOL IN PENNSYLVANIA, 1742

THE attempt to recreate in the New World a new Europe was constant and natural. Its achievements were often remarkable, but it was the tradition of the Europe one had left, or that one's father and forefather had left, that was remembered most vividly. This accounts for certain strange survivals in this country, such as the first Moravian School, at Oley, Penn. It was built in 1742; yet it is pure "medieval"

13　　From a photograph by H. Winslow Fegley

European half-timber in construction and appearance. Doubtless in the early towns of Massachusetts and Virginia many such half-timber houses — later covered with shingles for warmth — gave a "homelike" European atmosphere to the narrow streets.

14　　© Frank Cousins

OLD HOUSE ON MILL ISLAND NEAR BERGEN BEACH, LONG ISLAND

THE Schenck-Crook house, sometimes called the oldest house remaining in New York state, has little superficially that recalls the elaborate gables or the brick walls of the Amsterdam views. Yet analysis reveals, particularly in the roof forms, and the dormers that grow so naturally and frankly out of the roof, a feeling that it is unmistakably Dutch. The house was built in 1655; the porch is probably later.

CHAPTER II

THE FAR SOUTH AND THE SOUTHWEST

LONG before the English established themselves in America, Spanish conquest was proceeding apace. In Mexico Spanish power was most surely established and Spanish culture achieved its greatest American expression; and Mexico was the center from which Spanish influence radiated — northward into New Mexico, Arizona, Texas, California; eastward through Texas along the Gulf coast to Louisiana and Florida; westward over the Pacific to Manila and the Indies.

There was an enormous contrast between Spanish and English colonial methods. The conquest of Mexico was achieved by alliances with rebellious Indian tribes, and once the conquest was complete, it was found that the greatest wealth could only be won by coöperation with the natives. This commercial "coöperation" — often the most ruthless exploitation — was accompanied by much intermarriage, and the growth of a great body of mestizos. Moreover, the Indians of Mexico were among the most culturally advanced in the Americas. They were a town-dwelling, masonry-building, organization-loving people, with marked decorative ability. They had a highly developed art, whose use of surface richness was not unlike that of the Renaissance Spaniards themselves. As a result, they early became capable workmen in the new style of the conquerors, and added to it something of their own native exuberant originality.

These Spanish colonies in America were regarded as more than a mere means of producing wealth; they were great religious and missionary centers as well. To them flocked not only soldiers, adventurers, artisans, lured by dreams of wealth, but also in their train, priests, monks, clerical diplomats, eager to extend the power of the Church and the prestige of their respective orders. By dint of numbers and training they early developed a powerful influence in the Spanish new world. As they waxed rich, churches of great splendor and pure Renaissance character rose in every city. In Mexico the Jesuits found congenial territory; and in Mexico, through the development of Indian skill and the absorption of Indian influence, they attained to a new and lavish richness of style.

Meanwhile Spanish generals and Spanish missionaries were pressing north into the broader spaces of the American continent. First the Jesuits, and after their expulsion in 1767 the Franciscans, founded mission after mission in the Moqui, Zuñi, and Pima countries, and later along the mountainous coast of California. Tradition says that one at least of the missions still standing in New Mexico antedates by nearly a hundred years any building of European origin on the east coast of America. At a time when the New England settlers were content with modest framed houses in which Gothic tradition still lingered, missions were being built in the far southwest that followed as closely as possible the richness, the lavishness, the *baroque* love of swelling, broken line that characterized the last phase of the Spanish Renaissance.

The Englishman preserved his civilization in the new country by aloofness, by shunning native contacts, except as temporary alliances might prove profitable in a military way; the Spaniard preserved his by absorbing as large a body of the native population as possible. It is characteristic of the Spanish penetration of America that the Spanish were the only colonies whose architecture was modified by contact with Indian building methods. In that fact lies much of its peculiar vitality.

15 From Arnoldus Montanus, *Die Nieuwe en Onbekenae Weereld*, Amsterdam, 1671

PORTUS ACAPULCO

MONTANUS shows a view of the harbor of Acapulco in 1671, the same harbor from which the Manila fleet set out, and so later became an important link in the chain between the Spaniards in far-off Luzon and the mother country. But even in 1671 it has all the look of a Mediterranean port: masonry walls and tile roofs and occasional bits of thatch give the atmosphere of a settled European town, for by 1671 Spanish dominion in Mexico was already 150 years old. Only two Indian huts in the lower right-hand corner give evidence that the town is in America.

THE CATHEDRAL, CITY OF MEXICO

THE architecture of Mexico followed styles in Spain with remarkable accuracy, due to the enormous strength of the Jesuit and Franciscan organizations — comprising many trained designers — who were able to produce at an early date buildings of surprisingly good design and rich execution. The Cathedral of Mexico City with its neighboring Sagrario, begun in 1573, and not completed until 1811,

16 © Detroit Publishing Co.

bears marks of all the Spanish Renaissance styles, from the fine classicism of its conception, through the *Churrigueresque* (overloaded ornamentation) of the Sagrario, to the rococo classic of the eighteenth century.

17 From Sylvester Baxter, *Spanish Colonial Architecture in Mexico*, Boston, 1901, photograph by J. B. Millet

THE COURTYARD OF THE CASA DE LOS AZULEJOS, MEXICO

The courtyard of the Casa de los Azulejos, in Mexico, is a remarkable example of an earlier type of Spanish Renaissance domesticated in America. It is almost pure plateresque (the earliest style of the Spanish Renaissance), with an admixture of Mudejar influences — that is, with the polygonal and patterned columns, and the fine-scaled ornament of the frieze and architrave, which are the direct results of Moorish influence on Spanish art. The Moors add one more to the long list of traditions that contribute to American art.

ALTAR OF THE CHURCH OF SAN SEBASTIAN Y SANTA PRISCA

It was in the later developments of the *Churrigueresque* that the Mexican architecture, using native labor under clerical supervision, reached its greatest development. In this there is such massed and intricate richness — perhaps due to Aztec influence — that in daring *bravura* (elaborated brilliance) it surpassed anything in Spain. Such is the high altar of the Church of San Sebastian y Santa Prisca, in Tasco, where the intricate decoration of every surface, the sense of dramatic composition, and the resultant atmosphere of luxuriance outweigh occasional crudities of detail.

18 From Sylvester Baxter, *Spanish Colonial Architecture in Mexico*, Boston, 1901, photograph by J. B. Millet

GOVERNOR'S HOUSE, ST. AUGUSTINE, FLORIDA

In Florida, far to the east, Spanish influence left an indelible imprint, still evident in the Spanish character of St. Augustine. A view of the Governor's House in 1764 shows that the English governor merely took over for his residence a building of purely Spanish colonial type — the bracketed balcony and the engaged columns flanking the gate are full of Spanish atmosphere.

19   From the King's Collection of Maps, Prints and Drawings, British Museum

ZUÑI, NEW MEXICO

BUT it was in the west that Spanish development proceeded most rapidly and most romantically. Lured by legends of wealthy cities to the north, Coronado in 1540 and 1541 traversed much of New Mexico and the country northward to Kansas. The fabled cities he sought — and found all too disappointing — were the adobe villages, the pueblos of New Mexico. Zuñi pueblo (No. 22), with its white walls shadowed by the projecting tree-trunk roof beams, makes an impressive picture.

A BIT OF OLD ST. AUGUSTINE

AND to-day the stuccoed walls, hipped roofs and little balconies of St. Augustine have upon them a spell utterly Latin, a magic of the Mediterranean south. Here windows are spaced and proportioned, and broad surfaces of stucco gleam in the sun, with all that innate feeling for picturesque placing and quiet texture and austere simplicity which characterizes much of the smaller work in Spain itself.

SPANISH CATHEDRAL AT ST. AUGUSTINE

TO-DAY, too, the eighteenth-century Spanish Cathedral still dominates the square of St. Augustine. In it many of the characteristics of typically American-Spanish work appear. Such is the development of the open belfry, here used to crown the curved gable wall; and the peculiar mixture of rococo forms with cold classic orders in the doorway with its broken cornice and severe Doric columns.

21 From a photograph by the United States Department of Agriculture

THE PUEBLO OF WALPI

A VIEW of Walpi (No. 23), even to-day inhabited by Indians, shows precisely the kind of village the Spaniards found in the territory into which they pressed northward from Mexico. Walls of sun-dried brick, adobe, or stone; flat roofs supported by wooden beams that sometimes pierce the walls; tiny windows; entrances chiefly by ladders leading up to the terraced roofs; crowded picturesqueness — these are the characteristics of the pueblo.

THE "OLDEST EUROPEAN HOUSE IN THE UNITED STATES"

At Santa Fé, N. M., there is a house that tradition claims as the oldest house of European construction in the United States. It dates from the early seventeenth century. This house illustrates how the Spaniards, removed from the civilization of Mexico, in a country of few building materials, were forced to build in the native Indian manner, only adding larger doors and windows. The end wall shows the simple roof structure — a thick layer of clay resting on crude wooden beams.

REMAINS OF OLD SPANISH CHURCH, SIXTEENTH CENTURY

Earlier still were missions; for though the dream of wealth to the north was an illusion, thousands of Indians were there for political domination and religious conversion. Missions and *presidios* were founded in many portions of New Mexico, Arizona and Texas by the end of the sixteenth century. Few of the earliest buildings remain. In Alamo National Park, N. M., stands an old church, said to date from the sixteenth century, typical of the early Spanish adaptations of Indian building methods, a lonely monument to Jesuit missionary zeal.

25   From a photograph by the United States Forest Service

26   Courtesy of the Museum of New Mexico, Santa Fé

ST. JOSEPH'S CHURCH, LAGUNA, NEW MEXICO

Even by the end of the seventeenth century New Mexico missions still followed the same crude building methods. St. Joseph's Church, Laguna, N. M., built in 1699, is as crude as the earlier example, and the terraced buildings beside it are of pure Indian type. Only the decorative development of the parapet and the open belfry as a crowning motif show that an advance had been made.

SANTUARIO OF CHIMAYO, NEW MEXICO

In the church interiors of the time more of the Spanish Renaissance influence is observable. The church at Chimayo, N. M., is typical of many. Its crude roof beams have carved brackets of Renaissance type; arched forms occur; and the chancel railing has cut-out balusters. The gaily painted reredos is characteristic of the type of painted ornament devel-

27   Courtesy of the Museum of New Mexico, Santa Fé

oped by the Indians under the mission influence; full of their own native boldness and simplicity, but making rich use of the Spanish *baroque* influence with which it was in unexpected harmony.

CARVED DOOR OF THE MISSION CHURCH OF SANTO DOMINGO, NEW MEXICO

THE doors of the mission church of Santo Domingo, N. M., date from sometime in the seventeenth century. Quite different from the crudeness of the adobe walls, or the brilliant Indian painting of the interiors, these two beautiful doors, with their heraldic patterns so perfectly de-

28   Courtesy of the Museum of New Mexico

signed and so beautifully carved, must have been the handiwork of a Spanish monk who here found expression for a taste and skill for which his barbaric and arid surroundings furnished slight opportunity. The town and its church were destroyed by flood in 1880.

WINDOW OF THE MISSION AT SAN JOSÉ, TEXAS

THE greatest development of the Spanish colonial style came later and farther west. The Jesuits, who made their way up through Sonora and north into Arizona and east into Texas, were expelled in 1767, and their work was taken over by equally zealous Franciscans. The mission of San José Aguayo, founded in 1720 by the Franciscans, has a portal, with window above, whose scrolls and sculpture are full of the true *bravura* of Spanish colonial *baroque*.

29   From a photograph

30 From Rexford Newcomb, *The Franciscan Mission Architecture of Alta California.* © Architectural Book Publishing Co., 1916

31 From Rexford Newcomb, *The Franciscan Mission Architecture of Alta California.* © Architectural Book Publishing Co., 1916

SAN XAVIER DEL BAC, TUCSON, ARIZONA

THE church of San Xavier del Bac near Tucson, Ariz., like many of the Sonora and Arizona churches, has a dome; but it boasts a greater dome than its neighbors. On the interior as well, the dome is, in a sense, a climax; it is the only Spanish church in the United States now standing that has made any attempt to equal the richness of the *baroque* churches of Mexico. Its execution is simpler and more crude, but the *baroque* love of rich surfaces and the Spanish skill in composition broke up the lines of its pilasters and turned the spirals on its façade.

THE ALAMO, SAN ANTONIO, TEXAS

THE Alamo, in San Antonio, Texas, has a historical interest which has entirely obscured its artistic importance. Its picturesque front is perhaps the most striking example in the United States of the remarkable persistence of Spanish Renaissance forms. In it no trace of eighteenth-century classicism betrays its real date; instead, its composition is typical of Spanish *baroque* feeling, and its shell-headed niches, its flatness of ornament, and the flat wide frame of its central upper window are reminiscent of an even earlier style — the Spanish plateresque of the sixteenth century.

32　From a photograph by the United States Department of Agriculture

33 © Detroit Photographic Co.

FRANCISCAN MISSION, SANTA BARBARA

THE late eighteenth-century missions of California are the best known Spanish monuments in America to-day. Like the Alamo, they are remarkable survivals, in a distant colony, of the earlier fashions of the mother country. Santa Barbara, for instance, dates from 1787–1800, yet its double-towered façade and its arcaded cloisters, straightforward and beautifully proportioned, might well be a hundred and fifty years older.

BELFRY OF SAN GABRIEL MISSION, CALIFORNIA

THE same feeling for straightforward simplicity, for sure proportion, for picturesque and telling outline, shows in the famous belfry of the San Gabriel Mission, dating from the early nineteenth century.

34 © Detroit Publishing Co.

SAN CARLOS BORROMEO

OF the mission churches, San Carlos Borromeo (Carmel) most completely reveals the strength of that mighty tradition. Built 1773–1797, its curved gable end, its two unsymmetrical towers, its arched doorway, unusually elaborate for California, and its

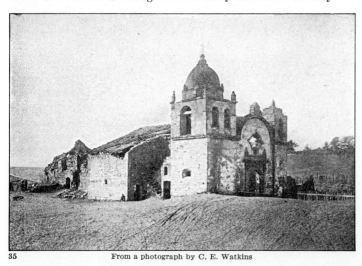

35 From a photograph by C. E. Watkins

strange *baroque* window above give it a sure effectiveness, Spanish and Renaissance, unmatched in California. Modern "restoration" has unfortunately robbed it of much of its original charm.

36   From Rexford Newcomb, *The Franciscan Mission Architecture of Alta California*,
© Architectural Book Publishing Co., 1916

SAN LUIS REY DE FRANCIA, NEAR OCEANSIDE, CALIFORNIA

ONE of the largest and most developed of the missions was San Luis Rey de Francia. Early travelers speak of its beauty; indeed as one came upon it suddenly, deep in the wilderness, its long white arcades, its court, its gardens, its chapel must have had an aspect truly palatial. It was finished in 1802; yet at that time, when all the East was under the sway of Adam delicacy or Jeffersonian classicism, in far-off California Spanish Franciscans were still building true to their vivid traditions of Spanish *baroque*.

37   Old Spanish Mission, 1731, San Antonio, Texas,
© Rau Bros., Inc.

CHAPTER III

EARLY COLONIAL IN THE NORTH

BY the middle of the seventeenth century, New England had grown into an ordered community. The coast was well settled; towns and villages had grown up along the shore where harbors or river mouths furnished convenient locations and settlements had already pushed westward into the interior. The white population had increased largely in the "great migrations" of 1630–1640; the sparse Indian population yielding grudgingly before the tide, with occasional outbreaks into open hostility. A number of colonies had been founded; Plymouth, Massachusetts Bay (which included New Hampshire till 1679 and Maine), Connecticut (with its center at Hartford), New Haven, Rhode Island — and all of them enjoyed early a remarkable degree of autonomy and independence of the mother country. In Massachusetts there developed a veritable theocracy, many of whose ministers were men educated in England. The strong cultural influence which they exerted upon the colonists under their sway was colored largely by English tradition.

The fine independence of the early New England settlers — all, or nearly all, of unmixed English blood — their hardy and persistent strength, and their ability to combine religious enthusiasms with an English zeal for political organization made them ideal colonists. Under the general system of town autonomy that prevailed villages grew up apace. In Massachusetts Bay the strict enforcement of an intolerant religious unity, while it was responsible for much bitter persecution which forced dissenters into other colonies, provided, together with the town meeting system of local organization, for those who conformed, an environment of order, security, and harmony admirably fitted to promote the rapid development of colonial culture.

As the villages grew, so did the few cities that served as market centers for the country behind. Artisans began to immigrate in increasing numbers; shops became numerous; greater and greater consideration came to be given to the amenities of life. Yet for the most part, throughout the seventeenth century, farming and fishing remained the chief industries, and the ministry the only profession. As a result, all sorts of home industries — spinning, weaving, quilting, and all the varied activities that a home requires — throve. Despite the growing importance of sea-faring, despite the growing number of skilled tradesmen, England remained remote and money scarce. Only that was bought which could not be made; the colonist of those times and his wife had to become true "Jacks-of-all-trades."

The rapid development of New England inevitably found characteristic architectural expression. As he learned the necessities of his climate and the possibilities of his main material, wood, the colonist put this knowledge to work in devising buildings that embodied his memory of those he had left behind in England. Casement windows, steep roofs, overhangs, gables were the forms he used; but he soon found that half-timber was impractical unless covered with shingles or clapboards to keep out the cold, and that shingled roofs were cheaper and better than the earlier universal thatch. The closest reproductions of English forms, such as the "Old Feather Store" in Boston (No. 51), were naturally to be found in the cities, where communication with England was most continuous. In more remote rural districts, as the settler's memory of his former home grew dim, and a local technique adapted to conditions of winter cold and to the abundance of timber gradually defined itself, the simpler forms were more and more developed, the complex forms less and less used. The Doten house in Plymouth (No. 46), with its simple gabled roof, is typical of this development. The Doten house, moreover, belongs to a growing class — the so-called "five bay house," with two windows on each side of a central door — which was the foundation of a powerful tradition that has dominated much American house design ever since.

The overhang, on the contrary, framed or hewn, as in the Capen house (No. 41), and the many gables of the Feather Store or of the "House of the Seven Gables" (No. 50) are but isolated examples of a fashion that died without architectural heirs. Similarly, in Dutch New Netherlands, simple houses like those of Old Hurley (Nos. 61, 62, 63, 64) set a type which was followed in houses along the Hudson for over a hundred years, while the more typically Dutch stepped gables of Albany and New York were replaced by buildings of a different type and are known to us only from old prints.

In church design the New Englander had few precedents to follow. His church must serve him as town hall and courthouse as well. Furthermore, at least among the earlier colonists, any resemblance to the hated Anglican forms was to be avoided at all costs. The result was the square meetinghouse; a direct and simple solution of the problem, whose influence, strange to say, persisted long in town hall and courthouse design, although in church design it was early absorbed and replaced by the classic influences of the eighteenth century.

To Pennsylvania the Quakers brought a culture more advanced and more sophisticated than that of the average New Englander. Their proprietor, William Penn, was a person of note at court. It was natural, therefore, that the Philadelphians, after their first cave dwellings and crude shelters, built in a style more affected by the growing English classicism that followed the return of Charles II to the throne; natural that the "Slate House" (No. 67) with its brick walls and hipped roof should be classic in spirit; and natural that in early English Pennsylvania it is almost impossible to find a single trace of that Jacobean character which distinguishes all the seventeenth-century building of New England.

But throughout New England, too, the classic fashion was bound, sooner or later, to penetrate. The continual immigration of artisans brought to colonial ports the current English fashions and techniques. The establishment of a royal government in Massachusetts in 1684 signified not only the passing of the old colonial charter; it meant as well an influx of many British officials, the marked tightening of the bond between England and the colonies, and the establishment of an Anglican church. Together with a tremendous increase of shipping and of travel that characterized the time, it meant the growing importance of the English fashions of the day as opposed to the memory of England of the original settlers; it meant, with the coming of the new century, the passing of the last vestige of Tudor and Jacobean tradition, and the final dominance of the classic Renaissance.

THE FAIRBANKS HOUSE, DEDHAM, MASSACHUSETTS

FOR the Fairbanks house at Dedham is claimed the honor of being the oldest house in New England. The oldest portion — a little over half the central block — may date back to 1640. In roof pitch and general character it is early work; but it must be imagined with casement windows. The left wing shows the gambrel roof of two slopes that was a later development.

38   From a photograph by the Halliday Historic Photograph Co.

39   From an engraving in *The Ladies Repository*, about 1840

THE WHITFIELD HOUSE, GUILFORD, CONNECTICUT

THE Whitfield house at Guilford, Conn. (Nos. 39 and 40), dates probably from about 1640. In its massive end chimney and its thick walls, it is unique in New England, and more characteristic of English types. It, too, undoubtedly originally had smaller windows closed with leaded casements. The little chimney is a later addition. This house erected at the beginning of the Guilford settlement is evidence of the substantial character of many of the settlers in New England.

40   From a photograph

41   © Topsfield (Mass.) Historical Society

THE CAPEN HOUSE, TOPSFIELD, MASSACHUSETTS

THERE are two types of overhang used in New England houses: framed and hewn. The Capen house is one of the most perfect examples of a framed overhang. This overhang with its great brackets and drops, the casement windows, and the large chimney, bespeak its English ancestry, and its charm of proportion the fine taste of its builder. Although built in 1693, well after the frontier period, its forms are those of England a century before. It is American Jacobean.

42   © Topsfield (Mass.) Historical Society

43   © Topsfield (Mass.) Historical Society

THE CAPEN HOUSE, INTERIOR

THE interior of the Capen house shows the same fine English simplicity. The beamed ceiling, the molded corners of the great girders — summer beams — and the simple board doors are all in the Tudor tradition; and the whole is a rare example of the surroundings in which the New Englanders of the seventeenth century lived.

The stair hall is full of the same fine primitive sincerity. Note the front door, on the left, made of several thicknesses of broad planks fastened with nails whose heads form a pattern.

WINSLOW HOUSE, MARSHFIELD, MASSACHUSETTS

IN the seventeenth century the sturdy English settlements took firm root in New England. The Winslow house at Marshfield dates from the last year of the seventeenth century, and the growing lightness of the balustrades and newels, and the use of paneling with moldings mitered at the corners, are indicative of the movement toward greater refinement, and the classicism and perfection that marked eighteenth-century work.

44   Courtesy of Winslow Associates Inc., Boston

THE BOARDMAN "SCOTCH" HOUSE, SAUGUS, MASSACHUSETTS

THE Boardman "Scotch" house at Saugus, Mass. (No. 45), is the earliest house that can be positively dated by documentary evidence — 1651. It was built for Scotch prisoners who came over as indentured servants to start ironworks at this place. Besides the chimney with its vertical strips, and the overhang, notice the break in the front roof slope, which is an unusual touch of refinement.

THE DOTEN HOUSE, PLYMOUTH, MASSACHUSETTS

MANY early houses are without overhangs, some but one story to the eaves. Such is the Doten house at Plymouth (No. 46), built near the end of the seventeenth century. With its four windows and a central door and plain roof, it is an early example of a type that persisted in New England for at least two hundred years.

45   © Halliday Historic Photograph Co.

46   From a photograph by A. S. Burbank, Plymouth

47   © Detroit Publishing Co.

THE PAUL REVERE HOUSE, BOSTON

Domestic architecture in the towns — Salem and Boston — was more English, more sophisticated. Even the Paul Revere house, built about 1676, clearly belongs in a city street. Its diamond-paned windows are restorations, but on almost certain evidence.

48   © Frank Cousins

THE MARIA GOODHUE HOUSE, DANVERS, MASSACHUSETTS

The Maria Goodhue house, built at Danvers, Mass., about 1690, is one of the most noticeable of the houses without overhang. The many breaks of the chimney are evidence of its English heritage; its general scheme is the familiar one with five bays on the front, and a lean-to behind, but it is unique in the plaster cove under the eaves, a charming and unusual touch.

49   Courtesy of the Essex Institute, Salem, Mass.

THE WARD HOUSE, SALEM, MASSACHUSETTS

The Ward house, built in Salem in 1684 and now restored and preserved by the Essex Institute, shows the many gables, the complex chimney of true English work. It is one of the best examples of the type there is.

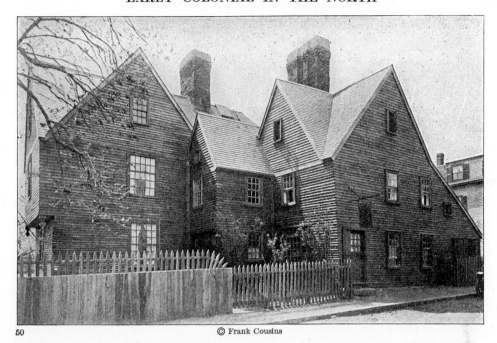

50 © Frank Cousins

THE "HOUSE OF THE SEVEN GABLES," SALEM, MASSACHUSETTS

THIS famous home of Hepzibah Pyncheon, dating from various periods between 1660 and 1700 or later, shows the complicated picturesqueness possible when the many gabled house is added to again and again.

51 From a print made in Boston about 1830

THE OLD FEATHER STORE, BOSTON

MORE English still, however, is the famous Old Feather Store, of Boston, now no more. It might have stood in Lincoln, or even in London. Its gables, its brackets, its overhangs, its picturesque outline are English, and English of the Gothic rather than of the Renaissance tradition. The decorations on the stucco are to be noticed, and the date, 1680, on the top of the gable.

GOVERNOR BRADSTREET'S HOUSE, SALEM, MASSACHUSETTS

THE many gabled English type reached an early climax in Salem in the Governor Bradstreet house, built in the middle of the seventeenth century and destroyed in 1753. Its nearly monumental size, its symmetrical dignity, its twin octagonal turrets that flank the curved-top, nail-studded door, all reveal a skill and wealth we are not accustomed to associate with Salem in that early time.

52 From a photograph by Frank Cousins of an original drawing

THE PETER TUFTS HOUSE, MEDFORD, MASSACHUSETTS

THE development of masonry building was rapid. One of the earliest brick houses in New England is the Peter Tufts house, at Medford, Mass., supposed to date from 1680. Its use of end chimneys is to be remarked; they later became common. The roof is one of the earliest gambrels, if not the earliest, existing in the country. Originally there were probably three grouped casements under the brick arches where are now two sliding sash windows. The dormers are modern.

53   From a photograph by the Halliday Historic Photograph Co.

THE SPENCER–PIERCE–LITTLE HOUSE, NEWBURYPORT, MASSACHUSETTS

ONE of the most remarkable of the masonry houses in seventeenth-century New England is the Spencer-Pierce-Little house, in Newburyport, Mass. Its arched doorway and windows, and the little niche above the door that looks as if it must once have held a statue or a bust, combined with its quaint mixture of stone, brick and wood, give it an old world appearance. This house was the creation of a people able to produce such vigorous literary work as Cotton Mather's *Magnalia Christi Americana* and also capable of such extraordinary mental aberrations as the Salem witchcraft scare.

54   From a photograph

THE PROVINCE HOUSE, BOSTON

ONE of the finest of the Boston mansions of the seventeenth century was the Peter Sergeant or Province house (No. 55), built in 1679. It has been recently ascertained that the house originally had stepped gables of thorough Jacobean character. The pedimented roof shown in the engraving is later.

55   From an engraving, about 1830

THE HUTCHINSON HOUSE, BOSTON

EVEN more classic, more sophisticated, is the Hutchinson house, dating from 1681–91. In it appear all the classicisms Sir Christopher Wren was using at that time in England — balustrades, colossal pilasters, a curved pediment over the central window. So extreme is the contrast to the earlier work that one wonders if this were not possibly built from designs brought over from England. It is prophetic of the century to follow.

56   From the *American Magazine of Useful Knowledge*, 1836

"THE OLD SHIP CHURCH," HINGHAM, MASSACHUSETTS

THE type of New England meetinghouse was early established — a simple square or rectangular building with a hipped roof and a belfrey rising in the center. The "Old Ship Church" at Hingham is a typical rectangular meetinghouse. It was begun in 1681, but did not reach the present size until the eighteenth century. It was primarily what the name implies — a meetinghouse, but it was also used as a church as well as for many other purposes.

57   From an old print in *Towns of New England*, courtesy of the State Street Trust Co., Boston

THE OLD BRICK MEETING-HOUSE, BOSTON

THE "Old Brick Meetinghouse" in Boston (No. 58) shows the same idea worked out in masonry on a much larger scale for a big city congregation. Its belfry was unusually delicate and important for the influence of its type on later towers and spires. The view is obviously a reconstruction.

58   Courtesy of the Bostonian Society, origin of the print not known

From a photograph by Soule. © Gramstorff Bros., Inc.

THE OLD STATE HOUSE, BOSTON

THE climax of the earlier type of masonry work is the Old State House in Boston, the oldest existing public building in New England. Its stepped gables and steep roof belong to the period that had passed; but its consistent and masterly use of classic detail in doors and windows, dormers and cupola, points to developments that were to come. Thoroughly English in its robust and sure strength, it is nevertheless a milestone in the development of architecture in New England. In it colonial architecture reaches maturity. Surrounded by the buildings of a great city it preserves the traditions of that distant day when Boston folk were subjects of the British king.

THE SENATE HOUSE, KINGSTON, NEW YORK

THE cultural tradition behind the Dutch of New Netherland differed somewhat from that of the English. The Senate House in Kingston, N. Y., is one of the earliest Dutch buildings still standing. It is built of rugged masonry; but instead of gables it has a hipped roof — sloped from all four sides — and the typical small slant-roofed dormers that are to be found again and again along the Hudson. It was originally a residence.

From a photograph by J. A. Glenn

61

62

63

64   From four photographs by George N. Nash, courtesy of the New York Historical Society

HOUSES IN OLD HURLEY, NEW YORK

OLD Hurley, N. Y., has preserved almost unchanged the spirit of the Dutch villages along the Hudson River. Built of the simplest materials, there was obviously no opportunity for the use of elaborate Dutch forms; the Dutch feeling here lies not in stepped gables or spreading roofs, but rather in a certain direct simplicity in the stone masonry, in occasional long sloping dormers like those of the McSperit house (No. 61), and in a long, low picturesqueness of composition.

65   © Frank Cousins

THE BILLOPP HOUSE ON STATEN ISLAND

The Billopp house on Staten Island, built in 1668, has preserved through an eventful history its old appearance almost unchanged. Its end chimneys, and particularly the treatment of the end walls with their copings raised above the roof, are typically Dutch. Originally the house probably had, like so many others, swinging casement windows. The doorway is later.

THE PROTESTANT DUTCH CHURCH, ALBANY, NEW YORK

Of the earliest Dutch churches, none is left. An engraving of the Dutch church in Albany, built in 1715, shows a character that is New England in type. In detail it is Dutch, notably in the tall windows with their brick tracery, and the coped and stepped gable of the little wing. Perhaps in some such building as this the worthy burghers in Dutch New Amsterdam thanked God for their deliverance from the tomahawk of the redskin.

66   From the *American Magazine*, Albany, N. Y., July, 1815

THE OLD SLATE HOUSE, PHILADELPHIA

The Pennsylvania settlement dates only from the closing years of the seventeenth century, so that but little of the work of this century is extant. But what existed is much more advanced than contemporary work in the North. The Slate house, about 1698, was considered the finest house in the province. In dignity and design, complexity of form, and permanence of materials it is certainly in advance of any known New England house of the day. It bears more resemblance to the English house than to typical American work.

37   From a print, about 1830, courtesy of the Ridgway Library, Philadelphia

HOUSE OF THE EARLY DUTCH GOVERNORS, ALBANY, NEW YORK

WE are fortunately not without veracious evidence of the appearance of the old Dutch city houses in America. J. Milbert published in Paris about 1828 a book of travels through New York and New England, illustrated with many beautiful lithographs that seem to be quite accurate. His view of the old Dutch Governor's house in Albany will repay careful study, for every line in it

68   From J. Milbert, *Itinéraire pittoresque du fleuve Hudson*, Paris, 1828-29

is saturated with Dutch feeling. Although Dutch rule finally ended in 1674 this view shows Albany, even in the eighteen twenties, still predominately Dutch in appearance.

69   © Rau Studios, Inc.

THE WYCK HOUSE, PHILADELPHIA

THE Wyck house is typical of the more usual form of large Pennsylvania mansion. Its stone walls, stuccoed front, and carefully placed windows show a spirit unsatisfied with makeshifts. Its total lack of ornament places it among the early types, and helps to give to it an air of austere yet welcoming dignity. It dates from before 1700.

THE KEITH MANSION, HORSHAM, PENNSYLVANIA

THE Keith mansion, Graeme Park, dating from about 1720, is as stark and unornamented as its predecessors. Complex chimney forms are also typical of the early period, despite its date. The roof, a queer form of gambrel found only in Pennsylvania, is due probably to other influences than English, for Pennsylvania was early a colony filled with a medley of nationalities. One hazards the suggestion that Swedish influence determined the roof forms.

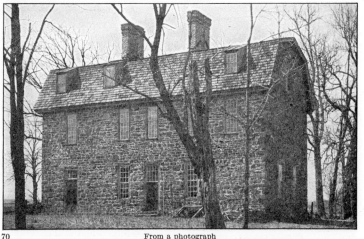

70   From a photograph

71   © Rau Studios, Inc.

THE STENTON HOUSE, PHILADELPHIA

In contrast with the Keith mansion, the Stenton house,
built 1728, is dominated by English classical influence,
noticeable in the bracketed cornice, the regular spacing
of windows, and the formal symmetrical composition.
There is, however, no ornament save the cornice. It is
a house bridging the
gap between the stark
simplicity of most of
the early work and
the dignified classi-
cism of the mid-
eighteenth century.

72   © Rau Studios, Inc.

THE OLD SWEDES CHURCH, WILMINGTON, DELAWARE

The Old Swedes Church, in Wilmington, Delaware (No. 72), bears, in
its masonry walls and the simplicity of its decorations, all the earmarks
of the earlier Pennsylvania style. (The upper part of the tower is much
later.) Its name is evidence of the mixture of peoples in the early colony,
although there is little in its design that can be pointed to as Swedish.

IMMANUEL CHURCH, NEW CASTLE, DELAWARE

Immanuel Church, at New Castle in Delaware, built, except the spire,
in 1704, is typical of all the early Church of England churches in this
region. Except for the transepts, which are much later additions, it is
a simplified rendition of contemporary English parish churches, with
many Gothic ideas still dominant, particularly the crenelated tower top.

73   © Frank Cousins

CHAPTER IV

EARLY COLONIAL IN THE SOUTH

A S the seventeenth century passed into the eighteenth the large plantation became more and more the striking feature of the life of Virginia, Maryland, and Carolina. This resultant of a combination of geographical and economic circumstances lent itself readily to an increase of ease, comfort and even luxury in living conditions. The vast distances between plantations, inadequately bridged by poor roads, necessitated the development of a complete social existence within the confines of each plantation. Hospitality flourished. The passing stranger was rare, and friends journeying by coach or horseback, on business or pleasure, made their stops with neighbors, even when only acquaintances, rather than at inns of which there were very few. Contemporary letters and books of travel give the impression of leisurely and comfortable country house life along the banks of the rivers. In a land where time was valueless and haste unknown, visitors stayed weeks and months rather than days, and the inevitable result was the stretching of the plantation homes to include commodious guest quarters, often in separate buildings.

In vivid contrast to the northern and middle colonies was the conspicuous absence of towns. In Virginia the sole exception was Williamsburg, founded in 1632, which, however, as late as 1750 boasted no more than two hundred houses, mostly of wood, and no paved streets. The absence of towns was the direct result of the self-sufficiency of the plantations, and their size was due, in turn, to the large individual grants of the Stuarts, made as inducements to colonization. The economic independence of the plantation is particularly noticeable in the method of shipping tobacco. The crop, which was the primary interest of the planter, was exported by each planter from his own wharf direct to England, the vessels on their return bringing such commodities as the plantation required. Thus the middleman and consequently the town was eliminated.

In Maryland, too, the town scarcely existed, the tidewater section consisting of a series of manors which were as self-sufficient as the plantations of Virginia, and which maintained many of the features of feudal England. Annapolis was only a village as late as 1750.

North Carolina, cultivating some tobacco in the north and some rice in the south, was, in its early days, scarcely more than frontier country into which the least prosperous and exemplary citizens of Virginia and South Carolina migrated. It was totally devoid of towns, with very few plantations or manors, and was populated almost entirely by small farmers living in rude dwellings.

South Carolina, though developing the plantation system, lacked the river facilities of Virginia, and a lucrative trade in rice and indigo resulted in the growth of a prosperous commercial center, Charleston, which had a population of 2,500 in 1680, ten years after its founding, and soon became the social and economic center of the colony. In this town, the single example of an urban community in the early South, many wealthy planters maintained town houses.

The center of southern colonial life, with this exception, was, therefore, and long remained, the country, and the life centers of the country were the great houses, the manors, the plantations, each, as far as possible, a self-supporting, self-contained, self-reliant entity. These, too, were naturally the architectural centers as well, and just as Boston and Salem and New Haven and Newburyport sought to become little replicas of English cities, so up and down the southern rivers the plantation builders erected imitations of the typical English manor of the period.

These imitations were at times remarkably close. With all the wealth of enormous plantations to support them, with abundant clay for bricks, with the finest of timber along the river banks, it was possible even in the seventeenth century to erect houses of a grandeur and a finish that New England or New York or Pennsylvania could not match till many decades later. Bacon's Castle (No. 74) is a salient example of the English Jacobean house in America; Fairfield, Carter's Creek (No. 76), is another; and without doubt, before the eighteenth century reconstruction which transformed so many of the plantations, dozens such stood along the rivers, representing in America some of the luxury of the England of the Restoration. Architecturally these houses show in their way, as early New England houses in theirs, the style roughly called Jacobean; a style in which Renaissance feeling is gradually creeping, leading sometimes to mere caricatures of the true classic, but which is still controlled by the Tudor Gothic tradition. Thus, in Carter's Creek there exist side by side a Tudor many-stacked chimney and a purely classic modillion (bracketed) cornice; similarly, in Malvern Hill (No. 80) with an exterior whose classic details belie its picturesque Gothic form, there was once, in the living room, paneling decorated with the Tudor linenfold. The same Gothic traditionalism finds expression often in the planning and composition of the manors, for the idea of the medieval Hall is embodied in several of the southern plantation houses, and in some there is a picturesqueness of outline and mass that is a direct legacy from earlier days.

Manorial in its houses, courtly and luxurious in its feudal social life, the seventeenth-century South could be nothing but orthodox Church of England in its religion. Parish churches were built, with the memory of English parish churches deep in the minds of the builders; no meetinghouses these, but obviously monuments of an official, sacerdotal, wealthy state religion. They are buildings primarily for worship, not for public meetings, often small in size, but carefully designed, expensively built, and frequently possessing the quiet intimate charm which characterizes so many of the rural churches of England. Of the early churches, Saint Luke's, in Smithfield, Isle of Wight County (No. 90), remains almost unchanged to show, in its Gothic buttresses and pointed arches, its quoined tower and little stucco pediment, that very mixture of quaint half-forgotten Gothic and erratic classic forms which proves that the southern colonies in church architecture, as well as in houses, remained for years true to the conservatism of their Jacobean tradition.

In the meanwhile, as plantations increased, the small tenant farmer and the small freeholder population increased also. For them, however, as the feudal plutocracy of the plantation area grew stronger and more organized, life became more and more difficult, and they pushed inland, pouring finally westward over the foothills of the Alleghanies, and south into the western portion of the Carolinas and even Georgia, there to mix with other English and Scotch and Irish and German immigration from the North.

The centuries have dealt harshly with their buildings; probably they were as simple, rude, and poor as the great houses were large and beautifully executed and rich. And as these people were gradually crowded out and sought for independence on the frontier, their places were taken by slaves, their cabins or huts fell into ruin and eventually disappeared; and the few that were left fell under the destructive waves of the Civil War. The architecture of the early colonial South is for us, therefore, inevitably an architecture of great houses and parish churches.

BACON'S CASTLE, SURREY COUNTY, VIRGINIA

In the time of Cromwell some English royalists came to Virginia where already successful men were beginning to enlarge their land holdings. In the latter years of the century an aristocracy was forming. Some large manor houses still stand in Virginia which show to what a high level of development seventeenth-century building was carried by the wealthy planters. Such

74　　From *Frank Leslie's Illustrated Weekly*, Sept. 8, 1866

is that strange structure, Bacon's Castle, built before 1676 (probably by Arthur Allen in 1654), whose chimneys with separate clustered flues, high roofs, and curved gable copings are all typical of Jacobean tradition.

BACON'S CASTLE, PLAN OF RESTORATION

A restoration, by Donald Millar, of the front of Bacon's Castle, reveals this medieval character more clearly than does the present condition. The sharp gable over the enclosed porch, with its little rectangular "ears," the simplicity of the brickwork, destitute of the least suggestion of classic ornament, and the mullioned and transomed leaded glass windows which were undoubtedly originally used in the large window openings, all have the look of Tudor England.

75　　Courtesy of *The Architectural Record*

FAIRFIELD OR CARTER'S CREEK, VIRGINIA

Another remarkable seventeenth-century manor was Fairfield, or Carter's Creek, Gloucester County, no longer standing. Built in 1692, it still retains the clustered chimney flues, set diagonally, the large roof surfaces, the rambling plan of an earlier century; but the classic modillion cornice shows how classic influence is beginning to seep in and modify the fine Tudor tradition.

76　　Courtesy of R. A. Lancaster, Jr., Richmond, Va.

Courtesy of the Charleston (S. C.) Museum

MIDDLETON PLACE, ASHLEY RIVER, SOUTH CAROLINA

MIDDLETON PLACE, on the Ashley River, S. C., is another of the old buildings whose form is reminiscent of the traditions and life of the England of James II. The curved gable ends were like those of many Oxford colleges. This large and imposing many-chimneyed house of a Carolina aristocrat is but one wing — the left — of the original plantation home. The rest was destroyed during Sherman's march northward from Savannah; and the whole must have rivaled in size many of the manor houses of England.

LANDGRAVE SMITH'S HOUSE, BACK RIVER, SOUTH CAROLINA

THE old Landgrave Smith Back River plantation house, built in the latter half of the seventeenth century, is another in which the struggle of Gothic and Renaissance ideals produces just that strange interest which attaches to English Jacobean work. A main building with stepped gables has a projecting porch wing, flanked by the lower one-story wings that may be later additions. It is all experimental, obviously transitional, but it has size and an elaborateness of conception that give it the true manor air, and remove it far from the simple rectangular schemes of most New England work.

78 From *Harper's Magazine*, Dec., 1875

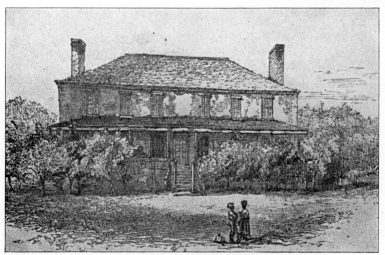

From *Harper's Magazine*, Dec., 1875

YEAMANS' HALL, SOUTH CAROLINA

FROM the Back River, Landgrave Smith moved to Yeamans' Hall, Goose Creek. Supposedly built before 1680, this mansion, solidly rectangular, with hipped roof and large end chimneys, is of much more developed style. Either because of the need for economy, or because of changing fashions in England, or both, gables and clustered chimney flues are abandoned, and a simple house is developed which is typical of the later, more classic eighteenth-century work.

MALVERN HILL, VIRGINIA

In Malvern Hill the development from the fine Jacobean of Bacon's Castle (No. 74) to the pure Renaissance of later work has progressed a step further. Chimneys are large, rectangular, simple. Cornices are of the classic type. Brick work is used in a careful sophisticated way, with that use of patterns which characterized early eighteenth-century brick work in

80   Courtesy of R. A. Lancaster, Jr.

Pennsylvania and New Jersey. Yet the L plan, with porch and porch chamber above, the simple arches of the porch, without moldings, the lack of columns or pilasters anywhere, are all in the older tradition.

THE MULBERRY, GOOSE CREEK, SOUTH CAROLINA

In the Mulberry, Goose Creek (No. 81), the Jacobean tradition found a belated and fantastic expression. It was built about 1714. Around a house of early eighteenth-century type, with double pitched roof, classic dormers, and a porch showing dawning classic influence, are grouped four square turrets whose fantastic and broken roofs, strongly Jacobean in character, with their curves and their tall weather vanes, give the whole a unique combination of monumental effect and picturesqueness.

81   From a photograph, courtesy of Ulrich B. Phillips, Ann Arbor, Mich.

THOROUGHGOOD HOUSE, YORKTOWN, VIRGINIA

For the Adam Thoroughgood house (No. 82) in Yorktown, Virginia, some claim a date of 1640, a claim that seems hardly possible, even if dormers and chimney tops of this house are considered later additions. Yet the crude taperings of the great end chimneys and the very high pitched roof are typically seventeenth-century English, and the type is one that became frequent in smaller southern work. Here lived the owner of a "tidewater" plantation, the master of slaves.

82   Courtesy of R. A. Lancaster, Jr.

THE "HOUSE WITH THE CUPOLA," EDENTON, NORTH CAROLINA

THE house built in Edenton, N. C., in 1758, by Francis Corbin, the agent of Earl Granville, the Lord Proprietor, is a strange monument to southern conservatism. Here, after the middle of the eighteenth century, is a fully developed Jacobean overhang, with a gable — a "lucomb"— in the center of the roof. It has the end chimneys usual in the South. It suggests that probably there were once in the southern colonies many such timber houses with the old English gables and overhangs.

83   Courtesy of the North Carolina Historical Commission, Raleigh

84   Courtesy of R. A. Lancaster, Jr.

BEWDLEY, VIRGINIA

BUT brick was not the only material of southern manors. Many were of timber, many resemble work in New England, but some are markedly different. Contrary to the general theory that steep roofs belong to

snowy countries, it was in Virginia that the height of peaked roof received its most astonishing development. Bewdley, Va., an early eighteenth-century building (except, of course, the obviously later porch) has a roof with two tiers of dormers, that give it almost a German appearance, and the height of the roof necessitates a strange and awkward lankiness to the crudely tapered end chimneys.

GUNSTON HALL, FAIRFAX COUNTY, VA.

THIS exaggerated roof height persisted occasionally until a late date. Gunston Hall, on the Potomac, has a roof whose height produces again the awkward lankiness of unsupported chimney, and makes its late date — 1751 — almost unbelievable. The porch, too, which seems to be original, is full of Jacobean feeling, and the only classic details visible are quoins and cornice and pedimented dormers. The building has been much altered.

85   From Martha J. Lamb, *The Homes of America*, New York, 1879

86   From a photograph by H. P. Cook

TUCKAHOE, GOOCHLAND COUNTY, VIRGINIA

MANY a southern planter journeyed to England and, returning to America, brought back the latest fashions of the mother country. Sometimes in their mansions are reflected the changing architectural taste that marked the passing of the style of the Stuart period and the introduction of the classicism of the Georges. In Tuckahoe, Va., built about 1730, Jacobean influence remains only in the H-shaped plan, in which the central bar of the H has on each floor only one large "hall" of the true old English type. In all exterior detail, classic influence is supreme. Tuckahoe is famous for its old hedged gardens.

87   From a photograph by H. P. Cook

STRATFORD, WESTMORELAND COUNTY, VIRGINIA

STRATFORD, famous as the birthplace of Robert E. Lee, was built between 1725 and 1730. Like Tuckahoe it has a plan of Jacobean character — a central hall with wings forming an H, and details in which classic influence is dominant. There is, however, Jacobean tradition here even in the chimneys — four separate flues in each carried up and joined at the top with classic arches. The simple brick detail of the pedimented door is carved out with great delicacy and skill. As usual, outside service buildings completed the composition; only one of the four symmetrically placed is here shown.

JENKINS' HOUSE, EDISTO ISLAND, SOUTH CAROLINA

The Jenkins' house, Edisto Island, S. C., by comparison with the houses that have preceded, is in a new style. Despite the early date, 1683, there are in it no signs of the Jacobean tradition, no visible elements of Gothic persistence. It is all in the newer Renaissance manner. Severely symmetrical, simply formal, with framed arched window on the stair-landing over a central rear entrance, with stone quoins (corner stones), and with classic cornice, its design bears eloquent witness to the new formalism and classicism that, in America as in England, marked the transition from the seventeenth to the eighteenth century.

YORK HALL (NELSON HOUSE), YORKTOWN, VIRGINIA

Somewhat similar in simple formality is the Nelson house — the headquarters of Lord Cornwallis during the siege — in Yorktown, built in 1740. But here classicism has gone one step further; windows are seg-

mentally arched, with stone keystones, and a gabled roof treated like a pediment takes the place of the earlier hip or more simply molded gable. The whole has been recently restored, and now one can obtain in garden and house some idea of the original state. No longer tentative, experimental, romantic, a lonely manor preserving a precarious grandeur in a wilderness, it is a great man's house in a well-established, civilized community.

ST. LUKE'S CHURCH, SMITHFIELD, VIRGINIA

If the Jacobean tradition is easily recognizable in southern houses, an earlier Gothic tradition is amazingly illustrated in one of the Virginia churches, St. Luke's, at Smithfield, the earliest brick church now standing in America. Stepped gables, Gothic buttresses with splayed offsets, a square entrance tower, and especially the pointed arched windows with true brick tracery, all are traditionally Gothic. Only quoins on the tower, occasional round arches, and a queer stucco pediment over the door give a hint of Renaissance. The whole has a strangely un-American look.

ST. PETER'S CHURCH, NEW KENT COUNTY, VIRGINIA

St. Peter's Church was built in 1703. Classic influence is more obvious than in St. Luke's, Smithfield. Buttresses have disappeared, round arches are more important, moldings of a semi-classic character are used to crown tower and church. Yet the projecting strips at the corners of the towers are strictly Gothic in feeling, and even the crude urns that top them are really Gothic finials in idea, though early classic in detail. Like St.

91   Courtesy of R. A. Lancaster, Jr.

Luke's, St. Peter's has the character of many rural parish churches in the English countryside.

92   Courtesy of the Charleston (S. C.) Museum

ST. JAMES' CHURCH, SANTEE, SOUTH CAROLINA

St. James' Church at Santee, built in 1768, is entirely in the classic manner. But the Wren influence is totally absent, and the brick columns with their crude brick capitals give the whole a tentative transitional charm that belies the correct classicism of cornice and pediment and round arched door and windows. This crudity is, however, the result not of any lingering Gothic tradition — that had passed away — but of the exigencies of local materials. Future building could only be in line with pure academic eighteenth-century traditions.

INTERIOR, CHRIST'S CHURCH, LANCASTER COUNTY, VIRGINIA

Christ's Church, Lancaster County, Virginia, built in 1732, preserves an almost unchanged interior unique in this country. Although the detail is Renaissance in character, the effect is full of Jacobean and Gothic survivals. The double arched reredos is Jacobean in character; the cross-shaped plan with complete transepts Gothic; the placing of the pulpit in the middle of the church, across the transept from the altar, is characteristic of medieval rather than Renaissance usage. Old square pews, little transept galleries with small paneled fronts, quaint woodwork, crude plaster vault, combine to give that surprisingly English character so often found in the South.

93   Courtesy of R. A. Lancaster, Jr.

CHAPTER V

LATER COLONIAL IN THE NORTH

ECONOMIC life in eighteenth-century New England is marked by steady commercial development. The peace and prosperity which followed the Treaty of Utrecht, 1713, together with a growing relaxation in the execution of the Navigation Laws, inspired an increase in the trade of England's American colonies, augmenting the intercolonial commerce along the coast of America and with the West Indies. Exportation of raw products to England increased greatly; in return there was an enlarged importation of various English manufactured goods that were demanded by the growing population. This increase in trade brought about an extraordinary development in the ship-building industry in New England, and in the growth and prosperity of the seaports and market towns. There resulted, inevitably, from all this, a rise in living standards and a new desire for luxury. Moreover, in 1684, the Massachusetts charter had been annulled, and in 1686 the royal governor had arrived; the beginning of the eighteenth century saw a great increase in the number of Englishmen of wealth and education who sojourned for a time in New England for official or commercial reasons.

All of this had a profound effect upon the building of the time. The royal officials wished to live in houses similar to those to which they were accustomed in England, where by this time, especially in the larger domestic work, the classic Renaissance ruled supreme. The Shirley-Eustis house in Roxbury (No. 103) shows how boldly and beautifully one of them — William Shirley, Governor, 1741–1749 and 1753–1756 — succeeded in realizing this wish, a success which wealthy citizens could not but emulate.

But more weighty than an importation of a fashion by great men from overseas was the development of the busy trade with England, and the opening of many shops in all the cities and important towns, dealing in all kinds of objects manufactured abroad. There were laces and silks and housekeeping necessities and jewelry for the mistress of the house, snuff boxes and weapons and buckles and watches for the master, and for the house itself clocks and mirrors and wall hangings of paper or cloth from France and England, and undoubtedly some furniture as well. There were books, too, for the New England public was a reading public, and among them were numbers of architectural books which furnished important models for the formation of the new architectural style. By them classicism was disseminated through the colonies, and mantels, cornices, doors, columns, and plaster ceilings were more and more patterned after the types shown in Swan's *British Architect* (1745), Batty Langley's *City and Country Builder's and Workman's Treasury of Designs* (1750), Kent's *Designs of Inigo Jones* (1727), Salmon's *Palladio Londonensis* (1734), James Gibbs' *Book of Architecture* (1753), Campbell's *Vitruvius Britannicus* (from 1717), and Ware's *Complete Body of Architecture* (1756). With such a body of English architectural literature present in the colonies soon after its English publication, it was small wonder that the classicism of the mother country spread swiftly, and found adequate expression in the colonial buildings.

Moreover, by the mid-eighteenth century the earlier Puritan fanaticism had largely burned itself out. The attempt to contain the growing and expanding life of New England within the rigid code that the early Puritan theocrats had sought to impose was proving a failure. The extreme Calvinism of the seventeenth century was getting out of adjustment with the needs of the eighteenth. The sceptical, intellectual humanism of eighteenth-century England was too powerful and too universal a movement not to have a deep influence on the English colonies. The disappearance of the most extreme forms of Puritanism at once opened the way for a great æsthetic development, for its departure left a deep seriousness of nature, an inquiring intellectual curiosity, and a high idealism that were admirably fitted to find artistic expression in works which evidence an almost universally sure, sane, and refined taste.

This new era of trade and increased shipping brought much wealth to New England, and upon it was founded during the century a new aristocracy; an aristocracy of ship captain and shipowner and merchant, who were seldom vulgar or ostentatious in their new-won power and wealth, because all alike were steeped in the background of Puritan intellectualism. And it was these men who filled New England, and especially New England port towns, with lovely houses of brick and stone and wood, and who furnished the money that built new churches to replace old and worn out meetinghouses — churches as rich and lavish as the meetinghouses had been plain and crude, and in whose design memories and perhaps engravings of the London churches of Sir Christopher Wren and James Gibbs played an always increasing, and finally completely dominant rôle.

Of importance in the development of New England architecture between 1725 and 1750 was a growing specialization of occupations. No longer was New England a country merely of farmers and fishermen and parsons; it had grown to be a fully developed commonwealth, with shopkeepers and innkeepers, skilled mechanics, printers, shipbuilders, carpenters, masons. The builders among them were trained men in the new style — the English classicism of Wren and his followers — trained either in England before their coming to America, or trained in this country by those who were English trained, to supply the demand for work in the current fashion. They were an alert and skillful lot of men, eager to learn, using the English builders' architectural books often and well. In the eighteenth century the names of men who were true architects begin to emerge.

So the classic Renaissance forms of the eighteenth century became common in New England, governed by English fashions and English taste, guided by English books. But the building materials were not English. The English built in stone and brick — preferably in stone. The New Englanders built in wood and brick, using stone sparingly. At first they merely strove to imitate the English stone forms in wood; later, as they grew in mastery of the classic forms, they were wise enough and skillful enough to modify these forms, where necessary, so as better to fit the materials at hand, just as they modified the planning of English types to fit the climate and local conditions.

The result was that mixture of solid substantial construction, dignified and classic detail, big simplicity of composition outside, and in the interior, paneling and mantelpiece and stairway, all characterized by a quiet beauty of composition and a delicacy and appropriateness of ornament, making eighteenth-century New England colonial Renaissance a style which moves the emotions of many people even to-day with a strength of appeal difficult to overestimate.

THE DUMMER HOUSE, BYFIELD, MASSACHUSETTS

THE Dummer house at Byfield, near Newburyport, shows classicism at last dominant. Pedimented dormer windows, bracketed cornice, decorative doorway, with its consoles and curved pediment, are all pure Renaissance. A new type of composition aiming at symmetrical dignity is evidenced, too, in the formal window scheme and the heavy end chimneys. Note that the ends of the house are masonry. The house dates from about 1715.

THE ROYAL HOUSE, MEDFORD, MASSACHUSETTS

IN the Royal house (No. 95), which had reached its present form before 1737, the formality is of a slightly different type. In the white panels between the windows and the white quoins at the corners there is an attempt to imitate in wood the stone forms of the English Renaissance, the natural result of the desire to make things as much like England as possible in a country where wood was the logical building material.

THE WARNER HOUSE, PORTSMOUTH, NEW HAMPSHIRE

IN the almost palatial McPhedris Warner house (No. 96), built about 1720, classicism reaches complete mastery. No longer tentative, as in the Royal house, it is here dominant, understood, carefully expressed. The broad chimneys are treated with skill; the dormers varied with alternation of curved and pointed pediments; and the whole topped with a fine balustrade at the break in the gambrel roof. The simple cupola is found in many houses built by wealthy shipowners in the seaport towns.

AN EIGHTEENTH–CENTURY DOORWAY

THE doorway of the McPhedris Warner house, in its simple dignity, its air of welcome, and the careful detail, is characteristic of many eighteenth-century doorways. The breaking of the cornice over the projection of the pilasters is typical of that *baroque* feeling of the Christopher Wren type of English Renaissance that was the chief inspiration of American eighteenth-century design.

97   From a photograph by Frank Cousins

98   From a photograph by Frank Cousins

A NEW ENGLAND SEAPORT MANSION, SALEM, MASSACHUSETTS

THE Cabot-Endicott-Low house (No. 98), built in 1748, shows another variation of the type of large mansion that filled the seaports of New England. It has the common gambrel roof, but the chimneys are not featured. Note the wood quoins, as in the Royal house (No. 95), and the typical pedimented dormers, with the central one slightly emphasized. The door, though correct in outline, is a modern reconstruction.

THE RICHARD DERBY HOUSE, SALEM, MASSACHUSETTS

THIS house, built in the final phase of the great French and Indian War, was a symbol of the growing economic and cultural life of the English colonies. In it the charm of red brick and white trim and green blinds and gray roof becomes a determining factor in the design. In the doorway note the imitation of stone joints in the wood trim.

99   From a photograph by Frank Cousins

THE JACOB WENDELL HOUSE, PORTSMOUTH, NEW HAMPSHIRE

THE Jacob Wendell house (No. 100), built in 1789, shows still a different treatment, with a hipped roof. Its cornice is particularly good, and its dormers unusually rich and large. Though smaller than most of the houses illustrated in this chapter, it is one of the richest; and the scrolled broken pediments of the dormers and the broken pediment of the door with its turned urn show unusually well the strength of the English *baroque* tradition. The smaller house beyond is an example of a simpler contemporary type.

THE MOFFATT–YARD–LADD HOUSE, PORTSMOUTH, NEW HAMPSHIRE

101   Courtesy of Rev. Alfred Gooding

THIS Portsmouth house (No. 101) is one of the few full three-story houses of the time in New England, dating from about 1761. The curved cornices of the windows are unusual examples of the ever continuing attempt to find simple, beautiful, and sincere wooden expressions for a tradition that originated in the stone forms of the English Renaissance. The simple dignity of the whole house is obvious. Note the little office building with its separate street entrance.

102   From a photograph by the Halliday Historic Photograph Co.

THE CUTTS, OR LADY PEPPERELL, HOUSE, KITTERY POINT, MAINE

THE house built after 1759 for Lady Pepperell has something of the official dignity which Sir William Pepperell so loved. In it the attempt to reproduce English stone forms in wood has become almost a vice. Yet the dignity of the pilasters, the richness of the door, and the simplicity of roof go far to make up for this deficiency. This house breaks away from the usual flat fronted five windowed scheme and the emphasis on a central motive is one more step on the road to monumental classicism.

THE SHIRLEY–EUSTIS HOUSE, ROXBURY, MASSACHUSETTS

THE Shirley-Eustis house, built about 1746, and later moved, carries the attempt to express Renaissance forms in wood to its logical conclusion. Its pilasters, coupled to emphasize the end bays of the house, its delicate round headed dormers, its crowning balustrade and cupola, and the heavy rustication of the door, lend weight to the tradition that the building was designed by an English rather than a colonial architect.

103   From a photograph by the Halliday Historic Photograph Co.

104   From a photograph by the Halliday Historic Photograph Co.

THE VERNON HOUSE, NEWPORT, RHODE ISLAND

THE Vernon Mansion, built in 1758 at Newport, reveals at its fullest development the desire to produce in wood the effect of monumental impressiveness. The wood walls, instead of being built of clapboards or shingles, are covered with boards cut and fitted to represent cut stone.

THE LEE MANSION, MARBLEHEAD, MASSACHUSETTS

THE Jeremiah Lee house was built three years after the Stamp Act. To study such a house, reproducing with beauty and a fine dignity the architectural taste of the mother country, is to get a vision of the cultural ties that bound the colonies to England. The war which broke out in 1775 found many Americans unable to espouse the Revolutionary cause and whose inherited loyalty to Britain remained unshaken.

105   From a photograph by Frank Cousins

OLD SQUARE WOODEN HOUSE, JAMAICA PLAIN, MASSACHUSETTS

THE love of balustrades as a crowning motif led eventually to the use of flat roofs, and the placing of the balustrade directly over the cornice. This is a type much developed in early post-Revolutionary days, and was accompanied by continually increasing refinement of detail and proportion. An early example of the quiet beauty of this type is shown by this house on the Moses Williams estate in Jamaica Plain.

106   From a photograph by Frank Cousins

THE GOVERNOR HANCOCK HOUSE, BOSTON, MASSACHUSETTS

UNIQUE in New England, the Hancock house (No. 107) in Boston, destroyed in 1860, was built throughout of coursed granite. Though early in date, between 1737 and 1740, it was one of the largest, most magnificent and most advanced in style. But however grand, it is of the traditional five-window, gambrel roof, end chimney New England type. The decoration of the central window and its bracketed balcony convey a richness that is rare.

107   From a photograph by the Halliday Historic Photograph Co.

108   From a photograph by the Halliday Historic Photograph Co.

THE OLDEST HOUSE IN HADLEY, MASSACHUSETTS

CHARACTERISTIC of the persistence of the early tradition in the Connecticut valley is the Porter house (No. 108), at Hadley, Mass., built before 1700. Here the overhang appears both at front and gable ends, and the scrolled pedimented doorway has a multiplicity of moldings and breaks which is anything but classic in spirit. The general type is in the new fashion, but every detail executed in the spirit of Jacobean work.

EARLY WALL PANELING, NEWBURYPORT, MASSACHUSETTS

THIS chimney wall of a room in the Swett-Ilsey house in Newburyport, built about 1670, shows already in the late seventeenth century the beginning of the simple paneling that later became such a characteristic of colonial interiors. This paneling, however simple, is a tremendous advance on the simple planks set vertically, with moldings at the edges, that had been the rule before.

109   From a photograph by Frank Cousins

110   Courtesy of the Metropolitan Museum of Art, New York

SEVENTEENTH–CENTURY WALL PANELING

THIS room wall, from Newington, Connecticut, shows how even in the "far-away" border rich paneling had come into use in the seventeenth century. With all the richness of china cabinet and pilasters, there is a quaintness and *naïveté* about the carving of the little flowers above the pilasters which give the whole an additional charm.

PANELED ROOM, BRENTON–COE HOUSE, NEWPORT, RHODE ISLAND

THE fireplace side of a Newport room shows the typical framing of the fireplace by pilasters set on pedestals. The use of a door trim of curved moldings, like the unusually rich panel molds, the rich chair rail that stops short of the trim and pilasters are all characteristic of the earlier type of paneling. The whole room is unusually rich. The fireplace was probably originally without a mantel shelf. The house dates from about 1720.

111   Courtesy of Louis B. McCagg, New York

112   Courtesy of Rev. Alfred Gooding

AN EIGHTEENTH–CENTURY PARLOR, PORTSMOUTH, NEW HAMPSHIRE

THE parlor of the McPhedris Warner house is perfect Georgian colonial. The fireplace with its Dutch tiles and heavy surrounding molding, the chair rail and the unusually rich projecting panel moldings are true to English precedent. The mantel shelf and mirror are of much later date.

INTERIOR, JEREMIAH LEE MANSION, MARBLEHEAD

THIS interior from the Lee house at Marblehead, built 1768, shows a later, more refined fireplace. The added richness of the cornice and the use of beautifully carved Corinthian capitals show a later date. The door trims of the flatter architrave type and the simple sunk panel molds are more usual in American work than the heavier moldings of the Brenton-Coe house. Note, too, that the fireplace wall is the only one paneled for its entire height; the side walls have wainscots only.

113   From a photograph by Frank Cousins

114   From a photograph by Frank Cousins

THE "MAHOGANY ROOM," LEE MANSION, MARBLEHEAD

The "mahogany room" (really painted and grained) at the Lee mansion is the most lavish of existing New England interiors. The unusually rich and complex fireplace carving shows that mixture of French *rocaille* (shell) and English forms which was popularized in England by Thomas Chippendale. Its design was taken almost line for line from Plate 51 of Swan's *British Architect*, 1745.

INTERIOR, THE LINDENS, DANVERS, MASSACHUSETTS

THE Lindens, built in 1752, rivals the Lee house in the richness and beauty of its interior. This interior, stained and waxed to show the beauty of the wood, is one of the finest, though not the most lavish, that eighteenth-century New England has left us. The decorative carving of the marble fireplace facing is noticeable, as well as the corner pilasters, the carving of the moldings and the lack of mantel shelf.

115   From a photograph by Frank Cousins

116   Courtesy of Rev. Alfred Gooding

AN EIGHTEENTH–CENTURY STAIRWAY, PORTSMOUTH, NEW HAMPSHIRE

IT was in stairway design that the eighteenth century produced some of its most noteworthy successes. In the Moffatt-Yard-Ladd house in Portsmouth, the hall has been developed into a real room, of which the stairs are the main feature. Like all these developed eighteenth-century stairs, this has rich turned balusters, decorated step ends, and the soffit (the underside), where it shows, is richly paneled in plaster.

THE MAHOGANY STAIRWAY, LEE MANSION, MARBLEHEAD

THE Lee house stair hall is as preëminent in its way as the "mahogany room." The richness of the openwork carved twisted newel, the combination of paneled step ends with carved scrolls, and the decoration of the walls above the dado with old wall paper, combine to make a whole that is remarkable for richness and dignity. A comparison of this with Nos. 43 and 44 in Chapter III shows the enormous advance made in design. The eighteenth century uses "open string," with balusters down to the steps; the seventeenth century the "closed string," with the step ends hidden.

117   From a photograph by Frank Cousins

From a photograph by Frank Cousins

KING'S CHAPEL, BOSTON

OLD King's Chapel, 1753, even without the colonnade, which is a later addition, had in its masonry walls, its stalwart tower whose spire was never built, and its simple hipped roof, all the monumental dignity which its position as the first official Church of England church in Boston demanded. This chapel was designed by one of the best of the early architects, Peter Harrison, of Newport.

INTERIOR, KING'S CHAPEL

THE interior of King's Chapel has not only dignity, but also great richness in Corinthian columns, the curved ceiling, and the lovely pulpit. The design of the interior follows Wren's London precedent more closely than does that of the exterior. Note the "Palladian" window in the chancel over the altar, and the box pews.

119 From a photograph by the Halliday Historic Photograph Co.

From a photograph

THE OLD SOUTH MEETINGHOUSE, BOSTON

THE Old South Meetinghouse, 1729, is one of the finest American churches of the eighteenth century. In it we get the beginning of the typical New England spire. This was a development of the church towers designed by Christopher Wren for London churches after the Great Fire; but in New England the tendency was towards greater simplicity, greater lightness, and greater importance for the spire proper, the topmost sloping section.

THE FIRST BAPTIST CHURCH, PROVIDENCE, RHODE ISLAND

THIS is perhaps the best of the developed colonial churches in the North. Designed by one Joseph Brown, it has a dignified simplicity of arched windows and pedimented doors, of quoined corners and well proportioned cornices, of tower and spire, soaring, rich and yet quiet, that rank it high among colonial buildings. It was built in 1775.

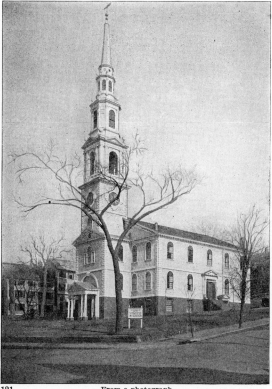

121   From a photograph

122   From a photograph

THE CONGREGATIONAL CHURCH, FARMINGTON, CONNECTICUT

THIS church (No. 122) is famous as one of the earliest to have the delicate white steeple on open arches that later became such a common feature of New England churches. It is most characteristic of the churches of the smaller towns, and represents a type which persisted well into the nineteenth century.

A STREET IN SALEM, ABOUT 1765

THE early official buildings of the northern colonies were simple and small, for the churches — true meetinghouses — served for all the larger gatherings. This simple gabled courthouse in Salem, built 1718, is typical. The one universal touch which distinguishes public from private buildings is the cupola. This sketch, made by a Dr. Orne about 1765, shows also the brick houses along the street, and with them earlier wooden houses. The large brick three-story house should be compared with that in Lincoln, England, shown in No. 1.

123   From Dr. Orne's contemporary water-color sketch in Essex Institute Museum

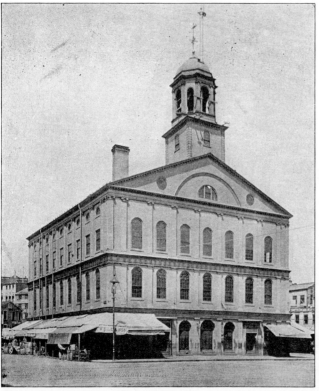

124   From a photograph

FANEUIL HALL, BOSTON

WHEN Peter Faneuil gave this great hall to the city of Boston, a form was chosen which was common in England; a public market on the first floor, a town hall for meetings above. It was built in 1742. The present state of the building is not exactly as it originally was, for the hall was burned in 1761, rebuilt in 1764 and enlarged in 1805. But the dimensions and the architectural quality were preserved. A corner of the original building shows in the view of the Old Feather Store (No. 51). Like all colonial public buildings it has the cupola, and despite its large size retains a simplicity of form that barely escapes monotony.

INTERIOR, FANEUIL HALL

THE interior of Faneuil Hall has the simplicity and classicism of the exterior. It is really simply an enlarged church interior; the gallery scheme is one found equally in churches. That the designer had not really appreciated the opportunities the large interior afforded is shown by the scale of the enormous rosette in the center of the ceiling. But despite that the hall has a simple beauty that made it a fitting frame for the stirring events that took place in it, and resulted in it being called the "Cradle of Liberty."

125   From a photograph by Baldwin Coolidge

THE OLD STATE HOUSE, NEWPORT, RHODE ISLAND

THE Old State House in Newport, built in 1739 and supposedly designed by Richard Munday, bears in the tiny scale of the stone quoins and arches and bands, in the awkward tops of its gables, and in the queer circular openings that crowd them, obvious evidence that its designer, confronted suddenly by a problem other than the typical house or church, was at sea. It is only when the problem is familiar, as in doors, the decorated window, and dormers, that the customary sureness of touch

126   Courtesy of the Society for the Preservation of New England Antiquities, Boston

is achieved. The front entrance with its balcony should be compared to that of the Hancock house in Boston (No. 107), which it closely resembles.

127   From a photograph

THE OLD CITY HALL, NEWPORT, RHODE ISLAND

IN the City Hall at Newport, built in 1762, the ascendant classicism of the eighteenth century reaches its triumphant completion. A composition so Palladian, so obviously the result of study not only of English but of Italian Renaissance, so correct in proportion and detail, seems "bookish," and lacks the vitality and vivid personality of earlier less intellectualized designs. It is almost more a formula than a living work of art. It was designed by Peter Harrison, also the architect of King's Chapel in Boston.

CHAPTER VI

LATER COLONIAL IN THE CENTRAL COLONIES

THE commercial development following the Peace of Utrecht which meant so much to New England, was equally marked in the provinces of New York. New Jersey, Delaware and Pennsylvania. New York had always been a trading center; the English government that had followed the Dutch, and the new prosperity of the eighteenth century did not change that. It is, indeed, astonishing that the change from Dutch New Netherlands to English New York involved so little break in the economic and social development. The city of New York, it is true, changed slowly from a Dutch to an English town, but Albany and many of the Hudson River settlements remained dominantly Dutch. The English, moreover, were scrupulous in preserving the Dutch property rights and the old Dutch manorial system was soon paralleled by a new English aristocracy. The persistence of Dutch names down to the present time is an indication of the strength of Dutch tradition.

Yet the new century brought to New York as to New England and Virginia new architectural ideals and forms. It is perhaps this change to the pure classic Renaissance of the eighteenth century which masks the change from Dutch to English architectural dominance. It is certain that the new classic inspiration was from the classic of England and not the continental rococo of Holland, although Dutch influence persisted long in certain traditions of roof type and dormer, and in certain quaintnesses of interior detail. Even the Dutch manor houses are English in design, while such houses as the Apthorpe (No. 137) and the Morris (Jumel) (No. 136) houses in New York, built by English families, are among the most classic and most monumental examples of English Renaissance that existed in the colonies. Only in out-of-the-way villages up and down the Hudson and around the bays of Long Island, Dutch influence continued long supreme.

Just as the English influence absorbed the Dutch in New York, so in New Jersey and Delaware and Pennsylvania it absorbed Swedish and German influences, or else pushed them back into the interior where large areas are still predominantly German. The *saals* of the German community at Ephrata in Pennsylvania show how typically Teutonic were many of the architectural forms. But along the coast and in the large cities, all was English.

During the eighteenth century Philadelphia became one of the great cultural centers of the American colonies, famous for its wealth and aristocracy. To Stenton and Graeme Park succeeded Cliveden (No. 146), the Morris house (No. 144), and the Bartram house (No. 145). It was a center whose close association with England, with aristocratic and wealthy England, is shown again and again in Franklin's *Autobiography*, and attested by the Tory attitude of many of its inhabitants during the Revolution.

It is typical of Philadelphia that there, in 1731, Franklin and some of his friends founded a subscription library — the Library Company of Philadelphia — that was to enjoy a long and prosperous history. The large number of architectural books it possessed early in its life shows how important a place architecture held in the mind of the educated people of the time — a fact borne out by the importance of architectural articles and

64

pictures in the contemporary *Columbian Magazine*. In its catalogue for 1770, for instance, the Library Company lists twenty-seven books purely architectural, including such diverse titles as Ware's *Palladio* (1738), Halfpenny's *Useful Architecture* (1752), *Perspective Made Easy* (1735), Ball's *Antiquities of Constantinople* (1729), Inigo Jones' *Stone-Heng* (1725), Montfaucon's *Antiquities of Italy* translated by Henley (1725), and even Stuart and Revett's *Antiquities of Athens*, Vol. I (1762). In the 1789 catalogue appears the great book of Robert and James Adam, *Works in Architecture* (1773); in that of 1794, William and James Pain's *British Palladio* (1790), and Soane's *Plans, Elevations, and Sections of Buildings* (1788). It is significant of the popular interest in architecture that when, in 1798, the Library Company put some of its volumes in circulation, a large number of these architectural books were included.

This naturally made a profound effect upon the architecture of the city. It gave birth to a spirit of dignified, established, European classicism strong at times to the point of heaviness. There was a sense of monumental composition elsewhere unknown; the provincial capitol building was the largest and finest state house in the colonies. Other public buildings in Philadelphia — Carpenter's Hall (No. 150), the Hospital (No. 231), the Market Halls — show an architectural quality equally marked. It is characteristic of Philadelphia that it not only had more paved streets than any other American city, and the earliest system of street lighting, but also a street plan carefully thought out and unparalleled in its regularity. It is the characteristic Philadelphia feeling for monumental effect which makes Christ Church (No. 154) one of the finest, if not the finest, of colonial churches. Philadelphia, moreover, was never completely subject to the tradition, so universal farther north, of the "five-bay house" — in the Bartram house or Cliveden, for instance, there is no trace of it — and the Philadelphia houses have therefore a variety and an English solidity that is peculiarly their own.

But Pennsylvania architecture was no mere copy of English work, although dominated by English fashions. Just as local traditions of planning and the local material, wood, modified the classicism of New England, so here local traditions and materials produced new forms and effects. One of the most important of such local peculiarities is the use of brickwork laid in Flemish bond. In this bond each course consists of bricks so laid that their long edges and short ends alternate, and over each long brick or stretcher the course above has the short end or header. This is a common bond, but in Pennsylvania work the interesting pattern to which it gives rise is emphasized by making all the headers either markedly lighter or markedly darker than the stretchers. The whole interesting color of such a wall is furthermore both relieved and accented by the universal use of solid white window shutters.

Another local characteristic even more important is the use of a projecting hood between the windows of the first and second stories to protect the lower windows and the entrance door from the weather, and furnish, as it were, a narrow porch without columns. This so-called "Germantown hood" is found in New Jersey as well as in the suburbs of Philadelphia, where it is exceedingly common.

But these local peculiarities, important as they are, in comparison with those of other portions of the country seem negligible. It is the English tradition that dominates; it is English Georgian classicism that is characteristic of the colonial eighteenth-century architecture in those regions that were under the cultural sway of Philadelphia.

128   From a photograph by John A. Wilson

A HOUSE UNDER THE PALISADES, NEW JERSEY

THE more primitive and simple the building, the less chance there is for the appearance of national characteristics. The main part of this little house under the Palisades bears a strong resemblance to some of the early houses of Massachusetts and Connecticut. But in the lower wing there is in the sweeping roof overhanging the porch a positive sign of Dutch influence. Such as this, undoubtedly, were the majority of the houses along the Hudson well on to Revolutionary times.

129   From a photograph by John A. Wilson

A HOUSE IN HACKENSACK, NEW JERSEY

A LATER, more developed, type of Dutch house is this example from Hackensack. The combination of masonry and frame construction, the low-pitched gambrel roofs, and the small square windows in the upper stories that are just above the floor, are all characteristic of much of eighteenth-century Dutch colonial work. The use of the Dutch type of gambrel roof persisted well into the nineteenth century.

THE DITMARS' HOMESTEAD, FLATBUSH, NEW YORK

A HIGHLY developed Dutch form is seen in the Cornelius Ditmars house in Flatbush. The sweeping curve of the roof which forms eaves so wide as to be almost a porch, and the use of very wide shingles for walls instead of the clapboards more usual in New England, are unmistakable. The lower slope of the gambrel

130   From a photograph by Frank Cousins

is about 45 degrees and the upper about 30 degrees. This is the universal pitch for Dutch gambrels, and easily differentiates them from others, whose lower slopes are much steeper.

131   From a photograph by A. V. Card

THE PHILIPSE MANOR HOUSE, YONKERS, NEW YORK

MUCH doubt exists as to the precise date of the Philipse Manor house at Yonkers. It was probably built some time about the middle of the eighteenth century. Its strong massive simplicity might suggest an earlier date, but the dominant classicism of its details, and the fact that Dutch influence has so completely yielded to the British influence make it probable that it is not much earlier. The glory of the house is its interior; like so many of the isolated manors, the exterior is treated in the simplest, starkest manner save for the door. Such were the houses of the great feudal aristocracy that in English as in Dutch times owned and governed large areas along the Hudson.

RECEPTION ROOM, PHILIPSE MANOR

THE reception room of the Philipse Manor house, with its lavish carving and decorated plaster ceiling so full of the broken curves that came into English architecture from French sources, expresses in every line of its rich decoration the courtly quality that characterized the feudal manors of the Hudson River. Here were held the stately functions of the past.

132   From a photograph by A. V. Card

133   From a photograph by Frank Cousins

THE VAN CORTLANDT MANSION, NEW YORK

THE eighteenth-century aristocracy cultivated restraint as well as good manners. The Van Cortlandt Manor house in Van Cortlandt Park, New York, is even more simple, more unassuming than Philipse Manor to the north. The only ornament is in the pedimented dormers, and in the strange grotesque masks carved on the keystones of the window arches. The porches, obviously an addition, with little artistic relation to the masonry walls, are the only elements that show Dutch influence. It was built in 1748.

SCHUYLER MANSION, ALBANY, NEW YORK

IN the Schuyler house in Albany we get the final absolute dominance of the English taste. Built in 1761, it has a "Chinese Chippendale" balustrade over the cornice, a classical modillion cornice, and the charm of proportion of the typical New England house. But it is longer, seven windows across the front, instead of five; and in its severe simplicity — for even the polygonal porch is a later addition — it shows the persistent love of exterior quiet that is evidenced at Yonkers and Van Cortlandt Park.

134   From a photograph by Rau Studios, Inc.

135   From a photograph by Frank Cousins

FRAUNCES' TAVERN, NEW YORK

Fraunces' Tavern shows to-day only what its brilliant restorer imagined to be its former and original state. In the main the restoration is probably accurate, and its appearance gives an idea of the New York of the period, a New York of red brick and white trim, of classic doorways, with here and there little persistent echoes of Dutch tradition, as here in the type of the dormer windows. The tavern was built originally in 1719, when New York was little more than an overgrown commercial village.

JUMEL MANSION, NEW YORK

THE Morris (Jumel) mansion that so proudly overlooks the Harlem River in New York is in many ways exceptional. Built in 1765, it anticipates post-Revolutionary development not only in the elaboration of its plan, but also in its full two story portico, which is the only example of such a porch that can be surely dated prior to the Revolution. The slimness of the column proportions is also ahead of the time. The doorway trim is of later date. Otherwise the front of the house is a typical five-bayed English type colonial house. This dwelling was eleven years old when Washington's battalions abandoned Manhattan Island to the redcoats.

136   © Detroit Publishing Co.

THE APTHORPE HOUSE

THE Apthorpe house (No. 137) that once stood in New York is another unusual house. Kimball calls it the "most architectonic of the group"; and certainly the use of pilasters and engaged columns, the subtle breaking out of the central bay with its pediment, and the unusually monumental effect of the contrast of small square windows above, with tall slim pedimented windows below, reveal a sophistication which is unusual in pre-Revolutionary work. The recessed porch should be compared with "Hampton" (No. 176).

137   From a photograph in the New York Historical Society

138   From *Harper's Weekly*, July 17, 1880

THE OLD SUGAR HOUSE, NEW YORK

NEW YORK long retained a mixture of English and Dutch characteristics. Even now an occasional gambrel remains in out-of-the-way corners. The Old Sugar house (No. 138), used as a prison during the Revolution, shows how much more striking these contrasts were forty years ago. The Old Sugar house has a coped gable like that of the Billop house (No. 65), and to the left is a two-storied building with pedimented dormers in the English tradition.

PHILADELPHIA BRICK

FURTHER south, in Delaware, southern New Jersey and Pennsylvania, it is the brick tradition of Philadelphia which rules. With English, Swedes, Germans and a few Dutch, that section of the country was the earliest "melting pot"; yet save in sporadic examples, the dominant English tradition of the metropolis, Philadelphia, was more and more the rule. This house in Dover, Delaware, built in 1728, shows the type; variegated brick walls, laid in Flemish Bond, a classic cornice, dormers with pediments, and solid wood paneled shutters. The glazed door with the hood is modern.

OLD HOUSES, SALEM, NEW JERSEY

THESE old houses from Salem, New Jersey, show similar spirit, but stucco takes the place of brick. The long hood or penthouse roof over the first story windows and door, forming a little porch, on the house at the left, is a common feature, particularly in Germantown, whence its common name "Germantown hood."

FRAME HOUSE IN IMITATION OF BRICK

THE Philadelphians were early

140   From a photograph by Frank Cousins

alert in matters of architecture. *The Pennsylvania Magazine* of 1775, for instance, reproduces from some London source an illustrated account of a new way of building frame houses so as to look like brick, by the use of a rebated tile. This manner of building is not known ever to have been used in this country; but the

space devoted to it reveals a cultivated popular taste. And the five-windowed three-story house, with quoined corners, is a type that was, with slight modifications, immensely popular. Fittingly Philadelphia, the largest city of the colonies and the home of a brilliant society, was in the forefront of the movement to introduce new ideas of construction and decoration from abroad.

COMBE'S ALLEY, PHILADELPHIA

PHILADELPHIA had early long rows of closely built streets, such as Combe's Alley (No. 142). Heavy classic cornices and pointed dormers and solid shutters give at once the Philadelphia atmosphere, but what contributes more than anything else is the typical Flemish Bond brickwork, where the headers — the brick ends that are exposed — are burned with a glaze so that they count strongly. Now down at heel and in disrepair, houses like these were once the home of most of Philadelphia's thriving population of merchants and professional men.

142   From a photograph by Frank Cousins

143   From a photograph by Rau Studios, Inc.

THE JOHNSON HOUSE, GERMANTOWN, PENNSYLVANIA

THE detail of the Johnson house doorway (1765–68) shows shutters, hood, pediment and the simplicity of the six panel door with its transom light above. The seats flanking the door add still more to the porch feeling that the pediment above indicates. Notice, too, the way the stone is laid; long narrow squared stones but laid in unequal courses, and of unequal length. This is but one of many beautiful ways in which this stone was used.

THE MORRIS HOUSE, GERMANTOWN

THIS lovely house, once Washington's headquarters, is a more sophisticated and highly developed example of Germantown work. The columns that flank the white paneled doorway, the carefully finished cornice, the unusually decorative dormers, with arched windows, all contribute to the classical feeling that distinguishes it from most of its neighbors. Its classicism is characteristic of the Philadelphia neighborhood, but its highly developed charm seems to owe something to influence from New England. This blend of dignity and intimacy constitutes the peculiar quality of Germantown work.

144   From a photograph by Rau Studios, Inc.

145   From a photograph by Frank Cousins

THE JOHN BARTRAM HOUSE, PHILADELPHIA

Of the great houses in or near Philadelphia the Bartram house shows how even in 1731 a truly urban magnificence was sought. John Bartram is supposed to have done much of the work on it with his own hands. This may account for its unusual plan and detail. He did not finish the carving till 1770. In its design there is evident a desire to reproduce as far as he was able the monumentality and the rather *baroque* richness of detail which characterized the English Renaissance of Wren and Gibbs.

THE CHEW HOUSE (CLIVEDEN), GERMANTOWN

Cliveden in Germantown (No. 146), built in the seventeen sixties, shows a further development of the Pennsylvania great house. In it classicism is dominant, monumental effect the end sought. All of the detail is heavier than is usual further north, and the doorway is framed with a Doric order of Vitruvian correctness. Windows are large in scale, and capped with cut stone arches. The dormers have scrolled consoles at the sides. The overheavy urns on the gables are awkward attempts to

146   From a photograph by Philip B. Wallace

recreate in America an English fashion. Such a house eloquently bespeaks the stability and the culture of a people whom an uncompromising British government drove to revolution.

147   From a photograph by Philip B. Wallace

A CLASSIC MANSION IN PHILADELPHIA

Mt. Pleasant, built slightly earlier than Cliveden, and having many similarities to it, is even more successful. The arched chimneys and the balustraded roof are better than the Cliveden urns in giving interest to the roof, and the charming contrast of brick quoins and stucco walls and white trim as effective as the ashlar of Cliveden. The Palladian window over the entrance is used with a beautiful sense of proportion and fitness. The blocks in the window arch, and the heavy keystones of the entrance door, are due to the general heaviness of the contemporary British tradition.

THE STABLE AT WOODLANDS, PHILADELPHIA

THE strongly Renaissance classicism which marks such great houses near Philadelphia as the Morris house, Cliveden or Mt. Pleasant, shows itself equally in their necessary service buildings. The stable of Woodlands, 1788, has a dignity of mass, a rugged strength of detail, and a bold treatment of its masonry that makes it seem almost Italian.

148   From a photograph by Frank Cousins

149   From a photograph by Rau Studios, Inc.

AN EARLY GEORGIAN PENNSYLVANIA FIREPLACE

THOUGH the exterior of Governor Keith's mansion, Graeme Park, is early in style, the interiors are in the style of the Georgian of the eighteenth century. The overmantel is of a highly developed type, with *baroque* influence showing strongly in the broken pediment. The curved frieze and the dentil course of the main cornice, which is of the double or fret type, are unusual details. The projecting "keys" or croisettes at the corners of the overmantel and the door trim help to give this room its strongly English character. It should be compared with the Mt. Vernon room (No. 182).

MT. PLEASANT, PHILADELPHIA, SECOND FLOOR

A ROOM end on the second floor of Mt. Pleasant is as characteristic of the *baroque*, highly architectural interior of the mid-century as the interior of Graeme Park is typical of the early century. In the "rocaille" (shell) work at the top of the central panel, in carved consoles and broken pediments, this room shows strongly the influence of such English books as those of Chippendale and Batty Langley.

150   From a photograph by Frank Cousins

151 From the original drawing in the Emmet Collection, New York Public Library

TRINITY CHURCH, NEW YORK, IN THE REVOLUTION

THIS old view of the ruins of Trinity Church in New York shows the interesting fact that the church which burned during the Revolution was not Georgian Renaissance in style, but rather the English Renaissance designer's idea of Gothic. The tower has slightly projecting corner buttresses and pointed arches in the top stage, and the main windows, though round arched, have masonry — probably brick — mullions which divide them into pointed lights. This persistence of the Gothic idea in connection with churches all through the classic eighteenth century is a most interesting phenomenon. Compare St. Luke's, Smithfield (No. 90).

ST. PAUL'S CHAPEL, NEW YORK

ST. Paul's Chapel in New York shares with Christ Church, Philadelphia, the honor of being the finest example of English Renaissance church design in America. St. Paul's, built in the seventeen sixties, is particularly famous on account of its tower and spire. The transition from square to octagonal is handled with peculiar skill by the use of the clock with the pediment over and the consoles flanking it. The decoration of the pediment end over the Broadway portico is both quaint and beautiful. The traditions of this fine old church run back to those long war years when New York was the G. H. Q. of the British army in America.

152 From a photograph by Wurts Brothers

ST. PAUL'S CHAPEL, INTERIOR

THE interior of St. Paul's Chapel has a completely vaulted ceiling that gives it an unusually spacious and monumental effect. The pure classic character of the detail and the large Palladian window give it a character extremely close to that of such London churches as St. Martin's-in-the-Fields.

153 From a photograph by Wurts Brothers

PHILADELPHIA'S LARGEST COLONIAL CHURCH

CHRIST Church in Philadelphia was, it is said, designed by an amateur of learning, a Dr. Kearsley, who certainly vindicated his right to be called architect. Built of the rich, colored Pennsylvania brick, it has a warmth and personal quality which St. Paul's may lack. The frank expression of the interior galleries by the two stories of windows and pilasters is to be noted. The whole design has close resemblances to several London churches.

154   From a photograph by Rau Studios, Inc.

CHRIST CHURCH, FRONT ELEVATION

THE chancel end of Christ Church (No. 155), with the fine Palladian window, the quaint shield and portrait over the keystone, and the rich, carved panel above, is one of its greatest beauties. Niche and window and pilaster are composed in a way that gives an unusually effective sense of scale and size. But even so clever a designer as Dr. Kearsley could not resist the temptation of using urns too many and too large, which detract from the dignity here as much as

155   From a photograph by Frank Cousins

they do in Cliveden. The church was begun in 1727, but the final completion of the spire did not occur until 1754. The fine iron railing and gates date from 1795.

INTERIOR, CHRIST CHURCH

THE interior of Christ Church shows the sturdy classicism of the exterior. The unusually large scale of the arches that are supported by the Doric columns gives a certain clarity and simplicity of effect that is an excellent foil to the quiet richness of the chancel wainscot and Palladian window over the altar.

156   From a photograph by Rau Studios, Inc.

ST. PAUL'S CHURCH, EASTCHESTER, NEW YORK

THE old church at Eastchester is the best example now standing of the eighteenth-century country parish church of the central colonies. Its unusually high simple tower, picturesquely crowned with a cupola, is admirably designed to fit the quiet beauty of its surroundings.

THE FIRST MERCHANTS' EXCHANGE, NEW YORK

THERE is little remarkable about New York public buildings prior to the Revolution. The City Hall was a simple, unassuming structure, and there was no state house worth the name. This is the first Merchants' Exchange, erected 1752. It has the ubiquitous cupola of the northern public building, and a broad gambrel roof. This type of building with open arcades below and rooms above has an interesting genealogy that leads back through English municipal buildings to the late medieval "Market Cross."

158   From W. A. Duer, *Reminiscences of an Old New Yorker*, 1867

159   From a photograph by Philip B. Wallace

CARPENTERS' HALL, PHILADELPHIA

CARPENTERS' Hall (No. 159), built in 1772, is a much more monumental and sophisticated building. The dominant classicism of its cornice, arched windows with the balustrades below to give them added height and dignity, and the arched door and pediment all show the true Pennsylvania spirit applied to a public building. Carpenters' Hall was used for a time for meetings of the Continental Congress. The Carpenters' Company, who built it, was a sort of guild that not only controlled general prices, but kept the standard of work high. It early possessed a good architectural library.

AN OLD VIEW OF SECOND STREET, PHILADELPHIA, 1799

BIRCH's view of Second Street, north from Market, shows in the foreground a market house, with the crowd around its capacious archway; a large gambrel roofed building beyond with shops on its ground floor, then houses and Christ Church. The market house type, like that of the New York Merchants' Exchange, is unmistakably descended from the old English "Market Cross". Rather open, but still close built and entirely urban, with a sense of established culture and prosperity; such was Philadelphia at the time of the Revolution.

160   From William Birch, *Views of Philadelphia*, 1799

THE STATE HOUSE, PHILADELPHIA, IN 1799

BIRCH's view (No. 161) of the state house, Independence Hall, shows it as it stood for a long time without the upper part of the tower. The elaborate *baroque* clock at the gable end is interesting; it is merely a colossal variation in masonry of the usual tall clock of the period that decorated so many homes.

161   From William Birch, *Views of Philadelphia*, 1799

INDEPENDENCE HALL, PHILADELPHIA

INDEPENDENCE Hall (No. 162) in its present state is merely the completion of the entire scheme as originally projected. It was undoubtedly one of the finest of pre-Revolutionary public buildings in the colonies, preëminent by reason of its size and the dignity of its composition of main building, connecting arcades and lower wings. It is an original adaptation of forms developed in connection with domestic and church work to a scheme perfectly expressive of official dignity and its public function.

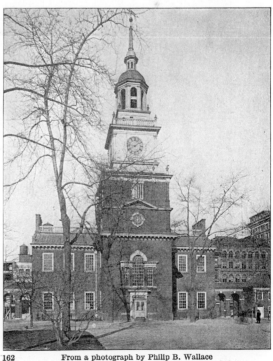

162   From a photograph by Philip B. Wallace

STAIRWAY, INDEPENDENCE HALL

THE interiors of Independence Hall are as fine as the exterior. In them, as no where else in the country, the full formal classic spirit of eighteenth-century English woodwork reaches its climax. Stair balusters are made heavier than in domestic work; great use is made of the full classic orders, but rich carving well applied takes away any purely impersonal coldness that the formality might otherwise have produced.

"DECLARATION HALL"

THE great panel or tablet over the dais, with its rich frieze carvings in the *baroque* style is a sufficient center for the room, and the twin fireplaces lead the imagination back to the time when the heating for the entire great room depended upon them. Outside and inside, the perfect unity of the building is a tribute to the skill of the architect, Andrew Hamilton, who probably had the assistance of Dr. Kearsley. The whole formed a fitting setting for that event destined to change the future of an energetic and capable people — the signing of the Declaration of Independence.

CHAPTER VII

LATER COLONIAL IN THE SOUTH

THE differences between the architecture of the North and the South during the eighteenth century are chiefly in matters of conception and composition; the similarities, on the other hand, are those of detail, particularly interior detail. It is not surprising that the common sources — English architectural books and English fashions — inspired similar details wherever their use was appropriate. The same paneling schemes, the same system of stair decoration, even the same molding profiles are found throughout the country; but general scheme and composition are affected by every change of climate or condition or material; and between New England and the Central Colonies and the South there were differences as vast in economic conditions and social systems as there were in climate.

The deeply founded aristocratic traditions of southern plantation life were not so much affected by the development of eighteenth-century trade as was sea-going New England or mercantile New York or Philadelphia. It was a culture innately conservative that was fostered in the manors along the James and the Potomac, the York and the Rappahannock. Changes came slowly. Aristocracy was so dominant, in fact, that there was continual internal friction between the planters of the coast districts and the poorer folk of the up-country; friction that even the winning of American independence could not dispel.

The governing aristocracy kept always in the closest touch with English developments. The proprietors of the great houses traveled frequently to England, and often their children went back to the mother country for their education More than one family of the Virginia and Maryland and Carolina plantations sent its sons to the English public schools and universities, and its daughters to London for a season or two. These young people, thus steeped at an impressionable age in English customs, traditions, and habits of appreciation, returned to the colonies keenly desirous of importing the best of everything they had seen and experienced in England. Moreover, the great wealth of many of the manors allowed the continuous importation from England of all sorts of objects of use or luxury. A quicker reaction to the growing classicism of English architecture than in the North was thus inevitable. This early classicism frequently conflicted with the innate conservatism of the locality; together with the separateness, the distance of one house from another, which made individualism of taste more important than community fashion, produced a strange condition that makes the dating of buildings, in the absence of written records, extremely difficult. So it happens that some of the houses of marked Jacobean character, shown in the last chapter, were built years after the completion of some of those of strong classical type that are shown later in this.

The eighteenth century brought to the South the real beginning of developed town living. Even the feudal conservatism of Maryland and Virginia and South Carolina could not forever withstand the economic pressure towards urban development which the inevitable commercial expansion of the time produced. Charleston, Baltimore, and Annapolis are particularly noticeable, and Charleston and Annapolis both produced local architectural types which are the direct result of climate and economic conditions. In low-lying Charleston, a house with a first floor set high was a necessity, and the warmth of the climate made a developed porch a desirable if not a necessary adjunct. In addition, the congestion of the fashionable residential sites along the Battery led to smaller houses more compactly planned, and size was gained by increased height. In more rural Annapolis, on the other hand, the desire of the house builders seems to be to reproduce the great houses of the plantations as closely as town conditions would permit. The result was a house with a large central block and low flanking wings closely related to it; a type to whose dignity and beauty many an Annapolis mansion bears witness.

The development of town life gave a new impetus, also, to church design and the construction of official buildings. St. Michael's Church, in Charleston, shows how in the cities the Wren tradition dominated eighteenth-century church building as completely in the South as in the North, just as Bruton Parish Church shows the persistence of the other more native, less formal and less urban tradition. Even the eighteenth-century public buildings in the South, with one exception, remained simple. In such a society, where government was so much a private and family matter, there was not the incentive that existed in the North for giving monumental expression to the idea of the state. Courts, however, were necessary, and Virginia is full of small colonial courthouses, whose charm is the charm of simple forms and a frank expression of the material. One of the exceptions to this universal simplicity is expressive of the popular interest in the government of Maryland. Through the vicissitudes of the proprietorship, and the sometimes successful and again unsuccessful efforts of the Crown to assume control of the colony, popular interest in the machinery of government never waned, and its continuous growth during the eighteenth century is typified by the much admired capitol. This famous Maryland State House at Annapolis can lay claim, along with Independence Hall in Philadelphia and the Old State House in Boston, to the honor of being the largest, the most highly developed, and the most architecturally beautiful of all pre-Revolutionary public buildings in the American colonies.

Meanwhile, far away on the Gulf coast, New Orleans was growing as the center of a new and different culture. Founded as a French colony in 1718, it never lost its dominant French character; the long years of Spanish control from 1762 to 1802 only served to give it a culture even more deeply Latin than before; it became cosmopolitan without losing its French traits, and even its change to American sovereignty by the Louisiana purchase in 1803 did little to alter it.

New Orleans architecture is, therefore, out of the direct line of descent; it seems almost a sport. Changed little by American tendencies, it affected American taste outside of its boundaries but little; New Orleans seems to-day a foreign city. Its buildings, like its heritage, are neither all French nor all Spanish. If in one place arched windows and mansard roofs and simple classic detail recall the provincial French towns under Louis XIV, the next corner with its iron balconies and stucco walls seems almost a bit of old Spain. Yet there is a consistency of character in it all; it is all pure Latin: it is the one great center in America of a style that might almost be called Mediterranean. As such its quaintness and its beauty are all the more valuable.

THE BRICE HOUSE, ANNAPOLIS, MARYLAND

THE Brice house at Annapolis, built in 1740, reveals the end chimneys and the high roof that characterize the great houses which were beginning to line the harbors of Chesapeake Bay. These are developments of earlier southern tradition, but classicism is beginning to show in windows and cornices, and the great size and end wings are evidence of the continued progress

165   From a photograph

in the eighteenth-century South towards the reproduction in America of the majesty and commanding dignity of the English manor.

A GREAT ANNAPOLIS RESIDENCE

THE Paca, or Carvel house, is of similar type, and in its setting of great trees, its warm red brick walls embody a charm that does not contradict the dignity of its size and rambling plan.

166   © Detroit Photographic Co.

THE CHASE HOUSE, ANNAPOLIS

THIS stately brick house shows that by 1771 town conditions had developed which rendered the earlier type with its spreading wings undesirable. Instead we get a fully developed, carefully composed building with a central projecting pavilion, capped by a pediment the effect of which is almost monumental. The doorway has become a dominating feature.

SHIRLEY, JAMES RIVER, VIRGINIA

THE great plantation houses of Virginia were even more direct attempts to recreate the atmosphere of an almost feudal English country. Everything is subordinated to the great house, the "place." The massive dignity of four-square Shirley (No. 168), with its hipped roof and its close ranked dormers, and its dignified lack of ornament (the porches are later

167   From a photograph

additions), show how far along the road of creating a suave, aristocratic environment Virginians had progressed even at the time of the building of Shirley, by some considered as early as 1700.

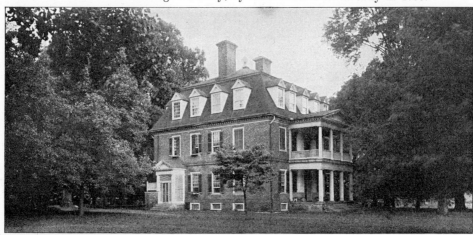

168   From a photograph by H. P. Cook

169   From a photograph by Frank Cousins

SHIRLEY — A CLOSE FRONT VIEW

A CLOSE view of Shirley (No. 169) shows not only the added double-storied porch that became common in southern houses of the latter part of the century, but also the steepness of the dormer roofs — sole remnant of Gothic tradition — and the beauty of the rich mottled brickwork, laid in Flemish bond (a "stretcher" or long brick, then a "header" or brick end), whose warmth of color and variety adds so much to the effect of these old tree-embowered places. All up and down the Virginia rivers the great brick houses stood proudly over their fertile fields; bringing into what had been so recently a wilderness something of the gracious aristocracy, the polish, the sophistication, of eighteenth-century England. White indentured servants and negro slaves served the masters of these estates.

ROSEWELL, VIRGINIA

THE eighteenth century saw the flowering of the aristocracy of Virginia. Of all the Virginia mansions before the middle of the century, Rosewell was one of the largest, most monumental, most English. Even in the disconsolate and stark barrenness of its semi-ruin here, the stone, window-arch keystones, the stone molded chimney caps, the white carved English door, show a formal grandeur such as was seldom attempted even at a later time. Rosewell dates from 1730. Note, by comparison with the figures at the door, the great height of the windows.

170   From a photograph by H. P. Cook

WESTOVER, ON JAMES RIVER, VIRGINIA

As Rosewell is one of the most monumental of Virginia homes, so Westover (No. 171), also built in the seventeen thirties, is certainly the most charming. In it English tradition and English detail have found an expression as sure as anything in England itself. End chimneys have become four, not two. The great hipped roof is made a striking feature of the house, and likewise the *baroque* doorway. Westover is the very quintessence of Virginia aristocracy, luxury, and polish, but not without a touch of austerity.

171   From a photograph by H. P. Cook

172   From a photograph by Frank Cousins

WESTOVER — A CLOSE FRONT VIEW

THERE are several interesting details in Westover that a closer scrutiny reveals. One is the dormers, with hipped roofs to help soften them back into the main roof. Another is the use of segmental topped windows. The eye is caught by the white stone band course. And finally the door, with Corinthian pilasters, scrolled and broken pediment, and carved pineapple between deserves study. The whole should be compared with northern houses (such as on page 52), to show what various expressions one style can develop amid differing environments.

MOUNT AIRY, VIRGINIA

In Mount Airy, built in 1758, the monumental
English formality reached a climax. The main
building and its dependencies are arranged around
a fore court. The steps are flanked by carved urns.
These, together with the use of cut stone ashlar
for the whole construction — unique in the South
for the date — give an aspect entirely calculated,
sure, and monumental. Even the studied lack of
ornament at entrances gives to the "rustication"
of the central motive the proper feeling of rather
aloof dignity. Mount Airy is the final expression
of southern aristocracy.

173   From a photograph by H. P. Cook

174   From a photograph by the United States Department of Roads

MOUNT VERNON

The most famous of Virginia mansions, Mount Vernon, reveals the elements of a southern estate in a peculiarly full and satisfactory manner. There is the central block, made more important by its cupola; there are
the flanking buildings, and a connection between of curved arcade. The large Palladian window at the end
of the main house expresses the size and monumentality of the great room inside.

Mount Vernon dates from various years between 1758 and 1786; the high porch is probably the last element
added, in 1786, though some authorities date it eight years earlier.

175   From a photograph by the United States Army Air Service

MOUNT VERNON — SEEN FROM THE AIR

An airplane view of Mount
Vernon shows that the house
with its wings is only the center
of a much larger whole, all carefully planned to give the finest
views. A lawn leading up to the
house, flanked on one side by
vegetable gardens, and on the
other by hedged flower gardens,
is the main element, but in the
whole composition are to be
found stables and ice houses and
barns and slaves' quarters. The
great plantation with its varied
population was a distinct social
unit. The mansion house symbolized and perhaps furthered
the planter's supremacy.

HAMPTON, MARYLAND

THE estate called Hampton, the seat of the Ridgleys, dates only from 1783, but it shows in its rich cupola, its carefully enriched dormers, the urns which crown its gables and pediments, and the large scale of all its details the culmination of the influence of the English Renaissance. It is a house that is large rather than great, polished rather than beautiful. Sophistication has slaughtered charm, and things are ripe for a new style.

176   From a photograph

177   From a photograph by H. P. Cook

DRAYTON HALL, SOUTH CAROLINA

THE South Carolina coast shows the same striving for the recreation of English country and big-place life that is found in Virginia, and frequently the same forms are used. In Drayton Hall on the Ashley River (No. 177), built in mid-eighteenth century, there is the high basement, the massive monumentality and the flanking service buildings that are common further north. There is, too, a two-storied portico, like that added at Shirley, and there is the same rich variegated brickwork.

A TOWN HOUSE IN CHARLESTON, SOUTH CAROLINA

THE famous Bull-Pringle residence (No. 178), built in Charleston in 1765–69, shows the same idea applied to a town house, where land was more valuable. The rather unusual richness of the detail of the entablatures of the double portico, based on a close study of English books, is an early example of the breaking away from strict classical forms that characterized the work of such men as Chippendale, and that played such an important part in New England work fifty years later. The house was originally owned by Miles Brewton.

178   From a photograph by H. P. Cook

179   From the *London Magazine*, 1762

A VIEW OF CHARLESTON, SOUTH CAROLINA

THIS old view of Charleston, from the *London Magazine* of 1762, gives something of the atmosphere of a prosperous southern seaport. The two church spires of St. Michael's and St. Philip's are shown at the right, and the range of closely built large houses stretching away to the left gives the whole a distinctly urban appearance. Among the more typical gable and hipped roofs appear two houses with decorative gable and copings; a form whose use here is due not to Dutch influence, but to the lingering Tudor tradition. Compare the houses in Chapter IV.

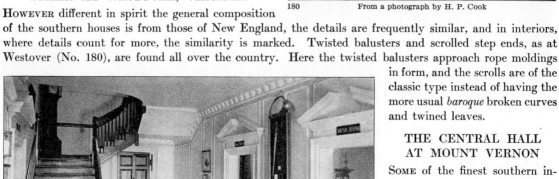

180   From a photograph by H. P. Cook

STAIRS AT WESTOVER, VIRGINIA

HOWEVER different in spirit the general composition of the southern houses is from those of New England, the details are frequently similar, and in interiors, where details count for more, the similarity is marked. Twisted balusters and scrolled step ends, as at Westover (No. 180), are found all over the country. Here the twisted balusters approach rope moldings in form, and the scrolls are of the classic type instead of having the more usual *baroque* broken curves and twined leaves.

THE CENTRAL HALL AT MOUNT VERNON

SOME of the finest southern interiors are to be found in Mount Vernon. The hall is peculiarly satisfactory with its pedimented doors, its simple painted paneling, and its wide inviting stairs. Even the simplification of the balusters of the stair rail helps the general effect of quiet and substantial beauty.

181   From a photograph by Leet Brothers

THE WEST PARLOR AT MOUNT VERNON

THE West parlor at Mount Vernon shows all the qualities of the developed colonial interior — simple paneling, door trims decorated with pediments and pilasters and a mantelpiece of unusual richness, whose duplicate could be found again and again in England. Mantel design became almost standardized in the eighteenth century through the wide

182   From a photograph by Leet Brothers

distribution of such books as Swan's *British Architect*, which contained many detailed drawings of such fireplaces, and evidently furnished the inspiration to builders equally in England and in her colonies.

183   From a photograph by H. P. Cook

ST. PHILIP'S CHURCH, CHARLESTON, SOUTH CAROLINA

ST. Philip's was an off-shoot of St. Michael's; but by the middle of the century it had grown to be so important a parish that it built a church to surpass its parent. This is an early view. Not satisfied with one portico, the architect has furnished three, but the tower is of a lower, stumpier type, and seems more a dome than a spire.

ST. MICHAEL'S CHURCH, CHARLESTON, SOUTH CAROLINA

IN Charleston, the influence of the Wren type reasserts itself. Some have even suggested that the "Gibson" referred to in an early periodical account as the designer of St. Michael's — built in 1742 — was really Sir James Gibbs, who designed the famous St. Martin's-in-the-Fields, London. The rather heavy stone portico and the detail throughout have a much more English atmosphere than is usual in the colonies.

184   From the *Gentleman's Magazine*, 1753

185   © Detroit Photographic Co.

THE NEW ST. PHILIP'S CHURCH, CHARLESTON

THE old St. Philip's was burned in 1835, but in 1836 a new church (No. 185) arose on its foundations. The lower part of the exterior was kept much the same, but tower and interior were altered. The tower, it is interesting to know, was designed to be as similar to that of St. Martin's-in-the-Fields as practicable. So, although this photograph shows work of only the period since 1835, below, it is a reproduction of the old, and above, it is carried out in a similar spirit.

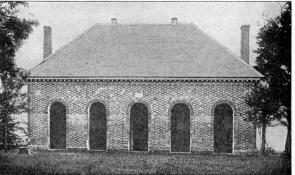

186   From a photograph by H. P. Cook

HANOVER COUNTY COURTHOUSE, VIRGINIA

THE Hanover County Courthouse, in Virginia, shows how the love of simple masonry forms affected the design of public buildings as well of houses. The high hipped roof, the classic cornice, and the fine simple arches are the only embellishments of this austere building. But interest is given to the somewhat bleak design by the variegation of the Flemish bond brickwork, with headers of a different color from the stretchers.

WILLIAMSBURG COURTHOUSE, VIRGINIA

THE Williamsburg Courthouse is a much more developed design. It is one of the many buildings in America whose design is traditionally attributed — but without foundation and contrary to all probability — to Christopher Wren. For years it stood without the columns that have been recently placed under the portico. In the picture the pediment looks like a huge projecting hood. This portico gives monumentality and a public character to a scheme otherwise almost as simple as the Hanover Courthouse.

187   From a photograph by Rau Studios, Inc.

STATE CAPITOL, ANNAPOLIS, MARYLAND

THE greatest of public buildings in the South is undoubtedly the state capitol at Annapolis. It is remarkable as being one of the earliest of American official buildings in which a dome plays the dominating part. It is thus one of the most important early buildings, as helping to set the domed type which has become almost universal in state capitol buildings. The chimneys shown in the photograph at either side of the pediment are modern additions.

188 © Detroit Photographic Co.

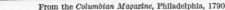

189 From the *Columbian Magazine*, Philadelphia, 1790

ANNAPOLIS STATE HOUSE

AN old print from the *Columbian Magazine* of Philadelphia in 1790 shows the Annapolis State House (No. 189) as it stood then with its accompanying minor buildings. The simplicity of the main rectangular building with its slightly accented central motive and its Corinthian porch is typical of eighteenth-century tradition, but the dome seems almost an afterthought; it sets awkwardly on the building below; and in its design itself seems rather the product of an inspired ship's carpenter than a trained architect. It was only later that this complex problem was satisfactorily solved.

190 From a print published at New Orleans in 1803. Courtesy of the Louisiana State Museum

A VIEW OF NEW ORLEANS, 1803

ROUGH frontiersmen from Kentucky or Ohio floating down the Mississippi in the early years of the nineteenth century moored their rafts and flatboats beside wharves of a strange city whose people spoke French and Spanish, and whose atmosphere was different from that of any town or city east of the Appalachians. Open-mouthed they gazed at French houses of masonry and at the great Spanish Cabildo (No 197).

AN OLD FRENCH COURTYARD

NEW Orleans atmosphere remains predominantly Latin. Dates of construction mean little; for except in minor details the spirit remained constant. This is an old French courtyard whose large arched casement windows and formal flower beds reveal at once the Latin origin. Only the dormer window is alien and English in feeling.

191 © Detroit Photographic Co.

© Detroit Publishing Co.

A STREET CORNER IN NEW ORLEANS

THIS typical New Orleans street corner, though every building visible is undoubtedly of nineteenth-century date, shows still in iron railing, colonnaded sidewalk, stucco wall and French window, a spirit which is as different from the colonial work of the Atlantic coast as can be imagined — a spirit which is neither all French nor all Spanish nor quite "American" — a spirit obviously Latin.

COURTYARD WITH GALLERIES, NEW ORLEANS

PREDOMINANTLY expressive of the warm South are the open galleries and wide brick arches and stone pavement of this courtyard. Less French perhaps is this than Spanish, or even Italian; but even so, in its mixture of influences typical of New Orleans.

193 © Detroit Photographic Co.

194 © Detroit Photographic Co.

THE OLD ABSINTHE HOUSE, NEW ORLEANS

THIS now famous landmark is another of the charming Latin houses which is neither all French nor all Spanish, nor all Italian, but French in the large size of its French windows, Italian, perhaps, in its first story arches; and predominantly Spanish in the atmosphere of its entire composition. This atmosphere pervades the buildings of all the old city; view after view in the lowlying streets is so similar to portions of some of the older cities in the West Indies, that the identity of the influences that formed them in their early days is obvious.

THE URSULINE CONVENT, NEW ORLEANS

AMONG buildings large enough to merit the epithet of monumental, the Ursuline Convent takes an important place. The queer stucco decoration on the façade of the central building, with its lyre forms, is exceedingly quaint. The convent shows its true Latin origin principally in the arcaded chapel with its scrolled gable at the end.

THE ARCHBISHOPRIC, NEW ORLEANS

IN the Archbishop's palace, with its high hipped roofs, the arcaded and rusticated porch with balustrade, the high brick wall and gate lodge and the tall windows with segmental trim, the French, the continental, character is most marked. The whole, almost without change, might be in some cathedral city of provincial France.

THE CABILDO (SUPREME COURT) NEW ORLEANS

THE Cabildo, built in New Orleans in 1795, shows how untouched the architectural character of New Orleans was even at this date by either the Adam tendency or the Classic Revival that were beginning to assert themselves in the East. The building, despite the crudeness of some of its detail, still remains pure Latin Renaissance in type. The ugly Mansard roof is an incongruous addition of 1850.

CHAPTER VIII

ARCHITECTURE IN THE NORTH, "LATE COLONIAL"

IT is easy to overestimate the cultural results of the successful completion of the Revolutionary War. It must be remembered that most of the thinking Revolutionary leaders considered it not so much an anti-English war, as a war to support old English liberties, founded on Magna Charta, against an unjust assumption of taxing power by the British Parliament. So, now that the war was over, there was no sudden abandonment of English architectural leadership; rather, on the contrary, for a time a still closer following of English ideals.

The early years of the republic saw many contrasts. Financial depression followed the inflation of the latter part of the war. The navigation system which governed commerce within the British Empire now operated in such a way as to exclude American with other foreign vessels from desirable trading areas. American mariners were forced to search over the world for new markets. Trade with China began to flourish. Depression in the seventeen eighties was followed by better times in the seventeen nineties and the first decade of the nineteenth century brought great prosperity. The Napoleonic wars were raging in Europe. America had the most important neutral merchant marine and until 1807 neutral trade brought larger and larger profits to America. New England ships poured into Salem and Boston and Portsmouth not only wealth, but goods of all kinds from all over the world as well. Every harbor was a port, and from the green shores of all the tidal backwaters rang the caulking hammer of busy shipyards, while the white walls of the square houses of rich sea captains rose out of clustering elms behind.

These houses, that were built in such numbers between 1780 and 1820, in the main followed earlier traditions. But the growing skill of craftsmen, the growing wealth of owners, and the growing command of natural resources made a richness and a delicacy possible that had been unknown before. Moreover, two fresh English influences were at work in all this building, both the result of the genius of one man — Robert Adam —: one towards a greater classicism, and the other towards an extreme and sometimes attenuated delicacy. The great inspiration of Robert Adam was the imperial work of ancient Rome. This Roman inspiration first appears in work strictly classical, almost archæological in its feeling, but later, as his skill developed, in a fresh note based on two of the less well known aspects of Roman art; one, the coarsened and simplified detail of the late Palace of Diocletian at Spalatro, which Adam had measured and published, the other, the exquisite and delicate richness of certain stucco reliefs that had been recently unearthed in the Baths of Titus. On this foundation, and borrowing perhaps also from the delicacy of the French work under Louis XVI, Adam developed a style that became universally popular in England. Its popularity was the doom of the earlier sturdy Georgian, and in the hands of less skillful imitators the style often degenerated into effeminacy and mere finicky prettiness.

The Adam style influenced the art of America quickly and profoundly, and its development in England is paralleled by a similar development here. So we find in the United States, first, a growing and more correct classicism, like that of the earlier work of the Salem architect, McIntire; and later, a sudden development of a love for forms of extreme delicacy, like McIntire's later porches, or the Portsmouth Athenæum (pp. 94 and 96). To make a unity of this dual tendency required all the skill of a great designer.

Such designers appeared. Samuel McIntire, originally a wood carver, became, before his death, an architect widely known, whose skill transfigured Salem. Charles Bulfinch, the son of a wealthy Boston doctor, starting as an amateur, developed into a professional architect of wide practice, whose brilliance was recognized when he was called to Washington to take charge of the National Capitol. In New York John McComb was producing designs and buildings that reveal a great talent. All these were working primarily on English precedent; the greatness of all lies in the brilliant manner in which they synthesized the classic tendency and the delicacy of the pseudo-Adam lightness, and in the skill with which they adjusted the forms thus developed to fit local conditions and local materials. It is this skill in modifying and adjusting that makes their work truly American; their influence and that of a host of other competent architects of the time — Alexander Parris, Peter Banner, and many others less well known — were the greatest element in the beginning of the divorce of American architecture from that of England. The progress of this movement towards a native American architecture was still further advanced by the publication in 1796 of *The Country Builder's Assistant*, by Asher Benjamin, which shows a great deal of detail that is not strictly classical or strictly English, and which influenced much of the current building in all the villages of New England.

Two other important influences were at work from an early period which conflicted with the underlying tendency still to base American architecture, like all American culture, on that of England. The first was the enormous popular impression which the friendship and aid of France had made upon the young country. In architecture, particularly in the North, this came gradually; for direct contact with French architecture was lacking, and, moreover, the large scale and lavish detail of the typical "Louis" styles were out of the question. It appears, however, in the New York City Hall (p. 106), in the design of which McComb had a French associate, Mangin, and which has a character distinctly Louis XVI. It appears in all the work which Major L'Enfant produced, notably in his plan of Washington, whose scheme is based on French garden layouts, and even more in the great Philadelphia house, never finished, which he designed for Robert Morris. Later, French influence was even more marked in the design of furniture and fashions.

The second influence which served to make American architecture a separate and individual style was a growing idealization of the classic world that became a sort of worship. The new republics of France and the United States both came to look back to the earlier republics of Rome and Greece for patterns and inspiration. A multitude of classic names for American towns and villages bears witness to this worship of antiquity, and the growing tendency to base American architectural forms on strict Roman models is just as natural a result as the carving of Washington in classic costume with a toga draped over his knees. But the story of that is centered particularly in the city of Washington and the South; classicism radiated north from there. Until the complete and final dominance of the classic revivals, which were nation-wide, the North, and particularly New England, remained largely true to that mixture of Adam and colonial influences that are so beautifully blended in the work of McIntire or Bulfinch.

THE PIERCE–NICHOLS HOUSE, SALEM, MASSACHUSETTS

THE later years of the eighteenth century were the years when one of the great "colonial" architects — Samuel McIntire — was beginning to set his stamp on Salem. In one of his earliest works, the Pierce-Nichols house, the great corner pilasters show his wish to be classic and monumental, but they reveal as well his ignorance at this time of how to produce his effects. The window spacing and decoration and the porch are, however, eminently quiet and right.

198   Courtesy of the Essex Institute, Salem

199   From a photograph by Frank Cousins

200   Courtesy of the Essex Institute

THE PIERCE–NICHOLS HOUSE — REAR

McINTIRE's peculiar personal touch is often a matter of felicitous detail, and in the rear court of the Pierce-Nichols house it shows to more advantage than in the front. The elliptical arches, the simplified pilaster capitals, the sure proportion and feeling of the whole, are typical of his work, and have a new kind of delicacy and individuality that is uncommon before his time.

THE PORCH OF GRIMSHAWE HOUSE, SALEM

IN the Grimshawe house porch, now in the Essex Institute museum, the love of simplicity and delicacy has progressed another step. The proportions of the "order" — pilaster and entablature — have been altered from the usual classical ratios; the entablature is lighter, its moldings more delicate, the pilasters more slim. Wall surface is treated in the flattest, simplest manner, and the only decoration is the band of delicate dentils in the cornice, and the accenting of the pilasters that flank the door by delicate fluting.

201   From a photograph by Frank Cousins   202   Front Elevation. From the original
drawing, photographed by Frank Cousins

THE DERBY–CROWNINSHIELD–ROGERS HOUSE, SALEM

OF the Derby-Crowninshield-Rogers house built in Salem, in 1800, it is fortunately possible to show not only an old photograph — for the house no longer exists — but also the architect's original working drawing (No. 202). Cousins and other authorities say the architect was McIntire; Fiske Kimball says the writing on the drawing is that of Bulfinch. Whichever it was, the drawing, though its indication of ornament seems amateurish, is accurate and sure in matters of proportion, and reveals careful study. Moreover, the executed building is so absolutely identical with the drawing that there can be no doubt that in this case at least — and probably in most houses built at the time — beauty and grace are not the result of chance, or rule-of-thumb methods of building, or of age, but of careful creative thought embodied in carefully prepared drawings.

The house itself shows more of the influence of the English Adam brothers than is usual with McIntire. Its order, and the arch treatment below, are both in the Adam manner.

THE GARDNER–WHITE–PINGREE HOUSE, SALEM

THIS house, built in 1805, shows the mastery McIntire had by that time achieved. Every superfluous ornament is omitted. Restraint, refinement and delicacy are the ideals that have taken the place of the earlier classicism and monumentality. A few windows, beautifully proportioned, with flat white arches over them, a delicate balustrade, a graceful cornice, and an exquisite semicircular porch make the house what it is. Salem waxed prosperous from the sea trade in the opening years of the nineteenth century. Merchants whose profits were mounting symbolized their success in stately mansions.

203   Courtesy of the Essex Institute

204   From a photograph by Frank Cousins

THE ATHENÆUM OF PORTSMOUTH, NEW HAMPSHIRE

PORTSMOUTH, in its old Athenæum, can boast of one of the most perfect American interpretations of the Adam style that the early nineteenth century has left to us. The treatment of the arched door, the elliptical marble pateræ, the slim pilasters, the light and delicate entablature without architrave, and the general elegance and refinement throughout are all in the Adam manner. The formal classicism is being eclipsed by a newer, freer classicism.

A TYPICAL OLD HOUSE, MAINE COAST

ALL through the coast towns that dot the harbors of New England, sea captains and shipowners, grown wealthy from a flourishing commerce, were erecting their white

THE LARKIN–RICHTER HOUSE, PORTSMOUTH, NEW HAMPSHIRE

AWAY from McIntire's influence simplicity and restraint developed more markedly than in Salem. A type common to New England during the first two decades of the nineteenth century subordinated everything to proportion, often disdained ornament, usually achieved dignity and grace, but sometimes became too stiff, rigid, unbending, and frequently lacked human atmosphere. Many such houses suggested a Puritanism austere and still imposing, but whose fires burned low.

205   Courtesy of Portsmouth Athenæum

houses. This is but one example, from Wiscasset, Maine; but it is typical of hundreds more. Pilasters, low-hipped roofs, often with a balustrade in the so-called Chinese taste, the traditional five-window front, and rich and delicate porch are the elements that create so much of the charm that is incarnate in Kittery, or Kennebunkport, or Bath.

206   From a photograph by Labbie

THE WEST PARLOR, PIERCE–NICHOLS HOUSE, SALEM

THE west parlor of the Pierce-Nichols house in Salem shows McIntire's transitional style in interior work. The paneling, fireplace, and door finish might almost date from thirty years before; and certain portions, such as the breaking of the cornice over the door at the right, show the same awkwardness that appears on the exterior.

207   From a photograph by Frank Cousins

THE EAST CHAMBER OF PIERCE–NICHOLS HOUSE

THE mantel, overmantel and cornice from the east chamber (No. 208), eighteen years later, show a different McIntire, who has mastered the Adam forms, and in addition certain features of unique decorative detail in wood that serve to distinguish much American work. The double or fret dentil in both cornices, the reeding of one molding in the room cornice, and the fluting of the central panel of the mantel are examples. More typically Adam is the use of papier mâché wreaths and foliage on the fireplace frieze.

208   From a photograph by Frank Cousins

DOORWAY FROM THE COOK–OLIVER HOUSE

A DOORWAY from the Cook-Oliver house in Salem shows an even more distinctive treatment. The broken flutes of the pilasters, the reeding of the door trim, the playful and original dentil course, all show at its highest McIntire's talent for re-vitalizing and liberating a tradition essentially classic. The mantel beyond and the wall treatment with its fine landscape paper are both also characteristic of the period.

209   From a photograph by Frank Cousins

210   From a photograph by Frank Cousins

CHESTNUT STREET, SALEM, MASSACHUSETTS

THE old towns of the first quarter of the nineteenth century had certain qualities that have fled forever. Established, without crowding; cultured, yet without snobbery; their architecture gave an expression, restful and charming, to the underlying unity that was their foundation. It is buildings as well as trees that give harmony and beauty to Chestnut Street in Salem; and behind that harmony of building was for a time at least a harmony of life.

INTERIOR DECORATIONS FOR ELIAS HASKET DERBY'S HOUSE

WE are fortunate in possessing a number of McIntire's drawings. This detail sheet for the famous Elias Hasket Derby house, Salem, with its studies for cornices, panels, moldings, and a plaster ceiling, shows that he gave quite as much study to interior details as he did to general design. But to him, as to all true architects, the drawing was but a means to an end; and the hard quality of the drawing was metamorphosed through craftsman's skill into modeled beauty.

211   From a photograph by Frank Cousins

212   From engraving by Sands after drawing by W. H. Bartlett, published at
                    London, 1839

MAIN STREET, NORTHAMPTON, MASSACHUSETTS

A VIEW of Northampton, Mass., published in London in 1839, shows the quiet breadth and harmonious beauty of this old Connecticut River town. Slim church tower and courthouse and embowering trees and wide openness are characteristic; even the bowed shop windows in the gambrel-roofed house across the street and the little columned porch from which the view is taken add their own note of refined restraint.

THE SOUTH CHURCH, SALEM

IN church design the opening years of the post-Revolutionary period show a progressive development of the tradition already established. The South Church in Salem (No. 213), by McIntire, is typical, and it is characterized by the same slenderness and delicacy of detail that characterizes domestic work of the time. It is from this period that most of our so-called "colonial" white church steeples date.

213   Courtesy of the Essex Institute

PARK STREET CHURCH, BOSTON

THIS church (No. 214), the final flowering of New England church tradition, designed by Peter Banner, was completed in 1819. The severely simple tower, flanked by the curved colonnade, emphasizes the lightness of three superposed stages of arched window, slim column, and the white slenderness of spire.

214   From a photograph by Baldwin Coolidge

CENTER CHURCH, NEW HAVEN

RATHER different are the influences behind Ithiel Town's Center Church at New Haven (No. 215), where the classic tradition is dominant. Here is little of the Adam-like delicacy of the time elsewhere; instead a rather heavy-handed monumental quality that reaches an ugly and awkward climax in the sprawling acanthus scroll in the pediment. But the tower and spire — carefully studied developments of types set by St. Paul's in New York and St. Martin's-in-the-Fields in London — are among the surest and best the period produced.

215   From a photograph by Pach Bros.

216   From the portrait by Mather Brown (1761-1831), in
                    the Massachusetts Historical Society

FIRST CHURCH OF CHRIST, LANCASTER, MASSACHUSETTS

THE First Church of Christ (No. 217) shows the peculiar combination of delicacy and classicism of Bulfinch's designs. The solid brick arches of the porch, and the simplicity of the tower were, for the time, daringly original; Bulfinch never let colonial tradition stand between him and the creation of beauty. He was one of the generation just preceding that which marked the intellectual flowering of New England. He was a forerunner of Emerson.

218   Courtesy of Rev. Charles A. Place

CHARLES BULFINCH, 1763–1844

CHARLES BULFINCH was one of the first Americans who devoted all his time to the professional practice of architecture. Born in 1763, graduated from Harvard in 1781, he spent several years in travel and study abroad, finally settling in Boston and starting practice in 1787. Distinguished alike by his delicacy of taste and his sense of monumental composition, he was the designer of state houses in Boston and Hartford, and was in 1818 called to take charge of the design of the capitol in Washington. An honored public figure, he was chairman of the Boston Selectmen for twenty years. His fine taste, his scholarly mind, his delicacy of feeling are well expressed in this portrait. He died in 1844.

217   Courtesy of Rev. Charles A. Place

INTERIOR, FIRST CHURCH OF CHRIST, LANCASTER, MASSACHUSETTS

INSIDE, the church is of great simplicity; delicately molded wall panels and exquisite pulpit are its chief features. It is interesting to note in works like those of Bulfinch, how the development of the individual professional architect, with the consequent opportunity for a personal expression, rather than communal expression, led to a new search for originality of form, a new fluidity of creative design.

THE BOSTON STATE HOUSE

THE Boston State House (No. 219) is one of Bulfinch's masterpieces. Built in 1798, it shows the result of his European study in its complete mastery of monumental scale, and the way in which the dome is made the dominating feature of the whole. The arcaded porch, the colonnade above with its brilliant emphasis of the end pavilions by the coupled columns, the dignified simplicity of the arched windows, and the full simple sweep of the dome are all new notes in American architecture.

219   © Detroit Photographic Co.

220   From a photograph

THE OLD STATE HOUSE, HARTFORD, CONNECTICUT

THE State House at Hartford (No. 220) is also attributed to Bulfinch. It was completed in 1796. It reveals a quieter, more restrained side of his taste, more definitely affected by the typical colonial tradition than the Boston State House; but the arcaded lower story with its open arched loggia, and the cupola, which combines a sense of monumental simplicity and restraint with the delicacy of detail he loved, are in the true Bulfinch manner.

COUNCIL CHAMBER OF OLD STATE HOUSE

A COMPARISON of the Council Chamber with the "Declaration Hall" of Independence Hall, Philadelphia (No. 164), shows the enormous difference between similar rooms, one treated in the typical formal English colonial style and the other expressive of the new ideals of lightness, delicacy and restraint of detail which under Bulfinch's influence characterized work of the North in the early years of the Republic.

221   From a photograph

222   From J. Milbert, *Itinéraire pittoresque du fleuve Hudson*, etc.   Paris, 1826

VIEW OF BOSTON FROM THE SOUTH BOSTON BRIDGE

THE Milbert view of Boston from the South Bridge shows how the State House, enthroned on Beacon Hill, dominated the city, no longer a colonial town, but already a city in its own right; a city of quality and per-

sonality, with soaring church spires pricking its sky line; a city that vastly impressed Milbert as one that "recalled to him more than once one of our cities of Europe."

Milbert found Boston a center of fashion as well as of culture. He commented on the eager-ness with which its feminine population awaited the arrival of each ship bringing goods from Europe.

223   From a photograph by Frank Cousins

DYCKMAN HOUSE, NEW YORK

NEW YORK in those early days of the nation still preserved evidence of the duality of its origin. Dutch and English influence were at work side by side in the city and its environs. The Dyck-man house, built in 1798, shows Dutch influence fully developed; the broad sweep of the gently sloped gambrel is carried still further down to form a broad porch. Once far from the city, in the center of broad acres; now the city is enclosing it, and it has only been saved by becoming a museum.

224   From the painting by Francis Guy, 1797, in the New York
Historical Society

TONTINE COFFEE HOUSE, NEW YORK

A VIEW of the "Tontine Coffee House," painted in 1797, shows New York at the time. In the Coffee House itself, at the left, there appears the same type of composition as in the Hartford State House, and Adam influence shows in the stone tablets between second and third floor windows. Down the street are a group of typical brick houses with white pedimented doorways. Dutch influence shows only in the gambrel roof of the old wooden building on the street corner.

GOVERNMENT HOUSE, NEW YORK

THE Government House in New York was primarily an official residence. Designed by John McComb, it shows in colonnade and pilasters, and pediment topped windows, the love of monumental effect which for so long dominated much architecture of the central states. But the ugly breaking out of the entablature over the columns and pilasters shows that at this time the restlessness of the English *baroque* still had its effect on American design.

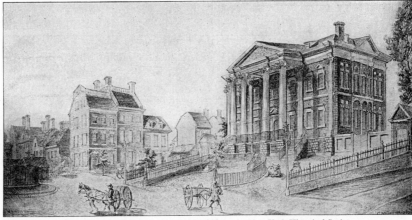

225   From the painting by G. Milbourne, 1797, in the New York Historical Society

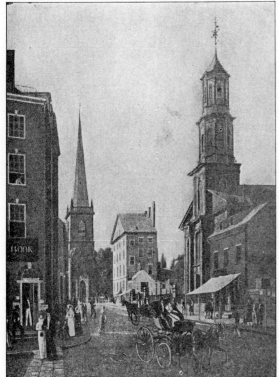

226   From a print in the New York Historical Society, after original by Burton, published 1831–32

THE MORRIS HOUSE, PHILADELPHIA

THE Morris house shows how closely early Republican work in Philadelphia followed the already powerful colonial tradition. Rich brickwork in Flemish bond, simple classic cornice, white shutters, a simply decorated doorway: all these are equally characteristic of work much earlier. Only the additional size of the windows and the marked slimness of the door and the delicate scale of its detail reveal the touch of post-Revolutionary influences.

TRINITY CHURCH FROM WALL STREET

THE view up Wall Street has for two hundred years and more had at its end the tower of Trinity Church; and for all these years that church tower has been Gothic — or the contemporary idea of Gothic — in type. Even the structure built after the Revolution followed the earlier building in style. Contrast the pseudo-Gothic of its angular windows and pinnacles with the Renaissance richness and grace of the First Presbyterian Meetinghouse to the right. The houses are of the restrained simplicity that was well nigh universal in the period.

227   © Rau Studios, Inc.

228   © Rau Studios, Inc.

LATE COLONIAL DOOR, PHILADELPHIA

THE detail of the period in Philadelphia and its neighborhood reveals a mixture of the delicate freedom that McIntire and Bulfinch both loved with the stricter formality and classicism popular in Philadelphia. This door has the slim proportions, the rich dentil band, the composition ornaments and reeding at the corner of the arch and trim that characterize the former trend, but also a certain straightforward simplicity — almost austerity — that is characteristic of the latter.

229   © Rau Studios, Inc.

LOUDEN, WAYNE JUNCTION, PHILADELPHIA

MORE typical of Philadelphia is Louden, Wayne Junction, with stucco walls and slim door; and in addition the dignity of a colonnaded porch with columns full two stories high. In these column capitals we find an early instance of the use of detail more Greek than Roman — a use which shows even that in 1801 American designers were feeling away from the close bonds of their tradition back to earlier styles for their inspiration.

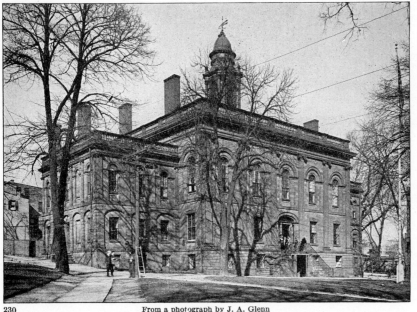

230   From a photograph by J. A. Glenn

THE ALBANY ACADEMY

BY contrast, the Albany Academy, designed by a famous Albany architect, Philip Hooker, about 1812, preserves intact all the quality of the pure colonial tradition, both in mass and detail; and only in the greater development of its classic decoration, and the greater slimness and delicacy of its ornament does it show the freedom of the new day. The Academy demonstrates the absence of a break in culture following the Revolution.

231   From a photograph by Frank Cousins

PENNSYLVANIA HOSPITAL, PHILADELPHIA

THE central pavilion of the Pennsylvania Hospital, built in the closing years of the eighteenth century, is full of the refined delicacy characteristic of Bulfinch. In it the slim monumental pilasters, the double-arched windows below, and the rotunda above, combine to form a whole that is perhaps the most perfect example remaining of the last and final flowering of "colonial" tradition, expertly molded to his will by a skillful and understanding designer. It is used to give just that balance of the official and the domestic that a hospital should have.

232   From a photograph by Wurts Brothers

ST. JOHN'S CHURCH, VARICK STREET, NEW YORK

ST. JOHN'S Church, once on Varick Street, built by John McComb, the architect of City Hall, and destroyed a few years ago to make way for the "Seventh Avenue Extension," shows how close to the pre-Revolutionary tradition early nineteenth-century work frequently was. It is almost a copy of St. Paul's (No. 153), but its aisle, ceilings and its chancel are richer. The destruction of this beautiful church was a tragedy.

233   From a print in the New York Historical Society, after drawing, 1826, by W. G. Wall, engraved, printed and colored by J. Hill

234   Courtesy of the City of New York Art Commission

NEW YORK CITY HALL IN 1826

THE New York City Hall, begun in 1803, was in many respects the most outstanding public building of the country at its time. Both a Frenchman, Mangin, — probably the original designer — and an American, the famous John McComb, who detailed and supervised its construction, were its architects. It is possibly to the character of Mangin's original scheme that the strong French (Louis XVI) quality of the whole is due. The perfection of its scale makes it effective even to-day.

ROTUNDA, NEW YORK CITY HALL

INSIDE as well as out, the New York City Hall is unusually distinguished in its detail. The rotunda, with its curving marble staircase, its ring of graceful columns, and its delicate iron rail of Louis XVI design, bears comparison with any of the work of the time in Europe, both in the sureness of the conception, and the delicacy of the execution.

VIEW OF EARLY CINCINNATI

CINCINNATI in 1835 had become a city. This old view shows brick buildings crowded together, without plan, little two-story houses remaining sandwiched in between larger neighbors. Arched doors and Palladian windows remind one of New York; but already the unity of the older, more

235   From a lithograph, *ca.* 1835, in The Historical & Philosophical Society of Ohio, Cincinnati

established cities is gone; haste in building and land speculation have produced in this Ohio city even ninety years ago the broken sky line, the helter-skelter quality which for so many years was and often still is the curse of American cities.

236   From Henry Howe, *Historical Collections of Ohio*, 1847

THE FIRST OHIO STATE HOUSE, CHILLICOTHE

OHIO reveals most strongly the imported, seaboard character of the early western towns. This old view of the first Ohio State House (No. 236) shows a square building with cupola and pedimented door that is as exact a reproduction of a New England meetinghouse as was possible. Beyond it is the white New England church spire. Ohio was full of New England people trying their fortunes on the frontier.

237   From Henry Howe, *Historical Collections of Ohio*, 1847

CENTRAL VIEW IN NEW PHILADELPHIA, OHIO

NEW Philadelphia, O., shows a courthouse exactly of the same type — the five-window front, the pedimented door, and the hipped roof and cupola that were used in almost every town in Ohio. The new settlers in the West tried to reconstruct the environment they had left behind, just as two centuries before the first English settlers on the sea coast had tried there to reconstruct the England they remembered.

238   From Herrmann J. Meyer, *Universorum*, New York, 1851

COURTHOUSE, INDEPENDENCE, MISSOURI

THE same thing is true even in far away Missouri. Independence, Mo., early had the ubiquitous square courthouse on a common or village green, and around houses of typical eastern type. The New England tradition still held true.

CHAPTER IX

ROMAN INFLUENCE IN THE SOUTH

THE architecture of the South suffered a greater change than that of the North during the decades immediately following the Revolution, but it was not the Revolution which produced the change. For even the Revolution did not break up the aristocracy of Virginia and the Carolinas, and the invention of the cotton gin and the consequent development of great slave-holding cotton plantations only strengthened it. The South, therefore, where it was untouched by other factors, continued long in accord with its old-time conservative traditions, erecting the same great manor houses in the English style. The factors which did produce great changes were, first, the foundation and building of the city of Washington, and second, the influence of the architectural learning and achievements of one great and popular individual — Thomas Jefferson.

The building of Washington was to the young country a concrete and moving symbol of its developing nationality. The creation from nothing of such a city was an imaginative undertaking of a scope which for the time was enormous. Into it went not only the best architectural thought of the day, but all the enthusiasm of leaders like Washington himself and Jefferson. The records show how close was the personal connection of these two men with the great undertaking; to both it was more than a vague dream; it was a concrete plan carefully thought out. Their foresight was fortunately matched by that of the designer, Major Pierre Charles L'Enfant. L'Enfant had training and imagination; he thought in large terms. But his training was French, and the design he produced necessarily French in every line, and accordingly utterly unconnected with any vestige of "colonial" tradition. Yet it was a plan almost perfectly successful both practically and æsthetically; it seized the imagination of the people; it became, as it grew, a vivid object lesson of the beauty which might be created without regard for English precedent.

The center of the Washington scheme was the great parked mall dominated by the capitol and the executive mansion. In order to obtain designs of sufficient dignity for these two buildings, it was decided to hold competitions for them. These competitions mark an epoch in the architectural development of the country, not only because they are the earliest official recognition of the architect as a professional designer, but also because in the judgment of the designs submitted, which ranged from the simplest expressions of colonial tradition to the most ambitious purely classical projects, a step was taken which determined the style development of the country for the next fifty years, and had effects which are evident even in the architecture of to-day.

To understand this judgment, which awarded the first prize to the design, now lost, of Dr. William Thornton, evidently of pure classic type, it is necessary to realize the energy, inspiration, and knowledge that lay behind Thomas Jefferson's enthusiasm for classic design, for his opinion had great weight in the decision. Jefferson was typical of much that was best in the young republic. A staunch, almost fanatical believer in democracy, he had, nevertheless, an innate and charming aristocracy of spirit that made him a born leader. He was above all else a scholar, a searcher, driven by a passionate intellectual curiosity into a continually growing interest in all sides of life. He early possessed a library of unusual scope; in it his interest in things architectural is revealed by the early presence of works by Palladio and Des Godetz, dealing mainly with Roman forms.

It is characteristic of him that this interest could not remain academic. He learned to draw, and as early as 1771 he was making schemes for the completion of his home, Monticello, that continued to be a sort of architectural laboratory for him up to his death. From the beginning his enthusiasm was for work in the classic vein, for his birth — he was from humble "up-country" stock — and his sympathies alike cut him off from the strong English traditions of the coast plantations. Palladio and Des Godetz became almost his sole guides and inspiration in matters of taste.

After the war, Jefferson spent several years in France. There for the first time he came into direct contact with Roman work; there for the first time, in the Maison Carrée at Nîmes, its large scale and the true grandeur of its simple direct greatness overwhelmed him, and, by contrast, made the delicate prettiness of much Adam detail and the heavy *baroque* of much of the earlier colonial seem alike petty, crude, undeveloped. From that time on the simple temple scheme obsessed him, to find expression first in the designs for the Virginia capitol (whose completion, after heart-breaking years, left only a cheap caricature of Jefferson's original plan, preserving the scheme, but little else), and later in parts of the University of Virginia. It was this classic enthusiasm of Jefferson's that played a great part in the early building of Washington, and so, through popular interest in the new capital, influenced deeply the architecture, and in particular the official architecture, of the country as a whole.

Moreover, throughout the Revolutionary period and the first days of the republic, as somewhat later in France, the Roman republic took hold of the popular imagination. More and more that blend of aristocracy and democracy which produced alike the imposing figure of Washington and the extremely human Jefferson seemed to recall the heroes of legendary Rome — Cincinnatus, the Scipios, Brutus. Jefferson's Roman taste was therefore singularly well designed to appeal to the whole nation.

Nor were trained architects wanting to express, interpret and spread this new classicism. A few were talented amateurs: Bulfinch; Thornton, the first architect of the national capitol; Jefferson himself. Many were truly professional: James Hoban, trained in Ireland, winner of the competition for the executive mansion; Benjamin Latrobe, trained in England; Stephen Hallet from France; Robert Mills and others trained in this country. Moreover, Hallet, Latrobe and Bulfinch all worked at various times on the national capitol, and so came directly under the spell of the classic enthusiasm which played such a large part in the early growth of Washington. All the conditions were therefore propitious to the rapid spread of this Roman Revival throughout the country. The Roman Revival was a symbol of the birth of the new nation; as such, its popularity was assured.

A TYPICAL FRAME HOUSE IN GEORGIA

FRAMED houses throughout the early nineteenth century bore a family resemblance to each other. A house in the village of Riceborough, Georgia, in 1829, had the long sloping-roofed piazza and dormer windows that seem almost like Dutch colonial work, and the heavy projecting end chimneys of the early Virginia tradition. Again

239   From Basil Hall, *Forty Etchings from Sketches Made with the Camera Lucida in North America*, Edinburgh, 1829

it is a case of the attempt to recreate forms to which the settler was accustomed.

240   From a photograph by H. P. Cook

THE JOHN MARSHALL HOUSE IN RICHMOND

To the older centers of culture in the South the end of the Revolution brought not only new prosperity, but two new architectural elements — one, the use of the developed Adam forms, and the other, an increasing classicism. The John Marshall house in Richmond bears witness in its quiet balance of white trim and red wall, in the broad low gable with its circular ornament, to the restraint that is a part of this trend, and in the combined delicacy and correctness of the moldings to the sureness of touch which is so characteristic of the time.

THE HOME OF HENRY CLAY, ASHLAND, KENTUCKY

HENRY Clay's Kentucky mansion, Ashland, was built in 1813 from designs by B. H. Latrobe. The projecting bay-like porch, crowned with a delicate iron railing, and the use of stucco on wall surfaces as an integral part of the design are characteristic of much post-Revolutionary work. But it is

241   From an engraving about 1870 by John Sartain, owned by Mrs. Thomas H. Clay, Lexington, Ky., after the painting by James Hamilton (1819–78)

interesting to see Latrobe, some of whose work is of pure "classic revival" type, even at this late date using the Palladian window and a pedimented central motif so true to colonial tradition.

From a photograph

HOMEWOOD, BALTIMORE, MARYLAND

THE light and delicate Adam type of Renaissance, such as was used in the North by Bulfinch and McIntire, was never as popular in the South; yet one of the finest examples of it is Homewood, in Baltimore, built about 1800. In perfection of proportion, delicacy of detail, in the white portico and quality of workmanship it rivals many houses of the time — even those in England. One important trend to be noticed, besides the finely Adam character of detail, is the attempt to make the house a purely one-story composition.

243   From a photograph by H. P. Cook

MONTICELLO, ALBEMARLE COUNTY, VIRGINIA

JEFFERSON'S large country house, begun as early as 1770, but not reaching its present state until fifty years later, shows a similar attempt to express but one story. But in every other way Monticello is the opposite of Homewood, for Jefferson, an architect and scholar and reader, despised the slim Adam proportions and was always trying for a return to pure classicism; first by means of using the "correct" proportions; later by actual study of ancient buildings. Monticello has a fine, correct Palladian Doric order.

ELEVATION OF MONTICELLO, AS DRAWN BY JEFFERSON

AN early study made by Thomas Jefferson for the treatment of Monticello shows it as a two-story building, with a two-story superposed portico of Palladian Doric and Ionic orders. It is a type of design which Jefferson got very directly from Palladio's published work; and Palladio was, prior to Jefferson's trip abroad, the closest connection he had with true classic form. But the drawing is interesting as showing that Jefferson, statesman and scholar, was, in architecture, though self-taught, much more than an amateur.

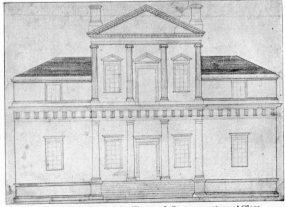

244   From the original sketch by Thomas Jefferson, courtesy of Clara Amory Coolidge (Mrs. T. Jefferson Coolidge, Jr.), Boston

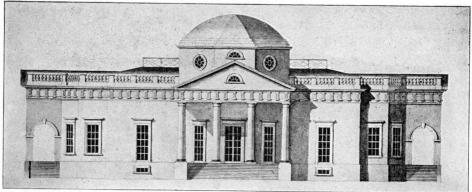

245   From the original sketch by Robert Mills, courtesy of Clara Amory Coolidge (Mrs. T. Jefferson Coolidge, Jr.), Boston

WEST ELEVATION, MONTICELLO

FOR a long period Robert Mills, who later became a well-known architect, worked under and with Jefferson on Monticello. The greater skill of his draughtsmanship is at once apparent. But the adoption of the one-story scheme, the dome, the severe classic spirit of the "order," pediment and other details are all due to Jefferson. There are even preserved large scale detail studies made by Jefferson for the treatment of cornices, windows, and the like.

MONTPELIER, VIRGINIA, THE HOME OF JAMES MADISON

THE monumental classical portico later became a typical feature of the southern mansions and manors. It was added to older buildings; Madison for instance, at the suggestion of Thomas Jefferson, added a Monticello-like portico to his great house Montpelier, giving it the greatest possible monumental dignity by keeping the steps inside the portico so that the columns could run clear down to the ground.

246   From a photograph by H. P. Cook

247   From a photograph by Gramstorff Bros.

LEE MANSION, ARLINGTON, VIRGINIA

ARLINGTON, across the Potomac from Washington, has the columned porch still more monumentally developed and treated with detail almost Greek — early Greek Doric proportions to the columns, but Roman capitals and entablature. The almost brutal strength is admirably designed to count for the most as seen from Washington.

A WASHINGTON CITY HOUSE

THE "Octagon" (Tayloe house) in Washington, designed about 1797 by William Thornton, the first architect of the capitol, shows the double tendency of Adam delicacy and strict classicism at work. The curved entrance bay, the delicate main cornice, the white panels between the windows show the Adam influence; the porch, and numerous interior details are purely classic. In this case much of the classic influence is Greek rather than Roman. The "Octagon" is now the national headquarters of the American Institute of Architects.

248   From a photograph by Frank Cousins

249   Courtesy of R. A. Lancaster, Jr.

A SOUTHERN STAIRWAY AND HALL

THE stair of the Valentine Museum in Richmond — formerly the Wickham house, built in 1812 — shows the attenuation of stair rail and baluster, the use of niches, and the love of curved stairs and landings which characterized stairs and halls both North and South in the early nineteenth century. The old Georgian *baroque* influence was dead; the severe classic of the Roman revival had not yet gained sway; between the two was a period when delicacy — delicacy sometimes carried to the point of effeminacy — was the dominant ideal.

THE CHARLESTON EXCHANGE

IN public work, too, the same twofold tendency appears. This old engraving of the Exchange in Charleston shows a building whose spirit is almost entirely Adam. But it is the more classic type of Adam design that is followed, and broad wall surfaces, an arched entrance loggia, and a pedimented motive above with engaged columns, all help to give that strong, simple classic formality, with every element of the *baroque* eliminated, which the people of the young Republic were growing to demand.

250   From Morris & Kenny, *The Philadelphia Album*, 1828

A CLASSIC CHURCH, RICHMOND, VIRGINIA

The Monumental Church in Richmond is perhaps the first attempt in church design to abandon the eighteenth-century tradition entirely and produce a building in strict conformity to the spirit of the pure classic revival. In detail it is a hodge-podge of Greek and Roman forms; there are elements also purely English and Adam; yet the whole, with its octagonal plan, its dome, and its porches, strikes what is obviously a new note.

251   © Detroit Photographic Co.

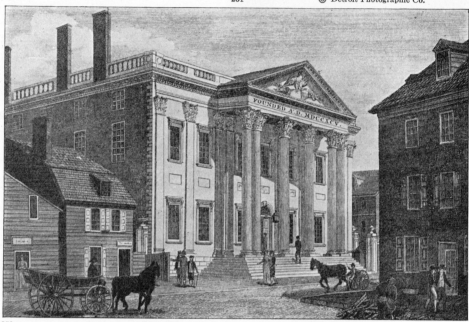

252   From William Birch, *Views of Philadelphia*, 1799

THE FIRST BANK OF THE UNITED STATES, PHILADELPHIA

One of the ironies of American history is that the managers of this bank, founded by Jefferson's arch political enemy, Alexander Hamilton, and bitterly opposed by the Virginia statesman, should draw the inspiration for their building from the Roman forms which Jefferson himself was doing so much to make popular. The first Bank of the United States in Philadelphia (No. 252), by Samuel Blodget, has a dignity of scale, a monumental grandeur that no building in the purely colonial tradition could ever achieve.

THE ARCADE, PHILADELPHIA

The Philadelphia Museum or Arcade shows the same desire to be monumental and Roman. Even the stark simplicity of the four large arches has in it a quality quite different from that generated by the colonial tradition. The use of the niche on either side of the main arcade is another evidence of study, if not of Roman examples, at least of such works as those of Palladio, in which Roman types were shown.

253   From an engraving by Fenner Sears & Co., London, 1831, after a drawing by C. Burton, New York

JEFFERSONIAN ARCHITECTURE

THE state capitol at Richmond marks an epoch in the history of American architecture. Thomas Jefferson was its architect, and the designs, prepared by him and under his supervision while he was in France, embody the results of much personal study of the Maison Carrée — that famous Roman temple in Nîmes. The capitol was the first American building to be modeled entirely on ancient classic forms, not only in detail, but in general form as well. Difficulties in construction and official poverty forced an unfortunate cheapening of Jefferson's original conception.

254   Courtesy of R. A. Lancaster, Jr.

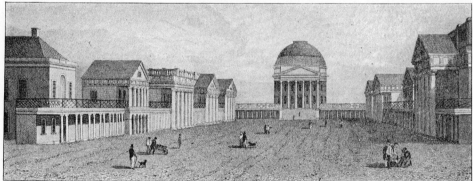

255 From an engraving by Fenner Sears & Co., London, 1831, after a drawing by W. Goodacre, New York

256 © Detroit Publishing Co.

THE UNIVERSITY OF VIRGINIA, CHARLOTTESVILLE

OF all the architectural work with which Jefferson was associated, the University of Virginia (No. 255) is the most comprehensive. An engraving of 1831 shows the main elements of the group: a quadrangle flanked by temple-like pavilions connected by colonnades, and at the end a great domical rotunda. All the orders used — Doric and Ionic for the pavilions, and Corinthian for the rotunda — were intended to follow the strictest classical canons in order to serve, as Jefferson put it, "as specimens of orders for the architectural lectures."

THE COLONNADES, UNIVERSITY OF VIRGINIA

THIS view along the one side of the quadrangle shows not only the temple-like pavilions that served alike as classroom buildings and faculty residences but also the lovely colonnades that connect them. All the detail is of the most severe and correct classical type.

THE LIBRARY, UNIVERSITY OF VIRGINIA

THE climax of the whole is of course the rotunda; and, like the state capitol (No. 254) it marks an epoch. In its direct simplicity of monumental form, the large scale and perfect classicism of its portico, and above all the purely Roman and Pantheon-like contour of its rounded walls and wide dome, nothing the least resembling it had ever been done before in America. Dignified, simple, graceful, strong, it still endures as a tribute to the important influence Thomas Jefferson had upon the development of architecture in the United States. It was restored after the fire in 1897.

257   From a photograph by H. P. Cook

VIEW OF THE CITY OF WASHINGTON

By 1834, Washington, despite its capture and burning during the War of 1812, had grown to be a thriving town, with the capitol and the White House dominating it. Cooke's painting shows the Navy Yard in the right foreground, with the capitol immediately above, and off to the left the rectangular mass of the White House. Already the rolling quiet hills of the site are being covered with houses and streets according to the plan laid out by Major L'Enfant (No. 259).

258   From an aquatint engraved by W. J. Bennett, 1834, after the painting by G. Cooke. Courtesy of I. N. Phelps Stokes, New York

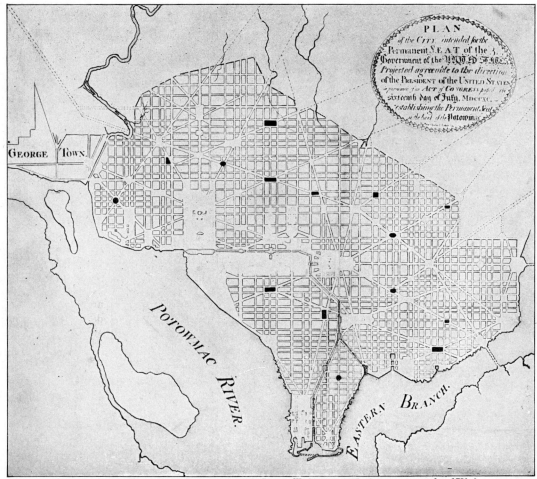

PLAN OF WASHINGTON, 1791

THE plan of Washington, laid out by Major Pierre Charles L'Enfant under the supervision of George Washington, is one of the great marks of the transition from colonial provincialism to national centralization. The garden plan of the great palace at Versailles was in some respects the original inspiration. In its magnificent use of monumental vistas, its radiating avenues and "circles," its monumental Mall, it was a piece of city planning not only unique in America, but an advance over any then existing city plan in Europe.

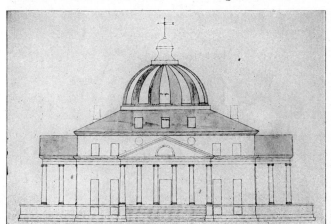

JEFFERSON'S DESIGN FOR THE WHITE HOUSE

THOMAS JEFFERSON submitted a design for the White House competition, under the name of Abraham Faws, which shows how strongly he was influenced by the Italian architect, Palladio, whose books were his constant inspiration. Jefferson's design not only resembles Palladio's work; it reveals as well how he loved simple, monumental forms, and especially domes and porticos.

THE FIRST ARCHITECTURAL COMPETITION IN THE UNITED STATES

THE decision to hold a competition for a design for a national capitol in the new city of Washington was a most important step in the architectural progress of the country. President Washington and Thomas Jefferson, both enthusiasts in their interest in the development of the national capital, and both interested in architecture, Washington officially as president and unofficially as a cultured gentleman, and Jefferson because architecture was his greatest hobby, realized that a building commensurate with their dreams demanded much more than the skill of the village carpenter. The need for

261   Front Elevation by Philip Hart, from the original competition drawings in the Maryland Historical Society

the professional architect was not only acutely felt; the very fact of holding the competition officially recognized it, and the results to-day certainly justify this early realization of the importance of good architecture.

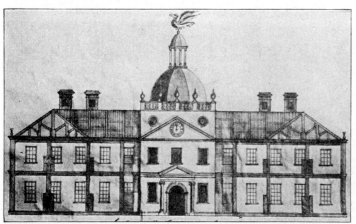

262 Section through Front by James Diamond, from the original competition drawings in the Maryland Historical Society

We cannot doubt that such a competition as this attracted the best architectural brains of the time; the designs submitted prove an invaluable evidence of the level of architectural taste at the end of the eighteenth century. The designs easily divide themselves into two groups; one, those which are obviously the product of carpenters and builders, self taught, and educated only in the native traditions; the other, those in which true architectural creative power plainly declares itself. Between the two groups is the design of Samuel McIntire.

The designs of Philip Hart and James Diamond belong of course to the first group. Hart plans a building purely colonial in type, but a sort of gargantuan colonial, enormously enlarged and exaggerated, without the slightest idea of planning or scale. James Diamond's design is more grandiose, but he was evidently a carpenter, preoccupied with such details as roof trusses; this design is complicated and unconvincing without even Hart's colonial character. By contrast McIntire's elevation seems a work of genius.

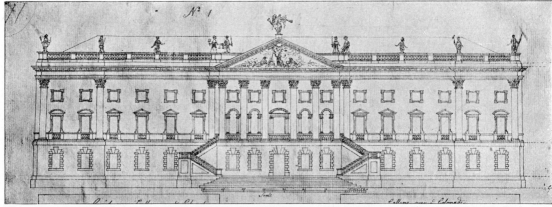

263   Front Elevation from the design of Samuel McIntire, from the original competition drawings in the Maryland Historical Society

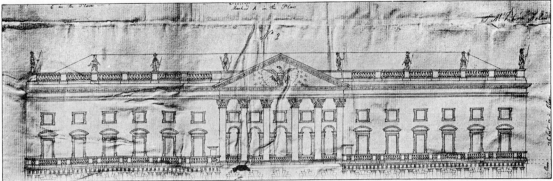

264   Rear Elevation from the design of Samuel McIntire, from the original competition drawings in the Maryland Historical Society

FROM COLONIAL TO ROMAN IN THE CAPITOL COMPETITION

YET even McIntire's design was not satisfactory. It is well planned and composed, and despite crudeness in the detail possesses dignity, good proportion, and a sense of the monumental. But its monumental character is purely English Renaissance after the manner of Sir William Chambers, and its interiors fine New England colonial; the correspondence between Washington and Jefferson shows that they were seeking something more classic, more Roman.

This element, new in American architecture, appeared in the designs of Samuel Dobie, Dr. Thornton, and Stephen Hallet. Dobie's design is a dignified piece of pure Palladian classicism, Thornton's design, now lost, which won the competition, was evidently a great classic temple; Hallet's, also largely lost, was even more monumental. But Hallet made many studies for the capitol, and all of them are far ahead of any other of the existing competition drawings in dignity, in scale, but particularly in monumental planning and a sense of what a great public building should be.

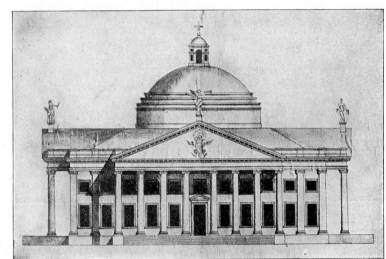

265   Front Elevation by Samuel Dobie, from the original competition drawings in the Maryland Historical Society

He won second place, and many of his ideas were incorporated into the final design of Thornton, whose assistant he became when the building was actually begun.

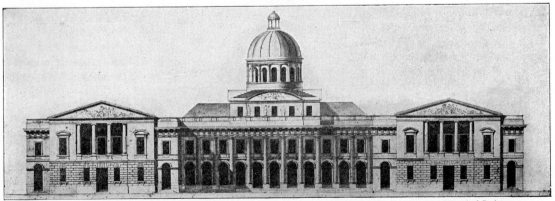

266   Front Elevation from a study by Stephen Hallet, from the original competition drawings in the Maryland Historical Society

THE WHITE HOUSE

OF the competitive drawings for the White House, that of James Hoban, an Irishman who had been trained as an architect in Dublin, was judged best; and the present White House in its general aspect is due to him. Latrobe added the colonnades at front and back after the War of 1812; but the pediment appears in the early designs, although then there were

267   © Harris & Ewing

only four engaged columns instead of the projecting portico. Here again the pedimented windows of the main floor and the elaborately decorated door show a Roman classicism that was new. The planning of Hoban was also markedly classic and carefully studied.

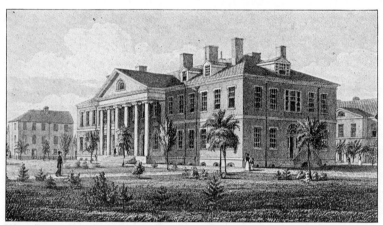

268   From an engraving by Fenner Sears & Co., London, published 1831, after a drawing
by C. Burton, New York

THE DEPARTMENT OF STATE, WASHINGTON, IN 1831

THE early building of the State Department shows a type intermediate between the extreme revival of classic forms and the colonial style which it superseded. The colonnade, to be sure, is monumental and correctly classical; but the body of the building has a straightforward simplicity and directness quite colonial in type. The whole resembles more the mixed forms

that Bulfinch used so charmingly in Boston than the true classic revival work that was to hold sway in America almost until the Civil War.

THE OLD GENERAL POST OFFICE, WASHINGTON

MUCH more Roman, and therefore much more truly characteristic of the Washington tradition, is the Post Office building. Later in date, it shows how strongly the classic style set by the capitol and the White House appealed to popular taste. Particularly noteworthy is the use of pilasters of monumental size to decorate a long wall, a scheme used alike both in buildings of Roman and Greek inspiration.

269   From Herrmann J. Meyer, *Universorum*, New York, 1851

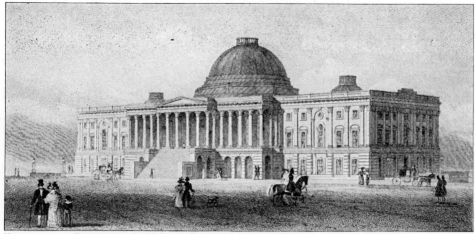

270   From an engraving by Fenner Sears & Co., London, 1831, after a drawing by H. Brown

THE CAPITOL OF THE UNITED STATES, 1831

THE United States capitol is the product of not one, but many minds. To Dr. Thornton, winner of the competition, is due the general scale and size of parts of the old capitol shown here in an old print. But Hallet, a Frenchman, modified details; Latrobe did much interior work, and finally Bulfinch, called to Washington in 1818, worked out new improvements in the manner of connecting the two wings. This calling of a New Englander to Washington is an early evidence of the break-up of local traditions that accompanied the growth of the young country, and the gradual development of a national art and culture.

STATUARY HALL, IN THE CAPITOL, WASHINGTON

STATUARY HALL — the former House of Representatives — in the national capitol is an early example of Greek revival work, by B. H. Latrobe, which combines with the delicacy of the Greek Corinthian capital a richness of dark marble shafts much more Roman than Greek.

271   From an engraving by J. Bentley, after a drawing by
W. H. Bartlett

THE CAPITOL, 1837, REAR VIEW

A BARTLETT view of the capitol in 1837 shows how beautifully the old capitol crowned its wooded hill, and how much more simple and easy to grasp its form was before the two enormous present House and Senate wings were added in the 'fifties. It was a building unique not only in America, but, according to Fiske Kimball, in the world; expressing the new ideas of the Roman Revival, but preserving the older direct quality that made it such a frank expression of its function and plan.

272   From a photograph by Rau Studios, Inc.

THE SUPREME COURT CHAMBER

THE present Supreme Court room in the capitol was once the Senate House. It owes most of its present delicate Greek revival form to Bulfinch, or perhaps to Latrobe, but as in so much of the capitol work, the Greek revival character is combined with much-domed coffered ceiling, arches, and various other Roman details.

273

From a photograph by Gramstorff Bros., Inc.

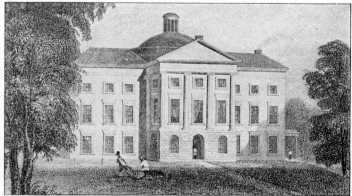

A NEW AMERICAN "ORDER"

B. H. LATROBE was not only a revivalist; he was also seeking that ever fascinating ideal — a purely American style. The Indian corn column designed by him for the Supreme Court stairway shows one of his attempts to combine classic logic and proportions with a symbolism altogether new.

275   From an engraving published by Tallis, London and New York, about 1840

THE CAPITOL OF NORTH CAROLINA AT RALEIGH

SUCH a building as the new capitol was bound to exert a profound influence upon all official American architecture. Embodying as it did so much thought not only of its architects, but of Washington and Jefferson, its style met with instant and wide-spread approval. Every state capitol thereafter must have a dome, columns, and a three part plan. This old capitol building at Raleigh, North Carolina, begun in 1794 — two years after the national capitol competition — was an early example.

274   From Glenn Brown's *History of The United States Capitol*, Washington, 1903

OFFICIAL CLASSIC IN NEW YORK

THE old Assay Office on Wall Street in New York, built in 1823, shows the wide spread of the Roman revival. It was originally a Bank of the United States. With columns, a pediment, framed and corniced windows, a rusticated basement — it shows all of these elements that were becoming so popular throughout the country due to the examples of federal building in Washington. It has now been rebuilt as the front of one of the wings of the Metropolitan Museum of Art.

276   From a photograph by Frank Cousins

THE POST OFFICE IN PORTLAND, MAINE

THE Roman type remained for many decades the usual model for post offices and other buildings of more or less official character. Typical of the later Roman revival post offices is that in Portland, Me. At a time when the general level of taste, creative ability and craftsmanship had fallen to deplorably low levels, the conservative Roman tradition for official work saved many a building from being an eyesore. Whatever its faults in detail, such a building — and their number is legion in this country — has something still left of dignity, quiet, repose, and academic beauty. Buildings like this kept the classic tradition alive during many decades.

277   From a photograph by W. H. Gay

CHAPTER X

THE GREEK REVIVAL—GOTHIC INFLUENCE

ENTHUSIASM for things classical, once started, could not be expected to stop with Rome. As early as 1770 the Library Company of Philadelphia owned Stuart and Revett's *Antiquities of Athens*, so that even before the Revolution there was some knowledge of Greek architecture among the *literati* of the country; but before the use of Greek forms became common, the Roman Revival was a necessary step to break the dominance of the colonial traditions.

During the early years of the republic, knowledge of Greek forms became more widely spread. Not only were these years notable because they brought into the country an influx of architectural books, but also because there was an increasing number of architects trained to use them. No trained eye can be entirely blind to the peculiar refinements of Greek detail; it is natural, therefore, that in the work of both Latrobe and Bulfinch in the capitol at Washington, Greek as well as Roman elements can be found, and that a strong Greek influence is discernible in some of the books of Asher Benjamin, colonial as, for the most part, they are. During these years, too, knowledge of many things was increasing rapidly; travel was becoming less difficult. Nicholas Biddle, for instance, in 1806 had traveled through Greece, and remained ever afterward a confirmed Greek enthusiast; in the *Port Folio*, a magazine which he owned, he published in 1814 an essay on architecture by George Tucker, in which Greek architecture was asserted to be the only type suitable for the new country.

But the true Greek Revival was in no sense merely the result of such aristocratic pressure. It was not imposed from above. On the contrary, it was in the widest sense a popular movement, deeply emotional, and despite its classic guise deeply romantic. It was but one phase of the world-wide romantic movement of the early nineteenth century; it fired all the western world with enthusiasm for the cause of Greek liberty; it was symbolized in the bringing of the Parthenon sculptures to England by Lord Elgin; it sent Byron to die at Missolonghi in 1824. Like all popular movements it had its proper architectural expression, and the American Greek Revival was one part of a world-wide Greek Revival. The American phase was not the mere copy of a movement already existing in Europe; it was an integral part of that movement, with which it was contemporaneous, and in some respects, America carried the use of Greek forms to a point which is unique.

But the Greek Revival was more than that. It was also a modified form of the age-old search for an Eldorado of the mind — a driving force hardly less powerful than that which made those years a pageant of humanity moving westward, pouring over the Alleghanies, over the Mississippi, filling the plains, at last topping the distant Rockies in the search for some promised wealth in the world of reality.

These two movements, the mental creation of an ideal Greece that was the Golden Age incarnate, and the physical search for an Eldorado in the West, had much to do with each other. For this period of growth was, for many, a period of all the hardships consequent upon the settlement of new land and upon pioneering; it was, moreover, a time of profound intellectual stirring, a period of maladjustment. There was a deep disillusionment because the ideals that had motivated the Revolution had not produced an immediate Utopia, and now the later Jeffersonian ideals were breaking down. There was political chaos; there was the ugly beginning of factional and sectional strife; and there was the so-called industrial revolution.

Already there had been, in the East, a remarkable factory development. Milbert, describing the suburbs of Boston in 1826, comments on this. Speaking of the lovely country houses that abounded, he says "their elegant architecture, their white walls and green blinds, make a striking contrast to the sombre appearance of the factories, which are recognizable by the brown color that they are usually painted." And he adds that Newton was "remarkable for its numerous factories of every sort, such as iron foundries, cotton mills, paper mills," etc. Wealth from this new industrial source was pouring into the country; but the development had been too rapid; the new industrialism merely added one more element to the chaotic thinking and feeling of the times. Such a period demands a Golden Age to dream about; and this Golden Age was Greece.

Books on architecture, showing Greek forms, began to be multiplied. Minard Lafever's *Modern Builders' Guide* is typical; it contained designs for various types of buildings, and details, beautifully drawn, of doors, windows, chimney pieces, in pure Greek style. This book, published in 1833, proved so popular that a second enlarged edition was required in 1841. It was by means of books like this that the use of Greek forms was spread over the country, filling Ohio, Missouri and even Michigan, as well as New England and the South, with the characteristic temple-shaped houses.

A style so popularized was necessarily a sentimental style. Greek detail was used not because it furnished particularly appropriate building forms, but because Greek enthusiasm was rampant. As a necessary result, it was a superficial style. It taught people to think of buildings not in terms of use or function or good planning, but in terms of details: columns, pediments and moldings of the correct Greek profiles. Use was everywhere sacrificed to looks. The Greek Revival has been widely condemned as superficial, artificial — perhaps rightly. It was superficial; it partook of the sentimental, romantic nature of its time (a time that produced both Poe and Longfellow) but it was not artificial, for it expressed a deep-seated, nation-wide emotion.

Moreover, the traditional instincts of native craftsmanship were soon at it, changing and modifying everywhere. Columns were made more slender; moldings were simplified; carved work was frequently omitted; new forms were worked out for window and door trims and the like, full of Greek simplicity and refinement, but yet typically of wood, typically native. Thus the Greek style suffered the subtle metamorphosis that had overtaken English forms in colonial days, and that to a lesser extent modified Gothic details a little later. It was these subtle changes, the result of a well-based craftsmanship working on the archæological material, which gave to the Greek Revival in America its unprecedented vitality, and which made it possible, as Fiske Kimball points out, for Greek temples to rise often side by side with the log cabins of the first settlers. The vitality of the American Greek fashion in building is proved by the way it subsisted beside, and eventually, except in church work, absorbed the Gothic Revival that followed. For the Greek and Roman Revivals made a Gothic Revival inevitable. Once the theory is adopted that the most vital and beautiful architecture is the result, not of creating anew on the basis of actual needs and materials, but of copying the work of past ages, any one chosen moment of the past may become as architecturally stimulating as another, and every increase in archæological knowledge may mean merely another style to imitate, another revival. And in this development, the beautiful Gothic monuments of Europe were too important to be neglected. The Greek Revival succeeded where the Gothic, except in church work, largely failed, because it was based on an emotion deep in the American mind, and because it lent itself more readily to such craftsman's modifications as took from it the curse of mere archæological copying, and gave it the status of a style almost new.

TO MILLWRIGHTS,

Carpenters, Cabinet-Makers, Ship-Builders, Masons, &c. who practice in their professions,

THE SCIENCE OF

Architecture.

Those who are desirous of learning the principles or theory upon which they are founded, according to Mathematics—as, Mensuration, Gauging, &c. together with drawing (as well as others, who wish to learn Mathematics, in particular, in all its various branches) are informed that WILLIAM SCHULTZ proposes, by the particular desire of some of his most intimate friends, to open a *NIGHT SCHOOL* on the 1st of October, 1813. To commence at 6 and continue till 9 o'clock in the evening. Private lessons from 9 to 12 in the forenoon, and from 2 to 5 in the afternoon. Price per quarter 10 dollars.

N. B To render the above learning easier comprehensible to all classes, they are respectfully informed that Draughts, Drawings, Paintings, &c. will be exhibited with that view, and consequently will render the knowledge easier known, and proficiency sooner acquired. It is hardly necessary to mention, that Mathematics, including its many branches, is the mother of invention as the principles are governed by philosophy, in application to the arts, &c.

Any further information may be had by applying at No. 5, Courtland-St. or at the New-York Free-School.

Printed by Hardcastle & Van Pelt, No. 86, Nassau-street.

278   From a broadside, 1813, in the New York
       Historical Society

"THE SCIENCE OF ARCHITECTURE"

A BROADSIDE of 1813 shows that in this early period there must have been not only a growing popular interest in architecture, but also a demand on the part of the mechanics for an education to fit them to supply the need of a great amount of new building. It was this growing interest in architecture which helped the spread of the Greek Revival.

A GREEK REVIVAL COUNTRY RESIDENCE

THE period of the Greek Revival was remarkable for the widespread knowledge of the style and the correctness of forms used everywhere. This came about through the wide distribution of carefully-made books showing plans, elevations, and details in the Greek style. Minard Lafever's *Modern Builders' Guide*, New York, 1833, second edition, 1841, was one of the best. The illustration (No. 279) is one of its plates which shows a large Greek Revival "Country Residence."

279   From Minard Lafever, *Modern Builders' Guide*, New York, second edition, 1841

THE FERRIS HOUSE, NEW YORK

IN execution, few Greek Revival houses are as rich or many-columned as the published designs. Given four Greek Doric columns, a pediment, and smooth walls, the result is the typical Greek Revival house. Windows, not being Greek forms, were sometimes difficult to handle. The Ferris house, Bronx Borough, New York, is a typical example of an attempt to be Greek.

280   From a photograph by Frank Cousins

THE BURT HOUSE, WORCESTER, MASSACHUSETTS

NEW ENGLAND, the West, the South, all fell victim to the fallacy that architecture is superficial form only, and thousands of Doric columns in wood supported porches the country over. The Burt house in Worcester, Mass., is one of the best. Designed by a famous Greek Revival architect, Elias Carter, it has unusual repose, dignity, and grace, and the Greek detail is sufficiently subordinated to the real demands of the straightforward, almost colonial scheme, so as not to appear forced or out of place.

281　　　　　From a photograph by E. B. Luce

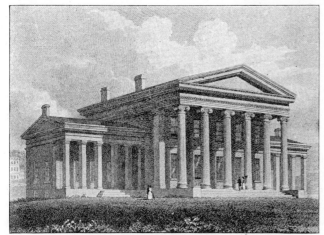

282　From an engraving, 1830, by Fenner Sears & Co., London, after a drawing by Alexander J. Davis

GREEK REVIVAL IN THE CONNECTICUT VALLEY

THE Bowers house, in Northampton, Mass. (No. 282), is a fine example of the larger, more monumental type of Greek Revival house with wings, and with Ionic columns instead of the more usual Doric. In this, as in so many others, windows, not the least Greek but still necessary to the building, are as far as possible hidden in porches behind columns. The old view was drawn by Alexander J. Davis, one of the most famous of early nineteenth-century American artists and himself an architect.

A COLONNADED SOUTHERN MANSION

THE Coleman house in Macon, Ga., shows how colonnaded forms were used in the South. Again and again southern houses of the first half of the nineteenth century were built with a colonnade two stories high running clear round the four sides of a central block. These high colonnades not only gave necessary shade, but conferred upon the houses they decorated a dignity and monumental character in keeping with the planter's aristocratic ideals.

283　　　　　From a photograph

THE SAMUEL DEXTER HOUSE, DEXTER, MICHIGAN

THE rapidity of the spread of Greek Revival details throughout the country is remarkable. Even in far-away Michigan, as Fiske Kimball points out: "Little after the log cabins of the first settlers, side by side with them in many instances, rose ambitious dwellings in the form of the temple." Such is the house (No. 284) built in the eighteen forties by Judge Samuel Dexter in Michigan when that state was still on the frontier.

284   Courtesy of Fiske Kimball

285   Courtesy of Fiske Kimball

THE SMITH HOUSE, GRASS LAKE, MICHIGAN

EQUALLY Greek, and based closely on one of Minard Lafever's house designs (No. 279), is the Smith house (No. 285) at Grass Lake, Michigan, dating from 1840.

286   From a photograph by Frank Cousins

A GREEK DOORWAY IN SALEM

EVEN when Greek ideas did not control the entire composition of a house, they appeared in details. This doorway from Salem (No. 286) shows a type of Greek Corinthian order that was exceedingly popular in just such porches as this. There is in it a tight-laced sort of austerity that seemed a natural reaction from some of the overwrought Adam detail that had preceded.

THE JOHN C. STEVENS HOUSE, NEW YORK

THIS house on Murray Street, New York, long since destroyed, shows a different and more elaborate treatment of the Greek Revival. The general composition is a type similar to that of the "Octagon" (No. 248), but all the details are of the richest Greek type.

287   From the original drawing by Alexander J. Davis in the New York Historical Society

288   From a photograph by Frank Cousins

A FRONT HALL IN THE GREEK SPIRIT

THE Greek spirit permeated interior work as well, as in the hall of the Daniel P. Parker house, Boston. But here precedents were lacking, the problem was new; and so new forms of trim had to be developed, in which little bits of Greek detail were introduced wherever possible; rosettes at the corners of the trim, frets in bands, frets or anthemions at the tops and bottoms of panels. Trim became wider than in the preceding period and occasionally heaviness resulted. But at its best, this work was dignified and beautiful and less tied to precedent than similar exterior work.

GREEK IDEAS IN ENTRANCE DOORS

THESE two designs for front doors (No. 289) by Minard Lafever, from the *Modern Builders' Guide*, show that the problem of applying Greek details to forms as un-Grecian as modern entrance doors had no terrors for the enthusiastic Greek revivalist. Greek fret, and anthemion patterns, and Greek consoles are used wherever possible, and architraves and bands decorated with rosettes, as in the Erechtheum doorway in Athens.

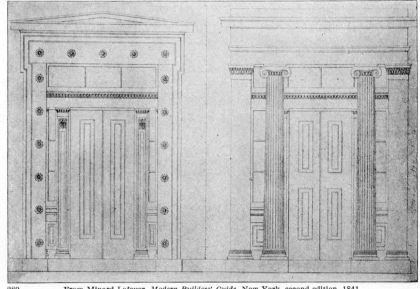

289   From Minard Lafever, *Modern Builders' Guide*, New York, second edition, 1841

290   A view of Leicester, Mass., from a print in the possession of the publishers

GREEK FORMS BLENDED WITH COLONIAL TYPES

The Greek Revival transformed hundreds of villages and towns. Built most frequently in wood, painted white, the Greek forms blended surprisingly well with older colonial types, despite the difference between the ideas that governed them. The view of Leicester, Mass., shows a Congregational church of normal colonial type; a town house of typical late Adam or Bulfinch character; a Unitarian church and an academy of typical Greek Revival style; yet all harmonize admirably.

291   From Henry Howe, *Historical Collections of Ohio*, Cincinnati, 1847

GREEK INFLUENCE IN OHIO, 1846

The same combination penetrated the Middle West at an early period. Ravenna, O., as drawn by Henry Howe in 1846, has a precisely similar combination; and although the western detail is often more crude and simple, the ideal sought was the same as in the older eastern towns. Such villages make clear the intellectual heritage of the Middle West.

A VIEW OF DAYTON, OHIO, 1846

Howe, in 1846, wrote that the Montgomery County Courthouse at Dayton was "the most costly and elegant in Ohio." Its elegance consisted, of course, in its accurate following of the fashion of the time: the Greek Revival. A colonnaded cupola, pilasters, columns in the front, a pediment — all the trappings of the Greek Revival building are present.

292   From Henry Howe, *Historical Collections of Ohio*, Cincinnati, 1847

BALLSTON SPRINGS, NEW YORK, 1840

BARTLETT's view of Ballston Springs, N. Y., shows a typical eastern town in the Greek Revival period. At the left is a four-story frame hotel with a colonnaded porch and a balustrade to hide its roof; behind it another balustraded façade, and at the head of the street a characteristic Greek Revival church, with its pedimented Doric porch, and above a tower which

293   From an engraving by J. Sands after a drawing by W. H. Bartlett, London, 1840

reveals as close an approximation to the Greek spirit as the demands of the universal "colonial" spire tradition would permit.

294   From J. Milbert, *Itinéraire Pittoresque du Fleuve Hudson*, etc., Paris, 1828–29

SARATOGA SPRINGS, AS SEEN BY MILBERT, ABOUT 1826

MILBERT's drawing of Saratoga Springs in the eighteen twenties shows the Greek Revival ideal applied to a large and fashionable hotel — and the result is a magnificent colonnaded two-story porch whose size and richness express the luxury that was afforded within. Faithfulness to the fashionable forms was absolutely essential here, for Saratoga was one of the first of the famous American watering places.

THE OLD TREMONT HOUSE, BOSTON

CITY hotels of this period were also naturally built in the height of the fashion for Greek forms. The old Tremont House at Boston was such: porch, cornice, corner pilasters, all pure Greek. Windows were, as usual, a puzzle: here they are rightly treated with the utmost simplicity. It dates from 1828.

295   Isaiah Rogers, architect; from an engraving, about 1830, by J. Archer after a drawing by J. Kidder

296   From a lithograph, 1834, in the New York Historical Society

A GREEK REVIVAL HOTEL IN NEW YORK

THE old Astor House on Broadway in New York City (formerly the Park Hotel) was another such luxurious and fashionable Greek Revival hotel. Great dignity is given by the pedimented porch and the pediment-shaped coping over the central motive. However illogical, there was in such building much of the beauty that comes from the sober dignity of the copied Greek forms.

THE CHARLESTON HOTEL, CHARLESTON, SOUTH CAROLINA

MOST rich of all the Greek Revival hotels was — and is — the Charleston Hotel (No. 297), at Charleston, S. C. The columns are pure copies of those of the Choragic Monument of Lysicrates, though much larger in size than the originals. In the cornice the architect has tried to combine the richness of the Roman modillion (bracket) with the purity of the Greek detail and has placed modillions in the dentil course itself; an attempt more original than successful. The Charleston Hotel reveals the beginning of one of the chief faults of much modern city architecture: it is too obviously a one-fronted building, with the other sides skimped or forgotten.

297   © Detroit Photographic Co.

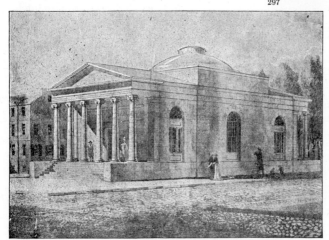

298   From the drawing by B. H. Latrobe in the Maryland Historical
                        Society, Baltimore

THE BANK OF BALTIMORE

B. H. LATROBE's design for the Bank of Baltimore shows Greek Revival forms applied to commercial use. It is also one of the very earliest buildings to use Greek forms, for it was built in 1799; and yet its portico is pure Greek Ionic from the Erechtheum. The composition as a whole is more original, logical and living than that usually found in later Greek Revival buildings and bears eloquent evidence of the talent of its designer. This is the architect's original sketch perspective.

THE TROY FEMALE SEMINARY, 1835

DURING the period of the Greek Revival in both East and Middle West there sprang up numerous schools, academies, seminaries, and colleges. To these the Greek Revival forms lent themselves readily. The Troy Female Seminary in 1835 shows a long dormitory of a type that was almost universal, with Greek feeling in details only. To the left is the Greek Doric porch of a church or chapel; to the right, behind the dormitory, another Greek colonnade.

299   From a lithograph, 1835, by Pendleton, Boston, after a drawing by T. Lee

300   From an engraving, 1831, by Fenner Sears & Co., London, after a drawing by Alexander J. Davis

EARLY COLLEGE BUILDINGS IN AMHERST, MASSACHUSETTS

THE chapel and dormitories of Amherst College, Amherst, Mass., as seen in 1831, show how the extreme restraint and simplicity that resulted from the poverty of many of these old institutions were themselves, æsthetically, often a virtue; changing and modifying the richness of Greek detail, molding all into a whole still recognizable as influenced by the Greek Revival, but with a robust vigor entirely American.

GIRARD COLLEGE, PHILADELPHIA

WHEN the institution of learning was rich, there was no such molding and modifying; the details and the forms, though perhaps recombined, were themselves copied line for line. The result, such as the main building of Girard College in Philadelphia, a fine Greek Corinthian temple, may be richer and more elegant, but it somehow lacks the vitality of the simpler, more native work. And yet such a building as this is a con-

301   From a photograph by Frank Cousins

stant æsthetic education to all who see it. Notice how completely the windows are hidden from the front.

302   From an engraving, 1831, by Fenner Sears & Co., London, after a drawing
by C. Burton, New York

THE UNITARIAN CHURCH, PHILADELPHIA

A LITTLE Unitarian church in Philadelphia shows one reason for the long continued popularity of the Greek forms; the fact that one dominating Greek Doric portico, if carefully designed, can in some magic way confer an appearance of dignity, a rather arid beauty, and even richness, to the building of which it is a part, however small or plain.

INTERIOR OF THE BROADWAY TABERNACLE

A TYPICAL church interior of the Greek Revival type is shown by this view of the old Broadway Tabernacle. Its amphitheater plan, with flat dome and no chancel save a projecting platform, was several times attempted in non-ritualistic churches. This was perhaps the most successful expression of the type.

303   From a lithograph, 1848, by Davignon, after a drawing by T. H. Matteson, in the New York
Historical Society

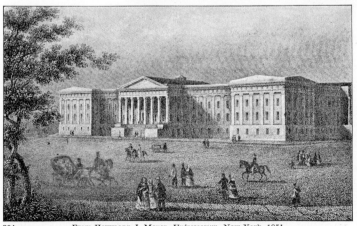

304   From Herrmann J. Meyer, *Universorum*, New York, 1851

THE PATENT OFFICE, WASHINGTON

DESPITE the strong Roman trend in Washington, the Greek Revival had its effect there as well. In fact, the largest and in some ways the finest of the Greek Revival public buildings in this country is the Patent Office. Its long ranks of pilasters, with the windows between, the range of triglyphs above, the strong end pavilions, and the central monumental porticos produce an effect that is extremely impressive.

THE UNITED STATES SUB–TREASURY, NEW YORK

THE old Customs House, now the United States Sub-Treasury, still lifts proudly its eight-columned Doric front above the traffic of Wall Street. Rather starkly simple, without color or ornament, its innate dignity of form and the fine sweep of its scale and size make it count more than many of its newer, richer, and more lofty neighbors.

305   From a retouched photograph about 1880 by Soule

306   After the original drawing in the New York Historical Society

THE ARCHITECT'S PERSPECTIVE OF THE SUB–TREASURY

THE designers of the old Customs House in New York (No. 306) were Ithiel Town, designer of Center Church in New Haven, and Alexander J. Davis, designer of the Stevens house (No. 287). Their original design made much of a large central dome that sits but oddly on the Greek roof below, and which hardly counts in the existing work. Columns, as the plan shows, are used even more lavishly inside than out; but the plan shows a real grasp of monumental arrangement.

THE OLD BOWERY THEATER, NEW YORK

THE front of the old Bowery Theater (No. 307) shows how the pedimented portico of the Greek Temple was used not only on houses, churches, customs houses, but even on theaters. There was obviously no attempt in Greek Revival design to express the *function* or the *structure* of buildings.

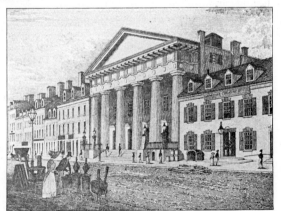

307   From an engraving by H. Fossette after a drawing by C. Burton

THE COUNCIL CHAMBER, NEW YORK CITY HALL

THE council chamber of the New York City Hall (No. 308) in the eighteen thirties shows a mixture of Adam, colonial, and Greek Revival forms to which only the big scale of the flat dome and the comparative simplicity of the general scheme give unity.

308   From an engraving by H. Fossette after a drawing by C. Burton

309   © Detroit Photographic Co.

THE CAPITOL, MONTPELIER, VERMONT

THE structure which was built in 1836, burned and rebuilt in 1857, is a characteristic example of the usual type in which the Greek element is much stressed. The use of a higher dome, on a drum, is an advance on the low dome squeezed down on a pedimented roof, such as the New York Customs House possessed, but the problem of combining forms so essentially Roman and so essentially Greek is almost insoluble.

THE TENNESSEE CAPITOL, NASHVILLE

MUCH more original in composition, and a much better solution of the problem of combining Greek forms with a high central feature is the capitol at Nashville, Tenn. This building (No. 310) borrows much from Jefferson's Virginia capitol (No. 254); larger, it has as well porticos in the middle of the long side, and for cupola a slightly modified replica, lovely in proportion, of the Choragic Monument of Lysicrates in Athens. The whole building with its four Ionic por-

310   © Detroit Photographic Co.

ticos, its simplicity and dignity of form, and the grace of its central tower, is one of the frankest, most logical, and most successful of all the Greek Revival public buildings.

211   From an engraving by John Poppel after a sketch by W. Heine, New York, 1850

THE TOMBS, NEW YORK

ONCE the door was open to the wide-spread copying of Greek forms, Revivalism could not stop there. Archæological discovery was proceeding apace, and the wonders of Egypt were beginning to make an impression on the popular mind. Hence there arise scattering attempts to revive Egyptian forms, of which the most interesting was probably the old "Tombs," court and prison, in New York City. It had dignity, scale, impressiveness; but the Egyptian forms were too foreign to American psychology, demanded too expensive material and decoration, and were too little understood to gain wide adoption.

DORSEY'S "GOTHIC MANSION"

THE English Romantic movement, which produced Walpole's famous seat, Strawberry Hill, in a sort of mixed Gothic, had little reflection here. There is, however, in the *Port Folio* for February, 1811, a view of an early Gothic mansion, in Philadelphia. It shows pointed arches, pinnacles, drip molds, and tracery, but all utterly misused. It is a unique American version of the "Strawberry Hill" school — Gothic as seen through essentially Renaissance eyes, like Chippendale's Gothic; possessing quaintness, and oddity, but little sense of essential consistency.

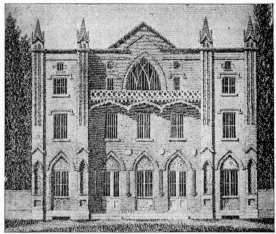

312   From an engraving by B. Tanner after a drawing by Mills in the *Port Folio*, Philadelphia, 1811

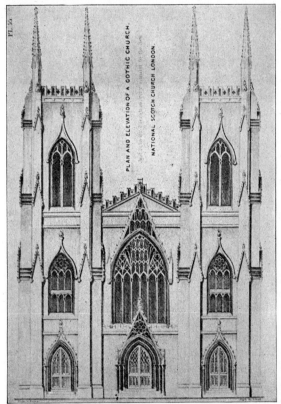

313   From Minard Lafever, *Modern Builders' Guide*, New York, second edition, 1841

DESIGN FOR A GOTHIC CHURCH

MINARD LAFEVER published a design (No. 313) for a Gothic church in the *Modern Builders' Guide*, "very similar to the new National Scotch Church, London," the only foreign element in a work otherwise utterly of the Greek Revival. It is an advance on Dorsey's Gothic mansion, but still reveals the study of Gothic forms in its infancy.

THE OLD MASONIC HALL, BROADWAY, NEW YORK

THE old Masonic Hall on Broadway, New York (No. 314), reveals, however, that even by 1830 much better Gothic than Lafever's *Modern Builders' Guide* church was being done in America. The Masonic Hall, in dignity, composition, richness and accuracy of detail, was unusually advanced for its date and will bear comparison with any English Gothic work of the same date. The off-setting of the walls, like buttresses, is, of course, an amusing misinterpretation; nevertheless the perpendicular tracery is good, and the lower story unusually full of the real spirit of late decorated English Gothic.

314   From an engraving, 1830, by Fenner Sears & Co., London, after a drawing by Alexander J. Davis

315   William Strickland, architect; from an engraving, by
Fenner Sears & Co., London, 1830, after a drawing
by C. Burton, New York

A FANTASTIC GOTHIC CHURCH

ORIGINALLY built in 1816 as a Swedenborgian Church (Church of the New Jerusalem), of whose governing body its architect was a member, this building was sold in 1826 to the Natural Academy of Sciences. With its strange classic dome and cupola, and its pseudo-Gothic entrance and pointed windows, it is typical of a chaotic and fantastic eclecticism which occasionally marked buildings of the beginning of the Gothic Revival. Its very *naïveté*, combined with its pleasant broad wall surfaces, is a tribute to Strickland's skill in finding new expression for the new sect.

THE NORTH CHURCH, SALEM, MASSACHUSETTS

IN New England Gothic ideas often found expression in a sort of homely simplicity that is frequently more akin to the true Gothic spirit than other richer and more pretentious works. The North Church in Salem is such a piece of simple Gothic work, and despite the absence of Gothic carving, despite elementary wooden tracery, the church has an effect of simple, dignified charm.

316   From a photograph by Frank Cousins

THE SALEM RAILROAD STATION

TYPICAL of the same spirit is the Salem railroad station, dating from 1847. However insufficient to modern needs and out of date to modern eyes, when it was built it was considered a masterpiece. Like the North Church, its authenticity as Gothic is *nil* but its total effect with corner towers and great pointed arch is effective, logical for the problem of a station as then understood, and expressive of the dignity of the times which produced it.

317   From a photograph by Frank Cousins

CHAPTER XI

PIONEERING AND THE GREAT EXPANSION

THE superficial quietness, sentimentality, and good manners that had characterized the decades that fostered the Greek Revival came soon to an inevitable end. The rumblings of bitter party strife, of sectional jealousies that were rooted in the question of the extension of slavery to the newly settled areas, were becoming continually louder, as the land west of the Mississippi was occupied and erected into territorial government. And the great westward push of the population which made this possible was itself an unsettling, complicating thing, for it brought with it tremendous new economic problems.

The discovery of gold in California and the rush of the Forty-Niners brought at last an American population to the Pacific; made the whole truly an American continent. Yet the settling of California was even more important as a symbol, a prophecy, than as an actual achievement, for large and valuable areas still remained unsettled, and pioneering continued a necessary process for thirty years more.

The effect upon architecture of this colossal westward growth, taking place in such a comparatively short time, with an intensity and rapidity of expansion almost unprecedented, was twofold. Obviously such a process — necessitating, as it did, the creation of thousands of new homes and new towns in localities where environment and materials were equally new — could not fail to make a deep impression on the building methods of the country. But there was a second more subtle influence, which was nation-wide, and extended even to the old-time centers of the East. For the adventure of pioneering, the working of liberal land laws, the early course of railroad development — involved with what the modern American would call graft — led to feverish and unhealthy economic inflation. Speculation in land and money was rife, great fortunes were being made and lost. The older quietness and leisure were gone. Pioneering itself entails a certain lack of permanence. It is here to-day and gone to-morrow; speed is its essential. Even staid Boston, and New York and Philadelphia, were affected; the atmosphere of those years throughout the country was hostile to tradition.

For the pioneer, tradition, or the lack of it, was at first of small moment. Shelter was what he needed. Despite Indians, despite forests, despite the almost treeless prairies of Kansas and Nebraska, he must make himself a home and at once. So history repeated itself; and throughout the country west of the Mississippi the pioneers built as best they could, using many of the same forms that their ancestors or predecessors had used in the forests and wastes along the Atlantic coast two hundred and more years before. So, in the forest, log cabins were built; for with one act two things were accomplished, the clearing of the land and the building of a house. The log cabin has come to seem the traditional pioneer house; its simple form has known little change from the earliest examples left to us almost down to the present day. So, too, in treeless countries sod houses and dugouts were built, just as long before the earliest settlers in Philadelphia had dug their houses into the river banks.

There was another similarity between the pioneer and the first settlers in America. Just as the Puritan in Massachusetts, or the planter in Virginia, tried as soon as he could to recreate in the wilderness a replica of the remembered home he had left, so the pioneer strove, often with a pathetic wistfulness and crudity, to recreate in his new environment old remembered forms. In the early days, it was the Greek Revival that was so remembered, and Greek Revival villages grew up to fill Ohio and Michigan; but later and further west these influences faded away, and the main result was that strange attempt to create an urban settled effect — the "false fronted" store or "hotel," where a front wall is run up to finish horizontally and mask the gable of the one-story building behind, and is often furnished with cornice and false second-story windows complete.

The pressure behind such pitifully disastrous attempts must be realized. The poverty of many of the pioneers was abject. Lawlessness was rampant, and lawlessness of life made lawless building. Moreover, the character of the pioneering population was strangely confused: adventurers, sharpers, thieves, solid farmers, bands of religious fanatics like the Mormons, the canny, hard working, rather ascetic Lutherans of Kansas and Nebraska and the Northwest — few or no artists, no wealth to spend on the luxury of design, and little wish for it. Yet there was the desire always to have a "town," a center to which one could go, where one could get the news, buy necessities, have a gossip, go on a spree — and a "town" meant buildings of more than one story, and flat roofs — so the false front arose, and lingers still, a silent memorial to those chaotic days.

But the false front was but one example of an ever growing disintegration of building ideals throughout the country. Land speculation in new or growing cities — and all the cities East and West were growing with continually increasing speed — was inevitable, and brought the ideal of cheapness into building as it never had been brought before. Cheap materials, cheap construction, speed, speed, speed, quick turnover and large profits — such an ideal leads to no great art. It breaks down the very foundations of creative design; it struck also the deathblow of the Greek Revival, and there was nothing to take its place. There began under this influence a decline of all artistic conscience — in strange consonance with a decline of financial and political conscience in the years following the Civil War, the results of which are, unfortunately, still all too apparent.

In these years of phenomenal growth, years which saw the building of the great West, which saw, rising slowly but surely, the specter of the Civil War, there were but two constructive, steadying artistic ideals, and they were rather imitative than creative; the persistence in some localities of the extraordinary Greek Revival influence, and the beginnings of the Gothic Revival. Otherwise new wealth, new materials — cast-iron and the like — were used only in the creation of chaos, cheapness, ugliness. It is perhaps because the country was so largely settled at this particular time, under these particular influences, that, since the Greek Revival farmhouse, America until very recently has had no rural architecture worth the name.

THE GOVERNMENT TOLLGATE

In the wake of the covered wagons that passed westward through Virginia and Pennsylvania and western New York came the turnpike. Tollhouses of simple but durable construction were built along them. The octagonal plan indicates a date in the early years of the nineteenth century.

318   From *Harper's Monthly Magazine*, Nov., 1879

319   Campus Martius, Ohio, in 1791, from a wood engraving in *The American Pioneer*, Marietta, 1842

A FRONTIER FORT

Campus Martius, at Marietta, Ohio, was built between 1788 and 1789. It was a carefully planned and well built fort, with dwelling houses within the walls, constructed of timber four inches thick, "nicely squared and dovetailed." It comprised also carefully planned bastions and stockades outside. From a little distance it resembled "one of the military palaces or castles of the feudal ages."

320   From a daguerreotype taken about 1855, courtesy of the State Historical Society of Wisconsin, Madison

FORT HOWARD, FOX RIVER, WISCONSIN

The typical military post of the period immediately after the War of 1812 was quite a different sort of building. The use of brick or stone for walls became the rule, and the design was based on eastern late "colonial" precedent. B. H. Latrobe designed houses for the Pittsburgh arsenal. Fort Howard appeared about 1855 as an enclosure in which houses and barracks and sheds have not only a sense of durability, but grace and quiet beauty as well. It was built originally in 1816.

FORT SNELLING, MINNESOTA

An early engraving shows, still further west, Fort Snelling, Minn., which was completed in 1822. It also is of sturdy masonry construction, simple, straightforward, but expressive of governmental dignity in a country still wild.

321   From C. A. Dana, *The United States Illustrated*, New York, 1852–53

A PIONEER LOG CABIN HOME IN OHIO

The early settlers west of the Alleghenies used almost universally the log cabin type, the typical American backwoods home. Travelers along the frontier found a crude and unlettered folk living in these rude habitations in the clearings. But they possessed a native strength and independence of spirit that augured well for the future. The engraving shows a cabin in Ohio about 1800.

322   From Henry Howe, *Historical Collections of Ohio*, Cincinnati, 1847

TYPE OF PIONEER HOUSE IN MISSOURI

Of the log huts of Missouri one existed (No. 323) until a recent date. The crisscross logs, the chinks between filled with mud, the tiny window, are all characteristic of the homes of the men who hewed a clearing in the forest and hoed a living out of the fertile soil between the stumps. But, rude as these cabins were, they sufficed to house the eager, adventurous pioneers who laid the foundation of America's westward growth.

323   Courtesy of the Missouri Historical Society, St. Louis

324   From a pen sketch made by J. D. Larpenteur, courtesy of the Minnesota Historical Society

AN EARLY LOG HOUSE IN ST. PAUL, MINNESOTA

The ground on which St. Paul now stands was almost a wilderness a century ago; one of its early log houses stood long enough to be preserved in this careful sketch, which shows its low-pitched, slab-covered roof, its lean-to shed, its low strong doorway. It was built in 1848.

A PIONEER FARMER'S HOME ON NEWLY CLEARED LAND

IN his book published in Edinburgh in 1793, one Mr. Campbell shows this naïve view of an "American new-cleared farm." Already the "dwelling house and wings" are of brick, although a log house is shown as well. This reveals the amazing rapidity of the process of settlement; but one step removed from the log cabin is the developed brick house and the established village. The view shows how forest became farm land; the tree stumps still cover the ground.

325 From Patrick Campbell, *Travels in the interior inhabited parts of North America*, Edinburgh, 1793

326 From Henry Howe, *Historical Collections of Ohio*, Cincinnati, 1847

SCENE ON THE AUGLAIZE RIVER, OHIO

HOWE'S sketch, "drawn on a pleasant day in June, 1846," shows a log house tavern dating from 1816. Its size and double construction mark it off from the simpler houses, although it much resembles the Missouri example (No. 323). Howe observes that "it has long been a favorite stopping-place for travellers, as many as twenty or thirty having, with their horses, frequently tarried here over-night."

A LOG TAVERN, INDIANA

ANOTHER English traveler, A. Welby, published in 1821 a view of a log tavern of more advanced type, the Lewis Tavern in Indiana. It boasts not only a sign, but also a porch running its whole length. Of its internal arrangements he says there was but one room, divided by a sheet, to accommodate himself and another gentleman with his wife, child, and nurse. Shelter and warmth were furnished; what more could one ask in the middle of the wilderness?

327 From A. Welby, *A Visit to North America and The English Settlements in Illinois*, London, 1821

A TAVERN ON THE OLD CUMBERLAND ROAD, MARYLAND

FURTHER east the taverns along the great roads were large, important affairs, almost hotels. This photograph of one on the old Cumberland Road in Maryland shows a stuccoed, masonry building with a long porch supported on high square posts of almost the Mount Vernon type. As the traveler proceeded into the less settled West, however, such luxurious resting places as this were soon left behind.

328 From a photograph by the Department of Roads, Washington

329   A First-Class Hotel on the Plains in 1867, from a wood
       engraving after a sketch by A. R. Waud

330   A First-Class Hotel on the Plains in 1869, from a wood
       engraving after a sketch by A. R. Waud

INFLUENCE OF THE RAILROAD ON BUILDING

CONDITIONS further west on the plains kept alive the primitive type of tavern another forty years, until the railroad was finally built. The "First-Class Hotel on the Plains" in 1867, before the railroad, is a crude log affair; the other two years later, a big wooden building in the full glory of Victorian fashion, reveals the effect of railroad development.

331   From Henry Howe, *Historical Collections of Ohio*, Cincinnati, 1847

COLUMBUS, OHIO, 1846

IN Howe's view of Columbus the state house is of the square, New England courthouse type, with hipped roof and central cupola. It was soon to be replaced by a Greek Revival building in stone. Across the street rises the five-story Neil House, and beyond is a vista of the uninteresting flat-roofed buildings of a highly developed city of the period.

VIEW OF TIFFIN, OHIO, IN 1846

THESE Ohio towns reached their first blooming at a time when the Greek Revival was at its height; and its impress is strong in Howe's view of Tiffin, with its colonnaded portico, its cupola, and houses beyond with arched doorways that are precisely like those built a little earlier along the Atlantic coast from Maine to the Carolinas.

332   From Henry Howe, *Historical Collections of Ohio*, Cincinnati, 1847

PUBLIC SQUARE, NEWARK, OHIO, IN 1846

THE broad square in this view is dominated by a Greek Revival Town or County Hall;

333   From Henry Howe, *Historical Collections of Ohio*, Cincinnati, 1847

the buildings around show anything but a "frontier" feeling; and only the bare and treeless expanse of the square shows the newness of the town. Like so many towns of early Ohio, it has a strangely "New England" appearance. Howe's sketch was done in 1846.

334   From Henry Howe, *Historical Collections of Ohio*, Cincinnati, 1847

PUBLIC SQUARE, HAMILTON, OHIO

THE white columns and cupola of the Hamilton Courthouse, sketched by Henry Howe in 1846, recall the grace of New England commons; so quickly did the crude log cabin of one generation yield in the next to the creation of the remembered and traditional eastern forms.

SLAB HALL, OBERLIN COLLEGE, OHIO

WITH the advance of civilization came education; schools and academies and even colleges were established almost in the forest itself. Oberlin College began in a slab hall in 1834; but twelve years later it had five well-built masonry buildings.

335   From Henry Howe, *Historical Collections of Ohio*, Cincinnati, 1847

336   From Henry Howe, *Historical Collections of Ohio*, Cincinnati, 1847

THE COTTAGE OF AN OHIO IMMIGRANT

OHIO was a center for other immigration than that from New England: Germans and Swiss came, invited by its hospitable fertility. Of this view, 1846, Howe says "it shows the mud cottage of a German Swiss emigrant, now standing in the neighborhood of others of like character, in the northwestern part of the country" [Columbiana]. Evidently its half-timber and chalet-like roof were not unique, but merely examples of a type once fairly common.

337   From the painting by George Caleb Bingham (1811–79) in the Mercantile Library, St. Louis

THE COUNTY ELECTION (MISSOURI, ABOUT 1840)

MISSOURI, owing to its favorable position on the Mississippi, was, like Ohio, settled early and had early lost its frontier quality. *The County Election* by George Caleb Bingham shows a typical Missouri street of the 'forties; the courthouse porch, with its square piers, is of the Greek Revival type, and the houses down the street in the background are those of a developed town.

THE FIRST DWELLING IN CHICAGO

THE beginnings of Chicago were of the humblest. Around the site of Fort Dearborn a tiny village grew up, was made a town in 1833, and by 1870 — a space of only 37 years — had over 300,000 inhabitants. Out of such log cabins as the Kinsie house, the first dwelling in Chicago, grew the second city of the United States. The view shows this house as it stood about 1820.

CHICAGO IN 1832

ANOTHER old lithograph shows part of the village (South Water Street) in 1832; a log tavern, a few log houses — that is all. But the situation of the city made it the natural outlet, via the Great Lakes, for all the fertile west country, and its growth from isolated trading center to thriving town was rapid.

338   From a drawing, about 1896, by C. E. Petford in the Chicago Historical Society, after a sketch by H. R. Schoolcraft, about 1820

339   From a lithograph in the Chicago Historical Society, after a contemporary sketch by George Davis

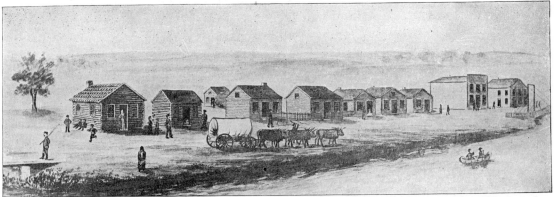

340   From a drawing by Justin Herriott, in the Chicago Historical Society, for W. H. Gale, *Pioneers' Tales and Pictures of Chicago*

THE LEVEE, CHICAGO, 1833

By 1833 the village of Chicago had grown to be an important trading center, and log construction had begun to yield to frame. The drawing of the levee at this period shows at the right an example of a new type that was destined to spread itself like an evil pest through the later Far West — the building with its gable end towards the street hidden by a flat-topped false extension of the front wall, to help give it, one supposes, a "citified" look.

A KANSAS SOD HOUSE

The early settlers on the great plains found little lumber, and log houses were usually out of the question. The sod house took its place — part cave, part hut built of tough prairie sods. Primitive in the extreme, it yet furnished shelter, and could be made a true, if temporary, home. This is an early sod house in the Swedish part of Kansas — Lindsborg — and dates from the late eighteen sixties.

341   From a photograph, courtesy of Rev. Alfred Bergin, Lindsborg, Kansas

342   From a photograph, courtesy of Rev. Alfred Bergin, Lindsborg, Kansas

INSIDE A "DUGOUT," KANSAS, ABOUT 1870

A little later the "dugout" took the place of the sod house. Still half cave, as a protection against the terrific Kansas gales and tornadoes, a wooden super-structure replaced sod for the portion above ground. The interior of such a "dugout" shows rough stone walls, unplastered, a folding table, rude stools and cupboard shelves. This was the bare and primitive environment in which lived hundreds of the hard working farmer families who opened up the great grain country of the West.

343　　　　　　From a photograph, courtesy of Rev. Alfred Bergin, Lindsborg, Kansas

McPHERSON, KANSAS

A VIEW of McPherson, Kansas, in 1873 shows the full glory of the pioneering town — a street lined with ambitious false fronts.

SETTLEMENT IN THE NORTHWEST

As the thrust of the growing country pushed the frontier further into the Northwest, economic conditions made pioneering more urban, less individual. Mining camps, logging camps, villages, replaced the earlier individual log house. A view of a new settlement in the Northwest shows such a village street with its simple

344　　　　　From Robert Brown, *The Countries of the World*, London, 1876-78

timber gabled houses, crude and cheap and close packed, and behind the crowding forest of Douglas firs.

345　　　　From Herrmann J. Meyer, *Universorum*, New York, 1851

NAUVOO, ILLINOIS

BY the middle of the century most of the Middle West had lost its frontier quality. Only occasional log cabins, like that in the foreground, gave evidence of earlier conditions; thickly-built towns were developing everywhere with mushroom rapidity. Nauvoo, seen from across the Mississippi River, shows such a town, dominated by the great Mormon Temple. Nauvoo was an important place in the Mormon migration, prior to the departure for Utah in 1847-1848.

346   From *Das Illustrierte Mississippi-Thal*, lithograph after a painting by H. Lewis, about 1849

ST. LOUIS, ABOUT 1849

A VIEW of St. Louis about 1849 reveals the urban quality it had already gained. Steamboat traffic made its position important and its crowded roofs, its many church towers, and the dome of its Greek Revival Courthouse show a city of size and importance.

SAN FRANCISCO, CALIFORNIA

TEN years from the time of the gold rush San Francisco was transformed into a thriving city. Its incom-

347   From Herrmann J. Meyer, *Universorum*, New York, 1851

parable harbor made that development inevitable, but the very rapidity of its growth kept it uncouth and prevented its achieving the finished urbanity of cities farther east, or the quiet dignity of the early Ohio towns.

JEFFERSON CITY, MISSOURI

THE new states soon expressed their pride in the importance they had so swiftly gained in state houses or capitols — which were often in their monumental grandeur so far ahead of their surroundings as to appear almost humorously inconsistent. Yet they were sincere expressions of an American respect for law and government that was manifested even on the frontier and of a mighty faith in the abounding promise of the future. Such was this capitol at Jefferson City, crowning the river banks.

348   From Herrmann J. Meyer, *Universorum*, New York, 1851

CHAPTER XII

CIVIL WAR STAGNATION—THE VICTORIAN ERA

THE disintegration of the Greek Revival — inevitable because of the sentimentality of the style and its lack of fitness to the multitude of uses the growing complexity of civilization required — left, in America, an æsthetic vacuum. The *Néo-Grec* Movement, that vitalized the Greek Revival in France, affected America only later, indirectly, and for the most part disastrously. There was not the artistic skill in any part of the country either to develop the like here, or to appreciate its subtleties. The Gothic Revival, which galvanized England into tremendous artistic activity at about the same time, had little effect save in church work until towards the end of the period. Colonial ideals were utterly dead: the result was an abyss of taste, a riot of ugliness, that is almost unique in history.

The deeper causes of this deplorable condition are various. Economic stress, the rapid development of the industrial system, political chaos, the Civil War and then more political chaos, a stridency of intellectual life that found refuge from its own inanities in its loud-mouthed devotion to the vaguest platitudes, all combined to make creative architecture an impossibility, just as in other fields of art it tinged the work of even such geniuses as Mark Twain, and embittered the youth of many a sensitive man — witness *The Education of Henry Adams.*

The economic life of the period was but a reflection of the speculation caused by the era of unprecedented western expansion that has been touched upon in the last chapter. To this development the Civil War and reconstruction were additional incentives; the economic history of the 'seventies, for instance, with its rings, its corners, its monopolies, its dramatic failures and panics, is not savory reading; a life so largely controlled by such forces was almost necessarily brutalized and materialized.

The Civil War's end marked the beginning of a new intellectual era. At last, for good or ill, the country found itself one country. This discovery, more it appears a deep almost unconscious sensation than an articulate thought, working on the materialism of the time, produced a sudden, unfounded national egotism that destroyed intellectual balance. The American became supercilious and condescending towards everything foreign. He traveled in Europe, saw hundreds of things better done than in America, saw a life more finished, better mannered, more urbane, saw beauty in art created and appreciated. To him the things better done were things merely laughable; the finish, the urbanity, the good manners were marks of underlying depravity, decadence, immorality; for him beauty in art was a book, if not closed, at least unreadable. If he secretly admired, publicly he abused. If he secretly felt himself, felt America, inferior, publicly he but made the eagle wave his wings with more violence, scream with still more eager stridency. He hid his envy under a cloak of hatred and scorn. And this scorn of things European came, inevitably, to be a public scorn of all art that was not merely pretty, vapid, ministering to the public's own vacuity, or else ostentatious, or loudly and brutally "comfortable." Plate glass, plush, jig-saw work. . . .

Into such an artistic atmosphere came two things which were of enormous importance — the development of new mechanical aids to building, and a new knowledge of the history of art. They were the final deathblow to what little straightforward work was still being done by conscientious and traditional craftsmen. Machined woodwork killed the traditions of workmanship; a new and vague knowledge of art history which the age was utterly unable to assimilate killed the last spark of the Greek Revival and all other indigenous traditional work.

It was not only the country districts which suffered from the horrible productions of new machinery. While band saw and lathe made wooden monstrosities for the village, brownstone and cast-iron assailed the cities disfigured by block after block of characterless houses and of coarsely detailed arcaded stores and offices. And each innovation was, with the strange hopefulness of the human race, hailed as a panacea for all architectural and business ills.

The "architects" of the time saw to it that their work was well done. It was an age of commercialism rampant, the beginning of the present age of salesmanship and advertising. The architects, with, of course, a few honorable exceptions, were quite up to the times; books of plans and details were broadcast, and their "villas" and cottages and residences, in which Roman forms and *Néo-Grec* incised lines and certain ideas seemingly Louis XIV in spirit, and others absolutely without precedent, are all mixed together helter-skelter without rhyme or reason, rose by the thousands from the Atlantic to the Pacific.

Yet in all this chaotic ugliness, there were still two hopeful signs. One has been mentioned already as a disintegrating factor — the growing knowledge of art history, such as is shown in Minard Lafever's *Architectural Instructor*, 1856 — a strange contrast to his *Modern Builders' Guide* published twenty years before. But any increased knowledge of art history eventually was bound to lead to dissatisfaction with the work generally produced, was bound to clarify critical faculties and stimulate artistic creativeness.

The other sign was the persistence in church work of the Gothic Revival — the only type of work of the time, save the completion of the National Capitol, and a small amount of public work under federal auspices — which can be credited to real architects, men like Richard Upjohn and James Renwick. (See page 311.) Here, still, beauty was sought. and, however academically, sometimes still achieved. Beauty of a more picturesque, romantic, less sure type was sometimes achieved in the many-gabled country houses of Gothic type. Sometimes beauty of a staid and weighty sort was even attained in the heavy quietness of the large square brick city houses of the early part of the period. Despite the horribleness of jig-saw work, of mansard roofs, of scalloped and patterned shingles, of the strange and awkward attempts of country church builders to imitate in sawn wood the forms of the Gothic Revival, despite the chaos of the time, the desire for beauty was never dead — it never can die — and little by little growing mastery of life, growing knowledge, prepared the way for a new dawning whose first glint was the immense popular interest in the Philadelphia Centennial of 1876.

349   From Minard Lafever, *The Architectural Instructor*,
            New York, 1856

SHERMAN'S HEADQUARTERS,
SAVANNAH, GEORGIA

CHURCH OF THE HOLY TRINITY, BROOKLYN

IN 1856 Lafever published a second book, *The Architectural Instructor*. It reveals the enormous leap made in twenty years; architectural history is sketched with fair correctness. But the charm of the Greek Revival is gone. Already the battle of the styles has begun. And already the Gothic Revival — and Gothic at last generally understood — is, in church design, supreme. A comparison of the Gothic of Holy Trinity Church, Brooklyn, with No. 313, designed by the same architect twenty years before, shows the difference, due partly perhaps to the work in this country of English architects like Upjohn, the designer of Trinity Church in New York (No. 762).

350   © Detroit Publishing Co.

MEANWHILE the country was filling with buildings whose Gothic Revival forms superseded the Greek Revival. With the Gothic Revival began the use of cast-iron as a building material. The house used as Sherman's headquarters in Savannah (No. 350) shows how purely a matter of superficial detail this Gothic Revival sometimes was. Battlements, oriels, and a cast-iron porch and piazza of generally Gothic detail are used on a house whose simple rectangularity and symmetry are indicative of classic rather than Gothic ideas. Here the mixture is so frank as to produce a great deal of charm. This style confusion is typical of the transitional period in which the house was built — a transition from the classic culture of the eighteenth century to the romanticism of the Victorian era.

351   From a photograph by John A. Wilson

THE HERMITAGE, HOHOKUS,
NEW JERSEY

THE Hermitage, once owned by the wife of Aaron Burr, shows a much more English type of Gothic Revival house, in which pointed gables, steep roofs, diamond panes, and broken silhouette give something of the romance and informal charm for which the true Gothic Revivalists in house design were always seeking. The heavy, wavy decoration of the gable end barge boards is typical of certain exaggerations of Gothic detail to which the early revivalist was prone.

A GOTHIC RESIDENCE AT IRVINGTON, NEW YORK

As time went on, the careful Gothic Revival details of the 'forties and 'fifties gave way to a freer, more original type — the true Victorian Gothic of the 'seventies and 'eighties. This is a view of the residence of John E. Williams, at Irvington, N. Y. *The Art Journal* said of it: "An old Warwick cottage modernized and Americanized, with a mild trace of the peaked turrets of Nor-

352   From Martha J. Lamb, *The Homes of America*, New York, 1879

mandy thrown in." But variety has brought incoherence, and freedom and originality of detail mean too often only a travesty of Gothic, with vulgarity and flippancy added.

353   From Minard Lafever, *The Architectural Instructor*, New York, 1856

THE TYPE KNOWN AS "ITALIAN"

In the late 'forties and during the 'fifties another type of house was developing a popularity that rivaled and in many places surpassed that of the Gothic. It was a type known as "Italian," though its relationship to Italy seems now very distant. But, based on ideas of the Renaissance, however distorted, using round arches instead of pointed, classic columns, and preserving something of the heaviness of the out-of-fashion Greek Revival, its products sometimes had a rather portly, self-conscious, righteous dignity that many "Gothic cottages" of the time lacked.

THE GROESBECK HOUSE, CINCINNATI

Typical of the houses built under the "Italian" influence is the Groesbeck house in Cincinnati. Large, stone-built, with capacious high rooms and big windows, with simple wall surfaces, with a pseudo classic porch and piazzas, it shows already in its mansard roof and cresting the tendency which was shortly to bring American architectural taste to its lowest levels.

354   From Martha J. Lamb, *The Homes of America*, New York, 1879

THE OGDEN RESIDENCE, CHICAGO

THE Ogden residence in Chicago (No. 355), dating probably from the 'sixties, shows another step in the decline. Frame takes the place of stone, jig-saw brackets and piazza posts of fantastic shape replace the simpler classicism of the Groesbeck house. The roof cresting is more elaborate, and placed on a cornice at the break of the mansard that projects unpleasantly. The classic modillion cornice is replaced by one with larger, formless brackets. Mere elaboration is beginning to be considered a means to beauty.

356   From a photograph by H. G. Dine

THE JEWELL RESIDENCE, HARTFORD, CONNECTICUT

THE most successful houses built under this type of influence were undoubtedly those square, wide-corniced, flat-roofed brick houses (No. 356), with cupolas, of which so many line the shaded streets of eastern towns and cities. They have a sort of quiet dignity, a capaciousness of windows, cornice, porch, wall surface, cupola, that has at least the virtue of consistency. In such buildings the inspiration is almost always primarily classic.

357   From a photograph by Soule

THE NATIONAL SOLDIERS' HOME, WASHINGTON

THE Library of the Soldiers' Home in Washington, built 1851, shows Victorian Gothic in wood at its worst. Roof slate laid in patterns, meaningless turrets and pinnacles, jig-saw brackets, and sharp gables filled with meaningless braces, show all of that restless incongruity, that complex awkwardness, that goes under the name of "carpenter Gothic."

THE ISAAC MARTIN HOUSE, FORT WASHINGTON

THE Gothic Revival had confused results. Typical of many of its better qualities is this old house at Fort Washington, New York. Its porch, its gables, the moldings over its windows are quite correctly in the English Gothic spirit, but the finials on the gable tops reveal that underlying restlessness of taste that so frequently hurts the best work of the period.

THE HOUSE–PLAN BOOK

THE decade following the Civil War brought an irresistible demand for expansion. Speculation, wild-cat schemes, sudden wealth, panics, destroyed the economic, artistic, and social traditions which the war

358   From a photograph in the New York Historical Society

had undermined. It was an era of vast building. It was a "boom" time for the distribution of house-plan books sold by "architects." The plans usually combined all the worst elements of "Italian" and "Gothic" and "Queen Anne," all flavored with a sauce of peculiarly ugly ideas developed from the heavier types of French Louis XIV work. The whole seems to us utterly tasteless; it certainly was, as this advertisement from a plan book shows, utterly commercial.

The above cut represents a

Design Patented by C. Graham & Son,

ARCHITECTS OF ELIZABETH, N. J.,

which may be applied to French roofs of any size or description, forming a great and acknowledged improvement in the ornamentation of French roofs—destroying the monotony of continuous slating, and presenting to the eye a beautiful, bold, and characteristic feature—particularly adapted for fronts of smaller cottages, as represented in cut.

DESIGNS FURNISHED

embodying said Patent in various designs. Also plans, specifications and working drawings for the same. Also the right to use said Patent designs on application to

C. GRAHAM & SON,

ARCHITECTS,

ELIZABETH, N. J.

359   From M. F. Cummings, *Modern American Architecture,*
New York, 1867

A TYPICAL DESIGN FOR AN "ELEGANT AND PICTURESQUE VILLA"

THE book of designs published in 1875 by G. B. Croff is a monument so full of typical material that the choice of an example (No. 360) for reproduction was difficult. The designer's object seems to have been to get the greatest possible number of different kinds of

Design for an elegant and picturesque Villa prepared for execution on a slightly bluff at Saratoga Lake The Shadows are intense and the effect very striking.

G. B. CROFF, ARCH'T.

360   From G. B. Croff, *Progressive American Architecture,*
New York, 1875

windows, to use the most varied possible jig-saw detail to frame windows or doors, and elsewhere to break every consistency and continuity of style or composition or line. Ostentatious and arrogant ugliness is the only possible result.

361   From a photograph by Perry L. Thompson

GOTHIC CHURCHES AT BATH, MAINE

THESE two churches (No. 361, and No. 362), both in Bath, Me., reflect perfectly the changes which historic and revival styles suffered at the hands of local builders. The first, the Gothic example, shows the use of vertical strips to cover joints in the vertical boarding of the wooden church wall — a typical "carpenter Gothic" trick. In mass the whole is strong and well-proportioned, but it reveals how futile it is to attempt to produce Gothic effect by the use of a little tracery and a few pointed arches.

The other church with its smoothly boarded front, its Gothic pinnacles crowning a nondescript whole, is evidently an attempt to be Romanesque. But it is all indescribably false. Both, with their absolute denial of the material in which they are built, contradict utterly the spirit of the styles they supposedly represent.

362   From a photograph by Perry L. Thompson

363   From *The Art Journal*, New York, 1879

"AN IDEAL HOUSE"

IN 1879 *The Art Journal* published a so-called "ideal house." The terrific ostentation and restlessness of the jig-saw houses of the plan books has passed. But the taste still lingers in the unnecessary banding and paneling, the use of curved-bottom shingles, and the observatory tower. But large panes have given place to small (some, it is to be feared, of stained glass), and the mansard roof with its metal cresting is no more. The detail is "original," but based more on the contemporary English "Eastlake" style than anything else. New men of wealth were appearing in America as industrial development after the Civil War made swift progress. Many of them lived in such "ideal" houses.

CHATHAM STREET, NEW YORK, 1858

As yet the city development, even on important thoroughfares, was ill thought out, and badly designed. Party walls plastered with advertising signs show the higher, uglier new buildings projecting above the quiet dignity of the old. Flat roofs became suddenly universal, forced by the economic pressure of city conditions. The era of box-architecture had begun. The awnings stretching out to posts along the curbstone are typical of New York at the date of the print.

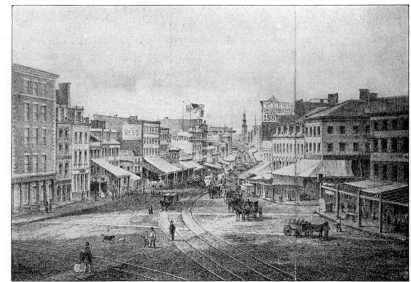

364 From *Valentine's Manual*, New York, 1858

THE PARISH HOUSE, FIFTH AVENUE, NEW YORK

THIS was the period, too, when builders and architects discovered and popularized the use of a soft brown sandstone — and in so doing shut color out of hundreds of miles of American city streets. The style was generally Italian Renaissance — at least at the time supposedly so — and individual houses are often not without dignity and a sort of charm. The Daniel Parish house is one of the larger examples of the type.

365 From a drawing by J. P. Newell, courtesy of the New York Historical Society

THE POPULARIZATION OF "ART" FORMS

FORMS fashionable in the big centers were soon broadcast over the country by means of plan books and books on architecture. This is a plate of details from such a book, published in 1875. Bracket, lintel, and arch forms appear in every possible combination with panels, scrolls and turned members; all covered with a decoration of incised lines, often gilt. Walnut was the favorite wood. So "art" was popularized, and ugliness made universal.

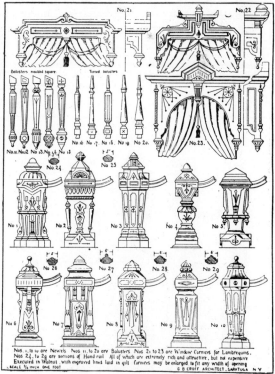

366 From G. B. Croff, *Progressive American Architecture*, New York, 1875

TYPICAL EXAMPLES OF PORCHES IN NEW YORK OF THE 1870's

An article in *The Art Journal* for 1876, published by D. Appleton & Company, on "Some Examples of the Porch in New York" shows a number of illustrations of porches of the brownstone and Victorian Gothic periods. The four selected are typical. The first (No. 367) shows the true brownstone "Italian" stoop that was fashionable for almost twenty years — Corinthian columns (probably cased in wire netting to keep birds away and incidentally utterly destroying the contour and effect) and leading up to them brownstone

367   From *The Art Journal*, New York. 1876

steps with balustrades often made from cast-iron painted and sprinkled with sand to imitate stone.

368   From *The Art Journal*, New York, 1876

The second (No. 368) shows the more "modernized" type of classic due to the influence of the French *Néo-Grec*. Great brackets take the place of an entablature, treated more like wood than stone, and the newels of the stair railings have undergone that enlargement and complication which has loaded so many American side streets with bulging obesities.

The third (No. 369), the porch of the Dry Dock Savings Bank, is a two-story porch of a type of rather flat Gothic — based mostly on Italian precedent — much admired in the 'seventies. In this Gothic work red and white

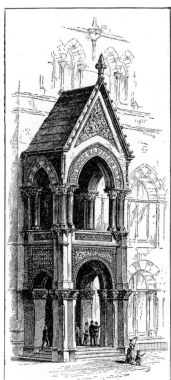

369   From *The Art Journal*, New York, 1876

stones were combined, flat carving takes the place of moldings, and all sorts of little splays and chamfers are used at corners. It was this type of Victorian Gothic which was responsible for much of the worst public, commercial, and ecclesiastic art of the period.

The fourth (No. 370), the porch of the Church of the Heavenly Rest —

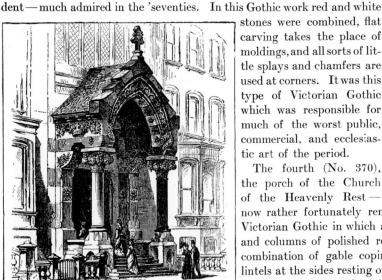

670   From *The Art Journal*, New York, 1876

now rather fortunately removed — is still another type of Victorian Gothic in which alternate stones of red and white and columns of polished red granite give the color. The combination of gable coping and arch stones and the cut lintels at the sides resting on fat capitals and fat brackets are examples of attempted originality which seem to us disastrous.

A HALL AND STAIRWAY OF THE LATE 1870's

EVEN the educated taste of *The Art Journal* was in 1879 almost as low. The hall and stairway (No. 371) reveal some of the elements seen in Croff's plate (No. 366). The door trim, with blocks at the corners, the stained glass panes in the stair window, the strange wainscot, the stair railing with its incised ornament — all reveal the wistful, hopeless striving of a people, their traditions killed by economic changes and immigration, towards a much-sought beauty whose secret they did not know.

371   From *The Art Journal*, New York, 1879

372   From *The Art Journal*, New York, 1879

AN ATTEMPT TO PRODUCE AN EASTLAKE INTERIOR

THE library for the same house (No. 372) shows, in addition to the vases and busts that decorate it, high "bric-a-brac" book-cases, whose strange semi-Gothic design is based on the work of an English designer, Eastlake. His own work, though possessing some of the qualities of the library shown, has usually more restraint and logic. The angularity and broken-up character of the bookcase standards are to be noticed, and on the shelves at the right the miniature curtains that depend from them.

THE OLD PUBLIC LEDGER BUILDING, PHILADELPHIA

THE 'sixties saw the introduction of cast-iron as well as brownstone as a building material. It was seized upon as the great hope of American architecture. Whole fronts of buildings were of cast-iron, in sections. Frequently it was used in ways rather French, as here, in the Philadelphia Public Ledger building opened in 1867. Mansard roof, French dormers, iron cresting are characteristic. Allowing almost continuous windows, cast-iron had its advantages; and many such buildings, nevertheless have not the incoherent ugliness of much other work of the time.

373   From Scharf and Westcott, *History of Philadelphia*, Philadelphia, 1884

374   From a photograph by Wurts Brothers

THE OLD A. T. STEWART BUILDING, BROADWAY, NEW YORK

THE old A. T. Stewart store in New York is an even simpler treatment of the cast-iron front. The endless repetitions to which it gave rise are fatal to any charm.

A PHILADELPHIA EXAMPLE OF AMERICAN GOTHIC

No cast-iron front could ever achieve the unique strangeness of this work in stone (No. 375), built in 1879. Like so much American Victorian Gothic, the sense of scale is absolutely lacking: what should be small is big, and vice versa. Structural logic — the foundation of Gothic — is forgotten. Stumpy polished granite columns; arches, cusped, pointed and segmental; offsets, brackets and meaningless gigantic moldings are piled together in astonishing ways. Such buildings are obvious proofs that the original is not always beautiful. It is tragic that the conscious desire to create beauty, which was vividly alive throughout this era, produced so little that was lovely; and created for so many an environment of such meretricious ugliness.

A VICTORIAN MUNICIPAL BUILDING

THE city hall of Buffalo, built in the same year as the Centennial Exposition, 1876, shows admirably the rather ostentatious grandeur to which the American public building of the mid-Victorian era aspired. A time that was characterized in political life by the

375   From Scharf and Westcott, *History of Philadelphia*, Philadelphia, 1884

excessive, overornamented, highfaluting oratory of the General Grant period, necessarily found architectural expression in buildings, such as this, where exterior complexity and ostentation governed the design rather than any direct and simple logic of form. High towers were common, and a heavy, ugly picturesqueness was often the result.

376   A. J. Warner, architect; photograph by Soule

A VIEW IN CHICAGO ABOUT 1870

A VIEW of State and Washington Streets in Chicago about 1870 shows the lack of unity, the hit-or-miss character of the typical American city of the period. Flat roofs, mansard roofs, gables — "Gothic," "French," "Italian," and plain no-style — are mixed together to give a total effect of chaotic confusion strangely different from the placid unity of the towns of fifty years before.

377   From a lithograph in the Chicago Historical Society

378   From a lithograph, about 1865, in the Chicago Historical Society

THE CHICAGO COURTHOUSE

THE Chicago Courthouse is a typical "Dark Ages" public building, borrowing from the so-called "Italian" rather than from the Gothic. But the tradition of the cupola on public buildings was so strong that it has a cupola as well; and one, strange to say, with rather a colonial look about it. The use of three arched windows in a close group, the central one larger than the others, is a frequent feature of this type of work.

DINING ROOM OF THE OLD FIFTH AVENUE HOTEL, NEW YORK

THE Fifth Avenue Hotel was at one time considered the finest hotel in the country. This view of 1859 shows its dining room, column-bordered, with great gas chandeliers and decorated plaster ceiling. The long thin columns might be considered Corinthian, but the entablature they support could be nothing but mid-century American. The combina-

379   From *Harper's Weekly*, October 1, 1859

tion of curved bracket forms above the columns with straight lintels between, the cornice with its big and little brackets, and the large scale of the ceiling decoration — all are characteristic of the blend of classic, *Néo-Grec* and purely new forms which characterized work of the 'fifties and 'sixties.

380   From *Frank Leslie's Illustrated Newspaper*, Oct. 3, 1868

INTERIOR, TEMPLE EMANU–EL, NEW YORK

REMARKABLE for its date — it was finished in 1868 — was Temple Emanu-el, designed by Cyrus Eidlitz. It reveals the beginnings of the oriental taste that was later to sweep the country; and its design shows an imagination, a grasp of scale and composition, and a true feeling for style quite unusual in work of the time.

381   From a photograph by Soule

THE GRAND CENTRAL DEPOT, 1871

THE Grand Central Station — Dépôt, as it was called then — was opened in 1871. It was famous for its size and monumental character. Built of red brick, stone, and cast-iron, it followed generally "French" inspiration, which appeared in the high curved roofs of the corner and central pavilions, in the pavilion dormers, and in the rather stupid classic character of its detail. Despite the smallness of its parts, its lack of compelling scale and distinction, the Grand Central Depot of 1871 was noteworthy for a grasp of big conception and monumental planning unusual in its day. Contemporary comment was all superlative praise — a strange indication of the taste of the time.

382   From *Harper's Weekly*, Feb. 3, 1872

TRAIN CONCOURSE, GRAND CENTRAL DEPOT

THE great concourse for trains was roofed with an enormous arched trussed roof of metal and glass. This type of train concourse, usual at the time and later both here and abroad, had a frank impressiveness that was truly creative. With smoke and steam rising into its dim vault, atmospheric effects were produced which were remarkable. But the difficulties of ventilation, the noise and the smoke, rendered this form at last undesirable, and it is no longer used, though many examples still remain.

383   From *Frank Leslie's Illustrated Newspaper*, Jan. 18, 1868

INTERIOR, PIKE'S OPERA HOUSE, NEW YORK

THE mid-century saw the development not only of more complex hotels and railroad stations, but also of large theaters. Pike's Opera House in New York, still standing, although altered, was the finest of the time. This view of 1868 shows the great rehearsal prior to the public opening. Multiplied galleries on cast-iron columns, the elaboration of the proscenium arch and its boxes, and the very rich ceiling, show the develop-

ment; but all is plastered over with coarse, ugly, and ill-designed ornament that is a typical travesty of classical detail.

SELTZER SPRING PAVILION, CENTRAL PARK

THE same year saw in Central Park the completion of numberless little buildings in pseudo-Gothic, mostly built of wood and cast-iron. Similar to much of the fashionable detail in houses, full of some of the incoherences of the plan-book architecture of the time, they had an effect more oriental than Gothic, and exerted considerable influence on popular taste. Many still

384   From *Frank Leslie's Illustrated Newspaper*, July 18, 1868

stand, and streaked with iron rust, with gaping joints and broken detail, reveal the essential unfitness of the materials as then used.

385   From *Valentine's Manual*, New York, 1864

FULTON FERRY, NEW YORK, 1863

THE blend of semi-classic and pseudo-Gothic forms that marked much of the iron architecture of the 'sixties is well shown in the Fulton Ferry house, built in 1863. The use of many long slim round arched windows is characteristic. The breaking up of wall surfaces by many small panels destroys any sense of repose.

© Detroit Photographic Co.

EXAMPLE OF A PSEUDO–GOTHIC COLLEGE BUILDING

It was in the pseudo-Gothic that college buildings of the period reached their fullest absurdity. The Princeton School of Science, Princeton, N. J., reveals the height of the movement. Gothic forms are travestied with an utter ignorance of their true character. Towers, oriels, variegated slate roofs in crude patterns mingle in that chaos of form known then — and loved — as "picturesque." And worst of all, planning is utterly absent, the building is a tortuous labyrinth, and a false door is used at a main entrance to give an impression of bigness outside where none exists within.

THE STATE CAPITOL, BISMARCK, NORTH DAKOTA

The tradition of bad building, the lack of æsthetic tradition in the great agricultural country of the plains, showed itself, even in public buildings, as late as the 'nineties. The capitol building at Bismarck, N. D., dating from the early 'nineties, shows the pseudo-classic detail, the small scale, the lack of any real composition, the use of "false" materials — galvanized

387   From a photograph by Underwood & Underwood

iron cornices and the like which in older and more established parts of the country were beginning, at least in part, to be superseded by a better standard both of design and execution.

© Detroit Publishing Co.

STATE HOUSE, HARTFORD, CONNECTICUT

At Hartford, Conn., a lavish state capitol was completed in 1880. It was designed by Richard M. Upjohn, son of the designer of Trinity Church (No. 761), like his father, a trained and enthusiastic Gothicist. With considerable dignity of mass, and decided beauty in some of its carved detail, beautifully executed, this building shows, in its attempt to treat forms essentially classic with detail essentially Gothic, that the full implications of monumental design had not yet been entirely grasped, even by an architect of training and distinction, in the wealthy and "cultivated" East in the advanced year of 1880.

CHAPTER XIII

BEGINNINGS OF THE AMERICAN
RENAISSANCE, 1880–1900

THE immense flood of popular interest in the art exhibits of the Philadelphia Centennial Exposition inaugurated a new phase in American æsthetic development. Here the American people first saw the best examples of European manufacture. In English furniture and china, French porcelains and textiles, and European silverware, they found such perfection of finish and execution, and despite fidelity to prevailing fashions, such a comparatively high level of design, that the contemporary American work appeared crude by comparison. Moreover, this discovery of the possibilities of artistic manufacture synchronised with a growing knowledge of art history and augmented an already nascent curiosity.

A deluge of art criticism, particularly on "Art in the home," followed during the late 'seventies and early 'eighties. The English *Art Journal* published an American edition. Books on interior decoration multiplied. Coincidently, a period of æsthetic ferment in Europe was marked by the height of Ruskin's influence, William Morris' heroic and magnificent zest for excellence of craftsmanship and straightforward beauty of design, and the vogue of pre-Raphaelitism. These were paving the way for Whistler and Impressionism, which penetrated the American mind and laid the foundations of modern popular taste.

At the same time with the awakened popular interest in art, architecture began to achieve a professional status. The examples of such great architects of the Gothic Revival as Upjohn and Renwick attracted to the profession young men, who soon appreciated the necessity of extended European travel and study. As early as 1850 Richard Morris Hunt had studied at the École des Beaux Arts in Paris, and had even worked on the Nouveau Louvre under Hector Lefuel. On his return to America he had first worked on the capitol at Washington under Thomas U. Walter, and later he had set up practice for himself in New York, where he was producing work which was revolutionizing American building by its scholarly use of French precedent, old and new, Francis I or *Néo-Grec*, and still more by the soundness of his basic design. A little later Henry Hobson Richardson followed Hunt to the Paris school, worked, like Hunt, in Paris offices during the Civil War, and returned to practice in America. The essentially personal influence of his style, a much modified Romanesque, colored American architecture long after his death.

The foundations of American architecture were laid by a long line of distinguished men who, like Hunt and Richardson, after foreign study, returned burning with artistic enthusiasm. The country was eager for their work. With the waning of post-Civil War materialism and inflation, a national spirit, abetted by railroads and steamship lines, was developing. Terrifically rapid growth and astounding prosperity, in spite of the panics and currency agitations, were founded on basic wealth and increasing natural industrial development. Though political crudeness, confusion and questionable dealings existed, constructive political struggles based on the domination of industry, and its demands for a higher tariff, stirred American life. Between 1870 and 1890 the conflicts of to-day, agriculture *versus* industry, labor *versus* capital, emerged. Civil service reform agitation and the beginnings of organized large-scale philanthropy evidenced the birth of social conscience. America became a modern state.

Such a time is admirably suited to the development of the building art. Growing wealth and growing expansion demanded an immense quantity of building; but there was not the terrific pressure of the preceding stage; there was less necessity for hurried carelessness; there was a new artistic conscience; there was a growing refinement of taste to serve.

Working in this favorable environment, the new generation of American architects established American architecture. To define this early Renaissance of American art is difficult. A battle of "styles" began. Hunt used *Néo-Grec* and Francis I; Richardson, Byzantine and Romanesque; McKim, Mead and White, Italian Renaissance, French Renaissance, American Colonial, the free picturesque; Ware and Van Brunt and Upjohn and Haight used Victorian Gothic; in Chicago, Louis Sullivan was working out his brilliant, purely personal expressions. The use of past achievements as a foundation for new creation is one of the great methods of human development. With the passing of native American Colonial tradition, of the Greek Revival, of the Gothic Revival, of the lathe and jig-saw monstrosities beloved in the 'sixties and 'seventies, there remained only Europe, for whose amenities the Centennial had awakened longing, where students had found inspiration and beauty. The battle of styles was inevitable.

But the new American Renaissance was characterized by a new psychology of style. Style became no longer an idol, as in the strict revival days. Historical style was an aid only, a means, to be used as the designer wished, freely or strictly. The character of the basic design — planning, expression, composition — that was the big, the deciding element. As historical styles were only a means, they could be abandoned entirely at will; some of the very best work of the period is work purely picturesque, purely non-historical, where the style is that which results from the necessary form, and not vice versa.

The new Renaissance was characterized by a new honesty and a new joy in the use of materials. Colors and textures began to be played against each other, made an integral part of the design. Terra cotta, *faïence*, glass mosaics, rough bricks, roof tiles, metal work — all were used, experimented with. Often an exaggerated, restless richness was the result, particularly in exterior work; yet the tendency served to set the artist free, to widen his field and broaden popular appreciation.

And one other underlying tendency ran through the period; a tendency that has its roots back in the years immediately following the War of Independence — a tendency towards the increasing use of classic forms. All through the Civil War the United States capitol dome had been growing — and the influence of that never stopped. All through the time of the Gothic Revival, of the artistic bathos of the 'sixties and 'seventies, some type of classic had seemed the accepted, the natural style for such monumental buildings as state capitols. And with the coming of the new Renaissance with its growing sense of restraint and dignity, its growing mastery of an eclectic classicism, this innate and natural love for classic forms could not but be enlarged. In the choice of a classic style for the World's Columbian Exhibition in 1892–93 the consulting architects only symbolized popular taste; in the actual creation of the tremendously impressive group of buildings with their ranked arches and columns they did more; they astonished, delighted, and fixed popular taste. The Chicago World's Fair was climactic as the Centennial at Philadelphia was epoch marking; one ushered in a period of gestation and growth; the other was the symbol of the arrival at full birth of that which may be called modern American architecture.

COUNTRY HOUSE IN JAMAICA PLAIN, MASSACHUSETTS

THE type of house shown in *The Art Journal*, (No. 363) was destined to remain popular long into the 'eighties. Its design was a product of the new interest in craftsmanship aroused by the Centennial in Philadelphia. Much talk of craftsmanship was in the air; much talk of "truth" and "sincerity" in design, but these principles were little understood. Although the turned posts and scalloped shingles and gable tops of the house in Jamaica Plain look out of date to us, its simplicity is a step in advance. The importance of restraint had at last been appreciated; because of that, development was inevitable.

389   W. R. Emerson, architect; photograph by Soule

390   Halsey Wood, architect; photograph by Soule

HOUSE AT ORANGE, NEW JERSEY

THE house at Orange (No. 390) shows not only these qualities of simplicity and free composition that were becoming more and more popular, but also another new quality: playful experimentation with surface textures. Its general form is based on French chateau types, as is frequent in this period. The large quiet wall surfaces are broken up by laying the brick in all sorts of ways and by making certain bricks project. But this new charm is compromised by certain reminiscences of earlier styles in oriels and balconies. Nevertheless, the advance over the houses shown in the last chapter is enormous, and the simplicity of porch arch and the round tower are significant signs.

391   McKim Mead and White, architects; © Architectural Book Publishing Co.

THE OSBORN HOUSE AT MAMARONECK, NEW YORK

THIS house shows how all of the new and promising tendencies were combined with a new mastery in the early work of McKim, Mead and White. The composition, with its use of the popular round French chateau towers, the simplicity, the feeling for materials and texture, and the lack of any superfluous ornament, combine to make a whole more truly a work of art than anything known ten years before.

THE EDGAR RESIDENCE, NEWPORT, RHODE ISLAND

ANOTHER important tendency in certain early work of McKim, Mead and White is the return to forms essentially Georgian. The house of Mrs. William Edgar shows how this Georgian trend was at first mixed with a rather contradictory trend towards the picturesque. The new interest in the "colonial," which here receives adequate expression, in the hands of others less skilled produced hundreds of dull, crowded designs.

392   McKim, Mead and White, architects; © Architectural Book Publishing Co.

393   From *Harper's Weekly*, January 26, 1889, after drawings by Harry Fenn

DOMESTIC ARCHITECTURE IN NEW YORK CITY

THESE sketches of 1889 show admirably the type of city domestic architecture which characterized the late 'eighties and the early 'nineties, strongly influenced by the Romanesque of Richardson, as well as the traditional Queen Anne, and assimilating neither completely. It was an architecture exuberant, picturesque, but incoherent, lacking in unity, with much ill-considered detail.

A WEST END AVENUE DWELLING, NEW YORK

MEANWHILE, in city work, the earlier brownstone Renaissance and later Gothic was superseded by work borrowing both from the love of the picturesque and the quasi-Romanesque that Richardson was popularizing. Such a mixture of influences is seen in this group of houses at West End Avenue and 75th Street, New York. The use of heavy, low, round arches of rough faced stone and of heavy corbelled forms is characteristic. Yet certain undesirable modern trends are apparent, too; the gables are purely false, and the sheet-iron cornice is used.

394   Lamb and Rich, architects; photograph by Soule

A MADISON AVENUE RESIDENCE, NEW YORK

THIS house (No. 395) reveals a mixture of details in themselves incongruous; but it shows also that Bruce Price was an architect great enough to rise above the demands of the then fashionable forms and impose upon them unity, restraint, and even charm, despite the obvious eighteen-eighty character of much of the detail.

395   Bruce Price, architect; photograph by Soule

396   Herter Brothers, architects; photograph by Soule

THE VANDERBILT HOUSES, FIFTH AVENUE, NEW YORK

THIS period was one full of the zest of architectural experimentation and the discovery of form. French influence was dominant in the best work; *Néo-Grec*, French Renaissance, French composition, but molded and changed to something fresh and new. One of the most talked of works of the time was the pair of Vanderbilt houses (No. 396) on Fifth Avenue. Bands of beautifully executed naturalistic foliage prove the new solicitude for detail; but as yet composition and the logic of style are not surely grasped; the design, however lovely in detail, is not "organized."

397   R. M. Hunt, architect; photograph by Soule

THE TIFFANY HOUSE, NEW YORK

THE Tiffany apartment house in upper Madison Avenue (No. 398) marks the climax of the free type of early non-stylistic design. Themselves pioneers in decorative art and responsible for a tremendous rise in the popular taste of the time, the Tiffanys chose McKim, Mead and White as architects, and the whole work, in its oddities, its originality, its use of materials (wrought iron and the like) and the powerful silhouette, is truly expressive of the artistic enthusiasms of the time and of the family for whom it was built.

399   Hunt and Hunt, architects; photograph by Wurts Bros.

THE W. K. VANDERBILT HOUSE, NEW YORK

IT remained for the two greatest architects of the time, R. M. Hunt, and McKim, Mead and White, to give final proof that American architecture had passed its apprentice stage. The W. K. Vanderbilt house, by Hunt, shows not only Francis I detail of a purity, delicacy, and sureness of execution before unknown, but also a whole carefully thought out, carefully organized, without a single note out of tune, where each bit of rich ornament is used not for its own sake, but in order to perform its definite task in the design of the whole. The house still holds its place as really beautiful, irrespective of its date.

398   McKim, Mead and White, architects

THE "MARBLE TWINS," FIFTH AVENUE, NEW YORK

THE "Marble Twins" show R. M. Hunt working in a vein purely classical and almost austere. All extraneous detail is absent; instead, we have a return to the classical feeling which motivated so much of American work eighty years before. Perhaps a little obvious and heavy-handed to modern taste, these houses nevertheless are in the modern, American tradition.

ITALIAN RENAISSANCE HOUSES IN NEW YORK

THE Henry Villard house (really a group of several houses) shows the same restrained Renaissance type. This time it is a simpler, earlier type of Renaissance; cornices, window treatments, the court arcade, the railings and gates are all based on the purest types of early Roman Renaissance, treated freely, so that the whole is not a copy, but a creation; only the material, brownstone, remains to place it as early as it is — 1885.

400   McKim, Mead and White, architects

401   McKim, Mead and White, architects; © Architectural Book Publishing Co.

THE CENTURY CLUB, NEW YORK

THE Century Association building, by the same architects, about 1890, shows another modern example of an inspiration essentially from the Italian Renaissance. It shows, too, the careful study of material, and, in particular, of the possibilities of terra cotta, a new material destined to play a large rôle. Here terra cotta is treated frankly, not in imitation of stone, but with a delicate modeled pattern on it, so that it shall obviously appear what it is — burned clay.

THE NEW YORK HERALD BUILDING

THE old New York Herald building is interesting, not only as being an excellent example of the architects' skill in using terra cotta to produce a vivid and scintillating richness, but also because it is one of the first modern buildings to be studied directly from an Italian Renaissance prototype, the City Hall of Verona.

402   McKim, Mead and White, architects; photograph by Wurts Brothers

403   L. Haberstroh and Son, architects; photograph by Soule

SMOKING ROOM, FLOWER HOTEL, BOSTON

In domestic interior work, the 'eighties were characterized by a blend of varying tendencies. One of these was a pseudo-Orientalism, sometimes Japanese, sometimes Arabic or Persian. The smoking room of the old Flower Hotel in Boston is typical of the Arabic variety — Arabic forms in the mantel, a tile ceiling, and walls of rich texture and color are relied on to give the Oriental touch. Although often manifestly incongruous, the Oriental taste sometimes resulted in an effect of rich, warm color.

FIREPLACE IN THE COURT OF APPEALS, ALBANY, NEW YORK

The love of color, particularly of iridescent effects, popularized by the Tiffany favrile glass, affected taste everywhere. Rich marbles were much used, painted plaster relief panels, sometimes insets of favrile glass or tile. This mantel (No. 404) by H. H. Richardson shows rich marbles combined with that type of free Romanesque and Byzantine ornament which was the special characteristic of his work.

404   H. H. Richardson, architect; photograph by Soule

HALL OF THE HENRY VILLARD HOUSE, NEW YORK

The hall of the Villard house (No. 405) shows the same love of color and surface richness finding expression in Renaissance forms. Mosaic forms a large element in the design, for mosaic design was being diligently fostered in this country, by the Tiffany Studios, the Lambs, and others. The beauty of the curving lines of the vault above counts all the more strongly because of the simplicity of the marble wainscot below. The fireplace has a beautiful mantel of the type that was developed in north Italy in the late fifteenth century, and helps to give this hall its rich yet restrained palace character. At its best, interiors of this period have a richness, a warmth of color and texture, an imaginative quality unfortunately frequently lacking in the more sober work of to-day.

405   McKim, Mead & White, architects

TRINITY CHURCH, BOSTON

THE work of one man — one of the few true geniuses of American architecture — gave to the Victorian Gothic its deathblow. That man was H. H. Richardson. Gifted with a great imagination, with a sure grasp of large informal composition, his enthusiasm was early fired by the Romanesque work of southern France. Trinity Church in Boston, his masterpiece, combines with certain fine Romanesque traits a bigness of conception, an originality of detail, and a perfection of careful execution that make it a true and noble monument.

406   H. H. Richardson, architect; photograph by Soule

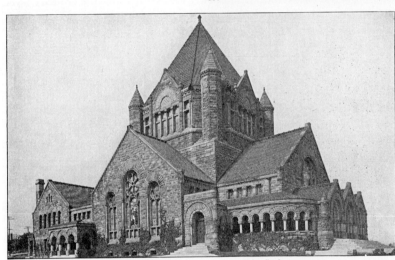

407   Halsey Wood, architect; photograph by Soule

CHRIST CHURCH, PITTSBURGH

THE style set by Richardson — Richardsonian Romanesque — swept the country. It was copied, adapted everywhere. Christ Church in Pittsburgh is a good example of the better type of adaptation. Its picturesque and forceful outline, the crag-like strength of the walls, the low and heavy porch arches are all in the true Richardsonian manner, but the pseudo-Gothic window tracery seems incongruous and forced.

INTERIOR, SECOND PRESBYTERIAN CHURCH, NEWARK, NEW JERSEY

IN church interiors the love of broken color and rich texture noticed before holds sway and combines with the large forms of Richardsonian Romanesque. The interior of the Second Presbyterian Church at Newark, N. J., shows the combination perfectly. Trusses of *The Art Journal* type of detail, heavy wood wainscots, round arches, and polychromed walls set the note. But the elaborateness of this type of decoration demanded more skill than was often obtainable, and cheap stenciled patterns, ugly and blatant, were sometimes used to spoil many quiet walls.

408   A. T. Roberts, architect; photograph by Soule

INTERIOR OF ST. THOMAS' CHURCH, NEW YORK

THE interior of the old St. Thomas' Church shows the same type of polychromy applied to a Gothic church interior. Here additional richness is given by the decoration of the chancel by John La Farge. In its combination of relief, painting, and mosaic, the whole is expressive of that love for textured richness which characterizes the whole era.

OLD MUSEUM OF FINE ARTS, BOSTON

STILL Victorian Gothic, but expressive of a new freedom and skill in design, is the old Museum of Fine Arts, Boston. Large plain wall surfaces, simple composition, panels of relief sculpture daringly used, and the continuous rhythm of

409   From a photograph by Wurts Brothers

the first floor windows gave this building a vitality, freshness, and power that set it above the ordinary level of Victorian Gothic work. It was built between 1876 and 1878.

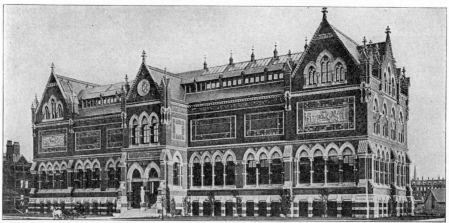

410   Sturgis and Brigham, architects; from a photograph by Soule

411   R. M. Hunt, architect; photograph by Wurts Brothers

THE LENOX LIBRARY, NEW YORK

THE *Néo-Grec* style found expression in a few public buildings, the most successful of which was the Lenox Library, New York. Forceful simplicity of composition complemented fine largeness of scale. The detail was gracious, restrained, delicate, well applied. Standing originally almost alone opposite Central Park, with but a few low houses in its neighborhood, the monumental character of the design lent itself peculiarly to the setting. It was destroyed after its collection had been removed to the New York Public Library.

412   Calvert Vaux and J. Wrey Mould, architects of part completed in 1880; Theodore Weston and Arthur L. Tuckerman,
architects of part completed in 1889. From a photograph by Soule

THE METROPOLITAN MUSEUM OF ART, NEW YORK

ANOTHER work of primarily *Néo-Grec* inspiration was the first enlargement of the Metropolitan Museum of Art. Its daring brilliant contrast of red — very red — brick and white marble was in accord with fashion, but its essential lines are quiet and well proportioned, and its detail — once its *Néo-Grec* ancestry is admitted

— sufficiently adequate, although to the modern eye strange and uncouth. But the whole has what most Victorian Gothic had not — *design*.

THE CRANE MEMORIAL LIBRARY, QUINCY, MASSACHUSETTS

THE Crane Memorial Library shows H. H. Richardson's work at its best. Good composition, free balance, rock-faced stonework, and detail of a Neo-Byzantine type are all characteristic; in this building the

413   From Mrs. Schuyler Van Rensselaer, *Henry Hobson Richardson and His Works*,
Boston, 1888, courtesy of Houghton Mifflin Company

picturesque quality is not forced, and the modesty of the whole has not permitted any of the eccentricities which sometimes detract from the effect of his work.

THE FRANKLIN McVEAGH HOUSE, CHICAGO

RICHARDSON's type of robust detail was manifestly less suited to houses than to monumental buildings. Nevertheless, his was too great a talent to fail at any class of design, and this house shows the picturesque and quiet character, combined with straightforward composition, which marks all of his work.

414   From Mrs. Schuyler Van Rensselaer, *Henry Hobson Richardson and His Works*,
Boston, 1888, courtesy of Houghton Mifflin Company

415 From Mrs. Schuyler Van Rensselaer, *Henry Hobson Richardson and His Works*, courtesy of Houghton Mifflin Company

HALL OF THE JOHN HAY HOUSE, WASHINGTON

THE hall of the house of John Hay shows Richardson's originality, imagination, and sense of picturesque composition applied to the design of a house interior. Using the popular richness of iridescent color and exuberant form, it is nevertheless quiet, dignified, and welcoming.

THE PITTSBURGH JAIL

THE Courthouse and Jail at Pittsburgh is undoubtedly one of Richardson's unique works. Particularly in the jail portion, with the "Bridge of Sighs" that leads to it, his love of simple wall surfaces, of the roughness of rock-faced stone, and his genius for the handling of heavy masses, found adequate expression. With certain elements — the bridge cornice, the pinnacle at the right, and the form of the central tower — betraying his love for South French Romanesque forms, the whole is nevertheless free, uncramped by archæology, and as vivid and fresh in style as it is successful in mass and composition.

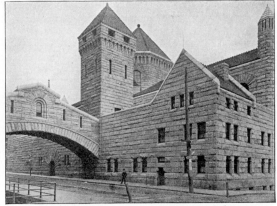

416 H. H. Richardson, architect; photograph by Soule

417 Holabird and Roche, architects; photograph by Chicago Architectural Photo Co.

THE TACOMA BUILDING, CHICAGO

DURING the 'eighties the skeleton frame building began to be common. Chicago was the center of the early development of "sky-scraper" design, and Chicago architects were the first to appreciate the peculiar æsthetic problems that work of this type necessitated. The Tacoma Building, 1888, was one of the first; but it shows how at once the problem had been grasped as essentially one of much glass and narrow piers. What ornament there is plays a subsidiary rôle. The conditions of the building itself determine its style.

THE AUDITORIUM BUILDING, CHICAGO

ONE of the most individual architects at work on the problem was Louis H. Sullivan. Not content with the novelty of general form, he felt that the novelty of the problem demanded absolute novelty of ornament as well, and out of a combination of geometric forms, Byzantine ideas, and some Richardsonian Romanesque details, he evolved an extremely rich and characteristic ornament. The Auditorium Building by Sullivan and Adler, 1889, is famous for its size, careful design, and the novelty of its decorative forms, in which, as is so frequently the case, originality unrestrained leads to disregard of structural logic.

418   Sullivan and Adler, architects

419   Burnham and Root, architects

THE MASONIC TEMPLE, CHICAGO

THE Chicago Masonic Temple, built in 1890, is by another great Chicago architect whose influence was fated to be broad — D. H. Burnham, then of Burnham and Root. Its enormous size, its simply gabled roofs, and the correct emphasis on tier after tier of glass make it still a landmark; only at the bottom the design — particularly of the great entrance arch — seems awkward, inconclusive, and inadequate for the simplicity and size above.

420   A. Belland, architect; photograph by Soule

THE POTTER BUILDING, NEW YORK

MEANWHILE, in New York, architects were striving to make the sky-scraper fit more conventional molds. In the early attempts the results were deplorable. Richardsonian Romanesque, Gothic, classic were tried, and failed. Such monstrosities as the Potter Building show how little the essence of the sky-scraper — simplicity and verticality — had been appreciated, and continual horizontal lines and bulging, meaningless ornament confuse the whole, and create restless ugliness.

THE NEW YORK STATE CAPITOL, ALBANY

THE varied history of the New York state capitol seems to prove that fashion is stronger than any abstract love of unity. Completed outside to the top of the second story from the competition drawings in a sort of harsh classic, above it suddenly breaks into Richardsonian Romanesque with hints of *Néo-Grec*, and above all the high metal crested roofs of the French Renaissance! Even Richardson himself, who did some work on it, could not by

421   © Detroit Photographic Co.

the charm of his detail redeem its hodge-podge character. Its high, crested roofs and towers, its chimneys, its richly decorated dormer windows belong in one category; the round arched windows of the third floor to another; the French Renaissance pilasters and columns and quoins of the lower portion to still a third.

422   From a photograph

THE STATE CAPITOL, SPRINGFIELD, ILLINOIS

IN general, however, the classic style with a dome, set by the national capitol, dominated state capitol design. The Illinois state capitol at Springfield, 1868–1888, shows the type; shows, too, how even in such a monumental building as this the pettinesses of fashion crept in, as in the curved mansards over the two wings, and the *Néo-Grec* pinnacles that flank the main portico. The detail is all too small, also, and destroys the monumental effect such a scheme should have.

CHAPTER XIV

MODERN AMERICAN ARCHITECTURE

MODERN industrialism means specialization; it replaces the village carpenter and the town builder with the contractor working with a large organization. A building to-day is the product of a multitude of trades, each furnishing its bit to the general result. This, in conjunction with the machine manufacture of building materials, has in time brought about a gradual disappearance of the old-time craftsman; more and more points that were formerly left to him to carry out are now settled in advance by the architect.

But specialization has not stopped there. It has joined hands with the tremendous railroad development to eradicate tendencies towards local styles, and, in newly developed country, to prevent their emergence. For specialization has led to standardization; it has led to specialized producing communities which supply materials for all the country. A building anywhere may have Hudson River brick from Haverstraw, limestone from Bedford, Indiana, sandstone from Brier Hill, Ohio, granite from Crotch Island, Maine, steel from Pittsburgh, Pennsylvania, plumbing fixtures from Trenton, New Jersey, slate from Bangor, Pennsylvania. Since the basis of local styles is twofold, in local materials and local climate, if buildings all over the country draw materials from the same specialized source, half of the reasons for local styles disappear.

So it is that the bank in San Francisco might just as well be in New York, the hotel in Los Angeles just as well in Chicago, the movie theater of Atlanta just as well in Detroit. A bank expresses the idea of American banking, the hotel, probably owned by a corporation that has hotels in ten cities, expresses the idea of American hotel life, the movie theater expresses the idea of a nation-wide industry.

The result has been that American cities, however distinct in character in earlier days, tend to grow more and more similar. For the industrialized specialization of life gives unity not only to buildings — it colors all material and intellectual life.

There has developed, then, from all these sources, a common building ideal that has made the American town or the American city a definite type, easily recognizable wherever it may be located. The illustrations in this chapter attempt to show the development of the type; the quaint colonial village yielding to the trim, prosperous town of the early nineteenth century; then the noisy crowding, the growing slums, the cobble pavements, the brownstone houses, the box designs of the late nineteenth century; finally the sky-scraper, the apartment house, the modern towered outline.

For this reason, any consideration of the modern development cannot be a matter for treatment by localities, nor chronologically; it must be a consideration of types. For a bank in Georgia of 1900 has more to do with a bank in New York in 1920 than it has with a church in Georgia in 1900. The general background for all modern American architecture is settled, uniform; localized traditions are, with three notable exceptions — the stonework of Pennsylvania, the "bungalow" of the Middle West, the Spanish Mission of southern California — extinct; the history of modern American architecture is necessarily a history of the development of specialized building types. For thus have modern industry and modern business, a standardized press and a standardized education forced upon us a uniformity such as no other country knows.

423   From the Ratzer Plan of the City of New York, 1766–67, issued in London, Jan. 12, 1776, by Jefferys and Faden

SKY LINE OF NEW YORK, 1766–67

THIS view of New York in 1766–67 shows a bustling city of low houses. Its most striking features are a fort and the group of church spires that prick the sky line. Trinity's Gothic spire shows at the left, St. Paul's towards the right.

424   From *Valentine's Manual*, New York, 1862

NEW YORK ABOUT 1790

A VIEW of lower New York just after the Revolution, 1790, shows crowded city houses lining Broadway, no longer detached but one against the other, with party walls. At the left behind the ship's rigging is the "Gothic" form of the rebuilt Trinity, and in the center the large and monumental mass of McComb's Government House. Early republican New York is still a city of houses and churches.

425   From J. Milbert, *Itinéraire Pittoresque du Fleuve Hudson*, Paris, 1828–29

VIEW OF NEW YORK FROM WEEHAWKEN

MILBERT'S view of New York as seen from Weehawken shows a city whose character is still given principally by houses and churches; a city of gabled roofs and steeples. But it is a true city; crowded shipping at the wharves; crowded buildings behind. St. John's, until recently standing on Varick Street, is the church farthest north (to the left); St. Paul's is the highest tower in the central group, Trinity the tower farthest south.

A PANORAMIC VIEW OF NEW YORK, 1834

HERE is revealed the beginnings of a change in character. Awnings over the sidewalk shelter numberless shops, flat or low pitched roofs over buildings of several stories are becoming common. Although there is still

unity of style, mounting real estate values are beginning to modify building forms. The city is already embarked on the commercial development which was later so radically to determine its character. Yet St. Paul's Chapel, in the foreground, is still the dominant structure in the scene. A strange contrast to the same location to-day, with St. Paul's lost in the midst of towering office buildings, a lovely reminder of the quiet beauty of times long past.

BIRD'S–EYE VIEW SOUTH FROM BRICK CHURCH, FIFTH AVENUE, NEW YORK, 1859

THE next twenty-five years brought to New York not only growth northwards, but the tremendous change due to the universalizing of the flat roof, and the beginning of the brownstone era. The view down Fifth Avenue from 37th Street shows the avenue lined with brownstone "Italian" residences, shows the cubic forms the flat roof necessitated, and shows still the continuing importance of the church spire.

VIEW SOUTH FROM BRICK CHURCH, 1925

A VIEW of the same locality to-day shows not only a change of character from residences to business, but also the inevitable development of the cubic forms under the influence of real estate speculation and steel skeleton construction; it shows a series of one-fronted buildings — save those on corners — with raked party walls, and a general sky line whose jagged thoughtlessness is perfectly expressive of the philosophy of almost unrestricted competition that gave it birth.

AN AIRPLANE VIEW OF MANHATTAN, 1923
But the full flower of the development in the metropolis is seen in lower New York of 1923. Serried towers, lavish, carefully designed, give a fairy, fantastic quality of piling, aspiring form. The unreality and romance of this great mass of office buildings furnish perfect, if unconscious, expression to those dreams, and that vague sentimentality, which so frequently underlie that American worship of business which made the whole possible.

429   From a photograph by Brown Brothers

430   From a wood engraving in the Chicago Historical Society

CHICAGO IN 1845, FROM THE WEST

We are fortunate in possessing illustrations that give a complete story of the growth of several American cities, their phenomenal change from primitive village to modern city. Chicago in 1845 has already grown mightily from the beginnings seen on page 146; church spires vie with masts of the lake shipping, and huge houses with chimneyed gables give already a sense of permanence, of prosperity.

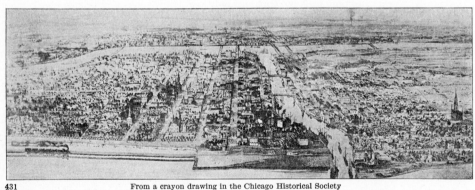

431   From a crayon drawing in the Chicago Historical Society

CHICAGO IN 1853

A bird's-eye view of Chicago in 1853 shows factories and grain elevators along the river, the rapid development of the checkerboard system of streets, the swift encroachment of the city growth over the surrounding country. But it shows, still, a city dominated by church spires; only in the crowded blocks next the river is the "modern" form beginning to grow noticeable.

432   From a contemporary lithograph in the Chicago Historical Society, Chicago, Ill.

MICHIGAN AVENUE, CHICAGO, ABOUT 1860

THE characteristics of the "brownstone" era are written large over the fine Michigan Avenue district by 1860. By that time the mansard roof and the flat roof seem to have eliminated the gable; Chicago has achieved, proudly, urban character.

CHICAGO BEFORE THE GREAT FIRE OF 1871

BY the time of the great fire of 1871 the change was complete (No. 433). Greenery and trees have for the most part

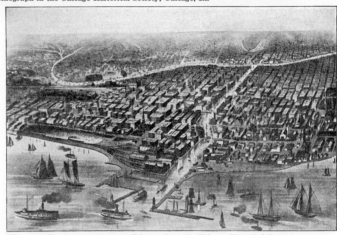

433   From a contemporary lithograph in the Chicago Historical Society

perished, the city spreading out crudely and thoughtlessly into the surrounding country. The play of economic forces uncontrolled has conferred on the city the blessings of trade, population, and the utter dreariness of growing miles of packing-box architecture, relieved here and there by a church spire.

434   From *Harper's Weekly*, June 23, 1888; after drawing by Charles Graham

VIEW OF CHICAGO, 1888

ANOTHER twenty years, and rising population and rising land values have forced the invention of the skeleton frame, piercing through the dull welter of dark and ugly packing-box architecture. Even industrialism, however, begins to seek and find certain vivid architectural expressions; but all is still, like the earlier growth, chaotic, thoughtless, inorganic.

AIRPLANE VIEW OF CHICAGO, 1920

THIS aerial view of the central part of Chicago shows the high building supreme. A comparison of this view with any of the earlier views shows, too, how the high building cuts light and air from the streets of a city; for, save Michigan Avenue in the foreground, built only on one side, not a street is visible, even from this high angle.

435   From a photograph by the United States Army Air Service

MARKET STREET, BALTIMORE, IN THE 1830's

A BALTIMORE street corner in the 'thirties shows buildings for the most part low and unassuming. Larger buildings of brick and stone are late "colonial," distinguished for their delicacy, simplicity, and austere restraint.

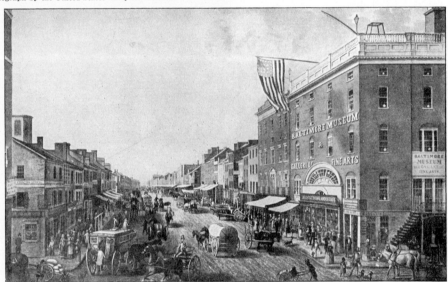

436   From a contemporary lithograph in the City Library, Baltimore

437   From a photograph by James F. Hughes Co., Baltimore

BALTIMORE STREET (FORMERLY MARKET), 1925

HERE is the same view to-day. Science has netted wires across the sky, put tracks on streets; commercialism has shot buildings up into the air; individualism has permitted each owner to build on his lot as he pleases, without regard to style or size of neighboring structures. Finance has put on the corner its classic temple, a bank; advertising has scrawled immense signs that dwarf any architecture across the naked and unkempt party walls where a building overtops its neighbor. It is all zestful, sharp; expressing economic struggle in every line.

438

PITTSBURGH IN 1871

PITTSBURGH in 1871 was a city on a hill that could not be hid even by the black smoke of its busy furnaces. Crowned with the domed and colonnaded dignity of official building, its gabled houses still retain something of the rather stuffy, quiet unity of ante-bellum days. But the enormous grain elevator at the left gives a hint of the future.

A PANORAMA OF TWENTIETH-CENTURY PITTSBURGH

THE Pittsburgh of the present shows the triumph of industrialism, not crudely or brazenly, in factories, but politely, symbolically, in up-shooting office buildings; the administration buildings of a whole countryside, "business" behind white marble based on — and concealing — the labor of mine and furnace. Only at the right the quiet roofs and Romanesque tower of Richardson's Courthouse uphold the dignity of official, communal effort. Behind, the stupidity of real estate speculation has driven parallel rectangular streets through the outskirts, up hill and down dale, a contradiction in usefulness as in beauty, of the whole character of the topography.

439

440   Raleigh, North Carolina. From a photograph by the
United States Army Air Service

441   Birmingham, Alabama. From a photograph by the
United States Army Air Service

TYPICAL AMERICAN CITIES

AIRPLANE views of Raleigh, N. C., Birmingham, Ala., Baltimore, Md., and Cleveland, Ohio, are here grouped together to show the unity that modern life has forced on American cities despite local conditions and traditions. The views of New York (p. 180) and Chicago (p. 182) are but additional evidence. Everywhere in the cities it is the tall building, and especially the office building, just as in villages it is the bank which dominates, shooting up out of the dull mediocrity of the earlier buildings. A glance at any of these views would show it to be an American city, but without personal acquaintance who could tell whether in the North, South, East, or West, on plain or mountain, by sea or far inland? And all show, too, the fallacy of one-fronted high buildings, with the street front only designed, the others, often in reality more important, left gaunt and harsh. All show the terrific expanses of chaotic, wasted roof-surfaces, disfigured with scuttles and tanks; and all show how it is chance that governs the development, and chance in the placing of buildings so insistent as sky-scrapers does not lead to unity of effect. But the Cleveland picture (No. 443) shows more, for in it is incorporated the beginning of a dream; the attempt to bring out of the chaos now, at great expense, a beauty and an order which could have been so much more cheaply and easily obtained at the beginning. The two large buildings at the top of the Cleveland view are to flank the beginning of a great esplanade to reach back to the square building in the center, and to be bordered by monumental and official buildings. The first of these, a great civic auditorium, is shown under construction. Little by little the buildings in the esplanade area are being condemned and removed. The Cleveland view is also interesting as showing over a large area perhaps the most helter-skelter character of them all. It is this condition of helter-skelter development — so obviously disastrous in so many American cities — that is one important factor in forcing the modern increasing adoption of municipal zoning ordinances. A certain amount of permanence in the character of a locality is a necessity for the healthy growth of a city. Zoning a city is an attempt to secure this permanence.

442   Baltimore, Maryland. From a photograph by the
United States Army Air Service

443   Cleveland, Ohio. From a photograph by the
United States Army Air Service

444 From a photograph by the United States Army Air Service

VIEW OF WASHINGTON, THE NATIONAL CAPITAL

ONE city alone in America has kept a unique quality of beauty all its own — Washington; for it was a city planned and built for the shrine of national government, and so freed from the pressure of economic conditions. It is still a city of vistas, of trees and green, of the broad low masses of classic, monumental government buildings, with the white dome of the capitol on its hill still dominant, despite the many storied hotels of the central portion.

445 Study by Hugh Ferriss of Maximum Mass possible upon a City Block under the New York Zoning Law

CHAPTER XV

BANKS AND BUSINESS BUILDINGS

IT is significant of the rapid development of American life that the type of building most characteristically American, the high business building, has a short history. Two things inspired it: modern centralized business organization and modern industrial financing. Industry is now directed in offices far from the factories. Industrial financing demands equipment for publicity, advertising, buying and selling credit, transactions in all sorts of symbolic paper — stocks, bonds, notes — and necessitates innumerable financial organizations requiring extended space. These tend to group themselves together, and close to the offices of the producing companies. The building types resulting from this industrial gregariousness are the product of the last thirty or forty years.

The ancestry of the modern bank building, however, is not new. Post-Revolutionary financial problems lent national importance to the banking business. An early and lovely architectural monument is Blodget's United States Bank of Philadelphia (No. 252). That type, roughly the classic temple, has remained constant, significantly, for more than a hundred years. Bank requirements led almost inevitably to some such treatment as this. A bank demands a large airy hall with sub-divisions into public and working space, and a treatment obviously monumental. The lavishness in banks, to-day, almost labels them our modern temples. Into them we pour our money to shape itself into a gorgeousness of material — marble, bronze, cut stone — into a richness of design, into a height and size and dignity that no purely practical element of the design requires. In thousands of towns the country over, it is the bank which is the one building with any architectural quality whatever, with any sign of a striving for dignity, space, glamor, the beauty of rich material or careful design. It is for the moralists and psychologists to determine the meaning of this symbol; whether it is the worship of Mammon, of success, or of financial probity and conservatism.

Recent signs indicate that the classic temple type is waning. Although in most cases the change has been toward a type resembling a Romanesque or Byzantine church, there have been two recent tendencies away from this pseudo-religious idea. One is the interesting attempt (No. 452) of certain "modernist" architects to produce a bank building expressing not so much the dignity or the lavishness of the financial power as the idea of the Safe — the *coffre-fort* — the people's communal strong-box. The other, so far more fruitful if less daring, is the tendency, particularly strong in the East, to use for the smaller banks some phase of the Georgian or colonial styles (No. 451). In these styles, of course, no pure temple expression is possible, and yet they permit that frank and dignified form which seems best to fit the problem of bank design.

Business buildings consist of two main classes, office, and stores or shops. The latter class developed early. The problems of department-store design were grasped as early as the 'seventies, and the change from cast-iron fronts to the restrained and classic style of to-day is only a matter of changing fashions. It is in the design of the smaller shop buildings that the greatest development has taken place. The shop window has come to be accepted as the controlling element; it has been treated playfully, joyfully, in a hundred ways: there are even signs of the eventual development of buildings fronted all in glass (No. 473). The possibilities as yet are scarcely realized.

To the foreigner, the high office building, the sky-scraper, seems the unique creation of American architecture. The geographical concentration of business and professional offices and the inflation of land values made height inevitable, and the perfecting of the elevator ensured the passing of the pitifully characterless and ineffective business "blocks" of the General Grant period. The development first of wrought iron, then of steel for floor construction, and finally the discovery that the walls themselves could be supported on steel columns embedded in them, set the architect free from any structural limitations of height. At once, then, in the late 'eighties, a new architectural problem had arisen. Its various solutions are an interesting comment on American architectural thinking.

It early became apparent that a masonry clothing for the steel skeleton was a necessity as a protection against both fire and weather. No purely functional expression in steel and glass, like the roofs of some armories or train-sheds, was therefore possible. While the architects of Chicago and the Middle West generally were experimenting with the simplest forms of wall and window, developing great unstable-looking boxes of glass and brick or stone or terra cotta, New York architects were usually floundering in useless attempts to treat the new buildings as they had treated smaller ones, with terrific results that are still all too apparent (see No. 420). But gradually the first of the successful solutions was being discovered — the triple treatment of base, shaft, and cap, the controlling idea of the design not only of the classic column, but of many old-world towers as well; and during the first decade of the twentieth century this was the accepted type. It had, to be sure, difficulties of scale, and the treatment of the cap, so high in the air, was often awkward, but it had the great æsthetic advantage of simplicity — such a building can be taken in at a glance — and it is still much used. The closer it approaches a tower in treatment, the more successful such a building seems to be. Among the finest of this type are the Municipal Building and the Metropolitan Tower, both in New York (No. 461 and No. 460). However, this solution, because it lacks close relationship between the structural frame and the decorative, protective shell, is not ultimate. Nor is it functionally logical. The offices, tier upon tier, are usually similar, and no one floor demands more decoration than another. Moreover, emphasis upon the vertical lines of steel columns seemed more expressive, and this emphasis, already used and discarded by earlier Chicago designers, led to the use of a Gothic style. In the Woolworth Building in New York, Cass Gilbert has produced one of the finest of this Gothic type, for its pre-eminence is due to its beauty as well as its height. And yet this Gothic idea often produced frivolous, overwrought, needlessly expensive detail, and moreover, the question of scale still remained a difficult one. Again the solution did not appear ultimate.

Meanwhile restrictive building measures were necessitated by the nuisances of congestion and of streets darkened by high buildings. This necessary municipal regulation of building heights inspired the third type of sky-scraper, which is stepped back as it rises, making an interesting silhouette against the sky, and using its own masses to build up powerful climbing buttresses for its central soaring tower. This new type with its return to the third dimension — to shadow, variety, mystery — is most important. Before the day of restricted measures, Harvey Wiley Corbett, in the Bush Building, New York (No. 466), showed some of the possibilities of this type. The same type predominated in the competitive designs for the *Chicago Tribune* building. John Mead Howells and Raymond Hood, in the winning design (No. 470), combined this type with the earlier Gothic, much modernized; unbroken sweeping verticals, an almost too exciting soaring characterized the second prize, a magnificently conceived tower (No. 471) by Eliel Saarinen; and a combination of block masses balanced against each other and decorated with frank surface ornament of mosaic was the conception of Bertram G. Goodhue (No. 472). These building restrictions have served more as a stimulus than a deterrent to the architect, and through them a new, typically American style is at last developing.

446   D. H. Burnham, architect

THE ILLINOIS TRUST AND SAVINGS BANK, CHICAGO

THE Illinois Trust and Savings Bank reveals the dignity and power that the full flowering of the classic tradition for bank design often secures. It is genuinely Roman in its simple grandeur and large scale.

THE COLUMBIA TRUST COMPANY BUILDING, NEW YORK

IT is difficult to say who first adopted the pseudo-temple scheme for the modern bank. Certainly one of the earliest of the really finished examples in America was the Columbia Trust Company's building (No. 447) (built for the Knickerbocker Trust Company).

Frankly denying story divisions by clever use of metal and glass, it obtained thereby—perhaps illogically, but certainly with power—a commanding dignity of scale, to which deep shadows and the beautifully designed and modeled capitals and frieze add their consistent Roman notes. It has since been much remodeled.

447 McKim, Mead and White, architects; photograph
by Wurts Brothers

THE GUARANTY TRUST COMPANY BUILDING, NEW YORK

A CONCEPTION more modern, because more definitely expressive of the difference between the bank itself and the offices above, is the Guaranty Trust Company's main building, on Broadway, New York (No. 448). A Greek rather than a Roman note is set in the detail, and the classic, temple-like character is strongly emphasized. Scale, dignity, massiveness, elegance of detail, classic restraint, are its characteristics.

448 York and Sawyer, architects; photograph by Wurts Brothers

THE SEABOARD NATIONAL BANK, NEW YORK

A SOMEWHAT similar treatment of bank and office building is the Seaboard National Bank (No. 449). Polished marble columns in the bank portion help to give that expression of rich and subdued lavishness which is a characteristic of much bank design. Large scale doorways and colonnades give variety, interest, and character to otherwise flat and stupid streets.

449   Alfred C. Bossom, architect

450   Alfred C. Bossom, architect

THE CHARLOTTE, NORTH CAROLINA, NATIONAL BANK

IN many a small town scattered over the length of the country the "Bank" is the one building to show any careful design or richness of material and execution. Even in many larger towns it is the most dignified, largest in scale, most monumental. Contrast, for instance, the simplicity and beautiful detail of this National Bank at Charlotte (No. 450), with the undesigned, slipshod, meretricious "stores" and "apartments" and "blocks" that line too many of our town and village main streets. Even the official buildings of the average town — courthouses, the post office, the city hall — are inferior to its banks in design, in richness and permanence of materials, frequently even in "workability." It is the bank that sets the architectural standard of the town; and even that standard is too often based on slavish copying of past styles.

THE COSMOPOLITAN STATE BANK, CHICAGO

EVEN the innately conservative force of established money power as expressed in the banks cannot prevent various protests against the temple form for bank use. One such is shown here in the Cosmopolitan State Bank building, Chicago. It shows a type generally Georgian in character, though Roman and Renaissance elements are present. It depends for its effect upon the simple brick and stone expression of the banking hall within.

451   Richard Schmidt, Garden and Martin, architects

452   Louis H. Sullivan, architect

THE PEOPLE'S SAVINGS AND LOAN ASSOCIATION BUILDING, SYDNEY, OHIO

A MUCH more emphatic protest against the whole panoply of the temple forms and classic tradition is shown in No. 452. Obviously an attempt to express the bank function not by a temple to enshrine finance, but by a form reminiscent of the safe or strong-box, it has distinction and power. As a matter of logic, the great arch over the little door, and the "applied" character of the window decorations seem as non-functional as classic columns and moldings.

BANKING ROOM OF THE GUARANTY TRUST COMPANY, NEW YORK

THE contrast of the richness of most banking interiors to the poverty and crowded meanness of some commercial, domestic, or public buildings is almost appalling. Very nearly the climax of modern classical richness is seen in the banking room of the Guaranty Trust Company. Here the rich Corinthian forms are used with perfect mastery of proportion, scale, and the placing of ornament; and all the fixtures, chandeliers, screens, vestibules, window gratings, and the pavement itself are blended into one impressive creation that is almost arrogant in its assertion of power and luxury. Here is the logical extreme of the temple idea; here is the American Temple — a bank.

453   York and Sawyer, architects; photograph by A. B. Bogart

THE FEDERAL RESERVE BANK, RICHMOND

THE Federal Reserve banks are of a different order; combining office building, bank, and public building functions. The most distinctive is the Richmond building (No. 454). Like that of the Columbia Trust Company (No. 447), it makes bold use of a monumental order of several stories. Its reserved and austere lower portion gives it a somewhat recondite and secretive expression; it suggests hidden mysteries, veiled *arcana;* but the picturesqueness of its simple mass and its power give it an element of true beauty.

454   Sill, Buckler and Fenhagen, architects

THE HARTFORD FIRE INSURANCE COMPANY BUILDING, HARTFORD

IF banks seem so frequently our modern American temples, our office buildings seem often to have an almost equal public and monumental character. Such, for instance, is the Hartford Fire Insurance Company building (No. 455). Size, material, restraint, the entrance colonnade, the dome above, combine to make this seem some great monument. Yet proportion, delicacy of detail, and large simplicity in design are always public property; the building is an ornament to its city.

455   E. S. Dodge, and Parker, Thomas and Rice, architects

456   Marcus T. Reynolds, architect

THE PLAZA, ALBANY, NEW YORK

MORE obviously an office building, the Plaza at Albany (No. 456), built for the Delaware and Hudson Company, still retains a strongly public and monumental character. Built in a free type of modernized Gothic, its picturesque mass borders the Hudson most effectively. A certain thinness of form bears witness not only to the steel framework within, but also to the difficulty of treating forms established by steel frame and large modern windows in a style developed under other conditions and for other purposes.

EARLY SKY-SCRAPERS IN NEW YORK

THE group (No. 457) showing the *Tribune* building at the left, by R. M. Hunt; the Tract Society building in the center, by R. H. Robertson; and the *Times* building at the right, by George B. Post, is typical of early sky-scraper design — all tentative, experimental, confused. Hunt essays a strange chaotic *Néo-Grec;* Post a Romanesque; Robertson a modified Renaissance. Of the three the Tract

457   From a photograph, about 1885, by Soule

Society building is the best because the simplest; it is an early example of treatment of a high building by reduplicating a *motif* several stories high. But again unnecessary horizontal lines interrupt what is, in the main, a pleasing simplicity.

458   D. H. Burnham and Company, architects

THE RAILWAY EXCHANGE BUILDING, CHICAGO

The later Chicago sky-scrapers, particularly those of the first decade of the twentieth century, are often deplorably thin; stability was there, of course, but no appearance of stability. The Railway Exchange building, built in 1903, is typical of this class of high buildings. It is a great rectangular box, filled so closely with ranked windows as to seem a work rather of cardboard than of steel and masonry; its stability is engineering rather than architectural; it is a work of efficiency rather than of fine art.

459   Ernest Flagg, architect; © photograph by Irving Underhill

THE SINGER BUILDING TOWER, NEW YORK

But if Chicago first tried simplicity in high building design, it was New York that first developed a modern expression for the tower type originated in Chicago by Louis H. Sullivan. The Singer tower (No. 459) came first, then the Metropolitan tower.

460   N. LeBrun and Sons, architects; © photograph by
                        Irving Underhill

THE METROPOLITAN TOWER, NEW YORK

The tower of the Metropolitan Life Insurance Company's building (No. 460) is one that is growing old gracefully; gleaming in the sun, gray in the dusk, or with its spire veiled in the wind-blown cloud fringes, the beauty of its silhouette and proportion, the bold simplicity of its shaft, the excellence of its scale, and its chimes and lights that flash the hour, have true poetry in them; they silence, somehow, all the criticisms of logicians, all accusations of plagiarism from the Italian Renaissance.

THE MUNICIPAL BUILDING, NEW YORK

THE Municipal building (No. 461) combines with the simpler treatment of a great flat-roofed building the rich lightness of a central tower, a massive screen colonnade and a triumphal arch connecting the two wings at the base. Adhering closely in detail to Roman and Renaissance forms, it is, nevertheless, in its simply and effectively grouped ranks of windows, in its emphasis on vertical lines, and in its whole conception and composition, truly an American building, whose beauty, despite classic columns and entablature, is a beauty of present day New York.

461　　McKim, Mead and White, architects

462　　Holabird and Roche, architects

THE CHICAGO TRADITION IN HIGH BUILDINGS

CHICAGO tradition has always shown a tendency towards a free and non-classical treatment of the high building. These two, the Monroe building and the University Club (No. 462), one (left) in a modified Romanesque, the other (right) in a most original and modern Gothic, reveal this trend. Both, too, have the tremendous artistic advantage of being buildings adequately and obviously roofed, not mere square boxes of masonry and glass.

463　　B. W. Morris, architect; Carrére and Hastings, consulting architects

THE CUNARD BUILDING, NEW YORK

ONE of the most monumental and lavish of recent New York high buildings, in which there is a similar attempt to gain effects by mass composition, is the Cunard building, whose piled stone façade, with its great crag-like Italian-palace-arched basement, dominates lower Broadway. Its four lower stories form a self-contained separate motif in themselves, and the relation of this to the great shaft above might, perhaps, be made more definite. This is a difficulty that is bound to arise in this type of treatment, and reveals the essential incongruity of this monumental Renaissance character with the necessities of a modern office building. Newer, freer forms avoid this mistake. But in scale and beauty of detail the Cunard building is worthy of study.

464   B. W. Morris, architect; Carrére and Hastings, consulting
architects

THE LIGGETT BUILDING, NEW YORK

New York was the pioneer city in the United States
to adopt zoning regulations, limiting, among other
things, the height of buildings. The particular type
of regulation adopted has revolutionized high building
design by necessitating set-backs, thereby making
mass composition of paramount importance, and
bringing shadows back into city architecture. A
simple type of set-back building constructed under
these regulations is the Liggett building (No. 465).
Verticality, simplicity of detail, careful mass composition are the chief elements in its beauty.

466   Helmle and Corbett, architects; photograph by
John Wallace Gillies

THE GREAT HALL OF THE CUNARD OFFICES

The most notable feature of the Cunard building is
the great hall of the Cunard offices, where marble
and bronze, rich relief and brilliant color serve
to make a whole delicate in detail and gorgeous in
subdued richness of color. The ceiling decorations
are by Ezra Winter, with decorative wall maps by
Barry Faulkner. To some eyes there is too sudden a
break at the cornice line between the absolute simplicity of the marble wall below and the rich vaulting
above. That is a detail; the whole is a delight and
a refreshing piece of loveliness.

465   Carrére and Hastings, and R. H. Shreve, architects

THE BUSH TERMINAL BUILDING, NEW YORK

The Bush Terminal building (No. 466) strikes at
the heart of modern sky-scraper design. It accepts
the problem in its entirety, even to the bare party
walls, and makes its effect by using precisely the
necessary elements: extreme verticality to express
the steel structure, and a polychrome brick patterning
of the party walls to make them contribute to the
tower-like effect of the whole. At night, when flood
lights set the delicate detail of the upper portions
agleam against the black sky, there arises the romance
of a new American beauty.

467 Cass Gilbert, architect; photograph
by Wurts Brothers

THE WOOLWORTH BUILDING, NEW YORK

To many people this building (No. 467) will always be the skyscraper *par excellence*, because it is the highest. The delicacy of its Gothic detail is a result of the use of terra cotta, here treated with beautiful appreciation of its limitations and possibilities. Certainly the bold vitality of the strong upshooting quality combines with grace and beauty of detail to create a beauty new, despite its Gothic detail, and truly American in its romanticism.

469 Bertram Grosvenor Goodhue, architect;
photograph of the architect's rendering

THE AMERICAN RADIATOR COMPANY BUILDING, NEW YORK

A NEW freedom has come over high building design in the last few years. Ever more daring experiments in form, in color, in texture are being attempted. Typical of these is the American Radiator Company building (No. 468), which so frankly develops the tower idea with a silhouette graceful and strong, and which clothes the steel with black brick, that the gold-leaf ornament may stand out by contrast. It is the most daring experiment in color in modern buildings yet made in America.

468 Raymond Hood, architect; photograph of
the architect's rendering

BERTRAM GOODHUE'S SUGGESTION FOR THE FUTURE

WHAT the future developments may be no one can tell. It is certain that the zoning law, with its necessity for mass composition, has been an architectural blessing. Bertram G. Goodhue, for instance, has published a scheme for a colossal convocation and office building in New York on the site of Madison Square Garden, whose piled buttresses, flanking wings, and soaring tower give some indication of what we may look for: buildings of great mass, power and graceful silhouette; strong, vital, new, romantic.

1922 COMPETITION
THE *CHICAGO TRIBUNE* BUILDING

THE competition held in 1922 for the new building for the *Chicago Tribune* was a landmark in American architecture. Aside from many variously impossible pieces of fantastic imagination, there were received designs showing almost every type of modern high building. The winning design is generally of modern Gothic, with verticals emphasized, somewhat similar in this respect to the Woolworth building (No. 467). Its rich and varied crowning motif, however, reveals that study of mass composition and silhouette which has been pointed out as a result of zoning ordinances. One of the best features of the design is its use — and expression — of the power of steel construction to allow many and large windows.

470 Winning design by John M. Howells and Raymond Hood. From a photograph of the architects' model

472 Honorable mention, Bertram Grosvenor Goodhue. From a photograph of the architect's rendering

THE second prize (No. 471) abandons the historical precedent of the Howells-Hood design. Its detail is purely modern, non-stylistic. Its emphasis on the vertical lines is daringly bold, and its silhouette of set-backs and breaks interesting, powerful, and well proportioned. It lacks the definite crowning richness of the first-prize design, but in some ways is more significant and realizes more of the undiscovered possibilities of sky-scraper design. Never have the vertical elements that steel construction makes possible received a finer or more inspiring expression than in this soaring and beautifully executed conception, whose simple, straightforward honesty is all too rare.

471 Second prize, Eliel Saarinen; Wallace D. Grenman, associated. From a photograph of the architects' rendering

THE design of Bertram G. Goodhue (No. 472), which won honorable mention in the competition, shows still another type of treatment; an effort to forget all detail and build a great composition of balanced, flat, crag-like masses. Here, too, the detail is free, and interesting possibilities in polychrome surface treatments are hinted at. Like the second-prize design it makes much of the change from rectangular plan to cross plan and back again. Goodhue was evidently less interested in the verticality implicit in sky-scraper design than in the opportunity the "set-back" idea furnished for developing conceptions that are romantic, lovely, endowed almost with a dream quality.

THE HALLIDIE BUILDING, SAN FRANCISCO, CALIFORNIA

ELEMENTS of great importance in modern commercial buildings are metal and glass. Few attempts have been made in this country to make designs stressing these elements. One such building, however, the Hallidie building in San Francisco (No. 473), reveals the delightful possibilities of this type of design — glittering, delicate, sunny, vivid.

473   Willis Polk and Company, architects

A MODERN DEPARTMENT STORE, NEW YORK

DEPARTMENT-STORE design has followed the general trend towards simpler, more monumental forms. The Lord and Taylor building in New York (No. 474) shows the feeling of restraint, elegance, and richness often sought. Show windows are made an integral part of the whole design; there is no appearance, so frequent in some buildings, of heavy masonry being carried on sheets of glass. The great entrance arch, the crowning colonnade, and the carefully designed cornice go to make a whole whose distinction is in itself an outstanding feature.

474   Starrett and Van Vleck, architects

THE ALEXANDER BUILDING, NEW YORK

THE problem of shop-front design for smaller shops is of very different type. The most usual and successful scheme is to treat shop window and door together in one large frame enriched with marble or the delicacy of wrought bronze. In the Alexander building (No. 475), *sgraffito* of Italian Renaissance character is used to give a quiet richness and delicacy that make even a narrow building distinctive and beautiful, so that it brings a welcome touch of color into the too usual gray of the modern city street.

476   George Ray, architect

A STUDY IN SHOW WINDOWS, WASHINGTON

THE store building on Connecticut Avenue, Washington (No. 476), shows a different working out of the same general type. The differentiation yet unity of the two show windows on the first and second floors is especially noteworthy, fitting so well into the simple stucco façade.

475   Carrére and Hastings, architects

CHAPTER XVI

PUBLIC BUILDINGS

ONE outstanding fact in the design of modern public buildings which strikes the most casual observer is the universal domination of the classic tradition. State capitols, city halls, courthouses, museums, libraries — all seem naturally to fall into classic forms; all show how the classic tradition, so firmly founded by Jefferson and his followers, lasting through the revivals, retaining an emasculated and sporadic vitality even through the horrors of the General Grant period and the vagaries of the Victorian Gothic, has come to new life and dominates modern monumental architecture. Another dominating and controlling though less obvious fact is the development of the art and the science of planning. It is this advance rather than an improvement in detail through increased archæological knowledge which is responsible for the general improvement in the quality of American public building design.

Planning is the art of arranging the various rooms, corridors, stairs, etc., that a building demands. As such its effect is most obvious in the efficiency with which a building "works." But it has other effects equally important; spaciousness, impressiveness, grandeur, on the one hand, or studied intimacy, coziness, and privacy on the other. Planning is therefore the art of relating the parts of a building together so that structurally, practically, and æsthetically all work toward a common end; all build into a common and composed unity. It is in the grasp of this conception that the basic merit of modern American public building design lies; it was precisely in missing this conception that the work of the 'sixties, 'seventies, and 'eighties so generally failed. Between the mean entrance and crowded stairs and dark indirect corridors of such a building as the old Post Office in City Hall Park in New York, and the magnificent openness of the grand stairs and the rotunda of the Missouri state capitol (No. 483) lies a gulf that reveals the advance in American architectural planning during the last sixty years.

Two tendencies have been at work in this growing mastery. One, purely French, called *logique*, comes from the École des Beaux Arts, Paris. It is the theory that the appearance of a building, outside and in, should express every function and important structural element of the building. The other tendency, Italian in origin, finds its inspiration in the planning of the great buildings of the Italian Renaissance. This theory maintains that perfection of proportion and beauty of details and general effect are of as great importance as the more formal theory of abstract expressionism.

Dangers beset both tendencies. *Logique* frequently produces complexity instead of simplicity and accents parts at the cost of the whole; and the Italian tradition, in making an exterior which is merely a mask for an interior, tends to lose true unity entirely. *Logique* demands careful thought, rigid analysis, prevents caprice and mere ostentation; the Italian tradition makes for quietness, careful proportioning of parts, and produces monuments to delight as well as essays to read. The greatness of American monumental architecture lies in its combination of these two tendencies, and in its consequent attempt always to make a building not only beautiful, but also straightforward, expressive, vital, yet never to sacrifice to an abstract theory any actual, visible unity and beauty.

Modern American classicism is not the classicism of the revivals. Neither is it that rather uncritical love of various Renaissance forms brought back from Paris by Hunt and his earlier American followers at the École des Beaux Arts. It is something much deeper. It is not a slave of periods, and its freedom is constantly enlarging. It is an eclectic classicism. It seeks æsthetic, not archæological harmony. In general it tends more to ancient, and particularly to Roman precedent, than to Renaissance, yet it uses Renaissance forms freely. The Detroit Library (No. 521), for instance, is neither Greek nor Roman, neither French nor Italian Renaissance, yet it is distinctly classic. The American designer in a classic style is seeking the essence of all those things which make the serenity, the dignity, the grand and simple scale of the finest classic work; he is using an alphabet of forms that the world has known and loved for hundreds of years.

The American architect has thus created a new sort of classic. He has wed Renaissance cleverness to the dignity of ancient Rome. He has treated a building with monumental planning, based on modern complex needs, perhaps with a Renaissance dome and stairways and windows, perhaps with a Roman colonnade, in a style which has, at its best, both Roman greatness of scale and Greek refinement of detail. He has used a vast number of materials boldly — steel and bronze, glass and stone, marble and baked clay — and made of them one unity. This is a unique thing; no other country has, with such complex problems and materials, produced a style so flexible, so free from archæological trammels, yet so dominantly and singly classic. This is not, however, an ultimate development. A new conflict has arisen from the very nature of this attempt to combine theoretically perfect planning with a beauty so obvious and so dear to the average person that it becomes a true communal expression — the conflict of pure design and modern structural materials. For steel and reinforced concrete have yet to find their true artistic expression. We are not accustomed to the forms they suggest; much less have we reached a point where we can play with these forms, vary them, create beauty with them. Now, too often we use these new materials to represent, even to imitate other forms; we build a structure and hang to it a bird-cage of wire lath on which we put our decorative surfaces of plaster that is sometimes jointed to appear like stone. Many a modern building seems less a building than a mere piece of stage scenery, exquisitely designed; and there is something in the architectural mind that will never rest content with this. Eventually a solution will be found, and new forms developed to fit the new materials. Already there has been a beginning. The Nebraska state capitol, by Bertram G. Goodhue (Nos. 486, 487, 488), shows a new expression of the classic tradition, and its beautiful interiors reveal a new vision of the tremendous possibilities ahead.

Modern America has developed a number of specific types of public buildings that need brief mention. First of all, there is the state capitol, usually domed, with two wings to express the two houses of the legislature; an idea based on the design of the national capitol, which, in its perfection, early inspired imitation. In the second place, there is the typical classic courthouse, frequently with a great colonnaded front to express the dignity of the law, and with lavish court rooms opening from a large central rotunda or monumental lobby. And then there is the railroad station, entrance, waiting rooms, concourse, train shed, all combined into one great building that forms a monumental gateway for a city. Finally, the public library, a monument to the American aim of universal public education, whose great halls, delivery room, principal and subordinate reading rooms — all often richly decorated — form one of the finest expressions of American democracy, a true people's house — built for them, owned by them, used by them.

The last two types, stations and libraries, are those in which America has contributed most to the stream of the world's monumental architecture. They embrace the two problems whose requirements are most uniquely American, and whose complexities seem particularly to require and to appeal to native ingenuity. The libraries of Boston, Detroit, Indianapolis, San Francisco, and the great stations of New York, Richmond and Washington, are true additions to the artistic wealth of the world.

477   From a photograph by Rau Studios, Inc.

THE OHIO STATE CAPITOL, COLUMBUS

THE capitol at Columbus shows that the accepted type of state capitol had been set early, prior to the Civil War: two wings and a crowning central motif. The austere Greek Revival style is well handled, if a little heavy, and the crowning circular drum is an interesting attempt to design what is really a dome motive in a Greek style.

478   William Thornton, Stephen Hallet, B. H. Latrobe, Charles Bulfinch and Thomas U. Walter, architects; photograph by
                                     the Halliday Historic Photograph Co.

THE NATIONAL CAPITOL, WASHINGTON

BUT it was the enlarged, completed national capitol which furnished inspiration to most of the more recent state capitol designs. Its dome is magnificent in silhouette, even though made of painted cast-iron, and its impressive length, with the two great Senate and House wings, is amazingly consistent in view of the length of time its construction occupied, the completion of the dome occurring at a time when taste was at a low ebb.

479   Minnesota State Capitol, St. Paul, Cass Gilbert, architect; © Detroit Publishing Co.

480   Indiana State Capitol, Indianapolis, Edwin May and Adolph
Scherrer, architects; © Detroit Photographic Co.

481   Rhode Island State Capitol, Providence, McKim, Mead
and White, architects; © Detroit Publishing Co.

482   Arkansas State Capitol, Little Rock, Cass Gilbert, architect;
© Underwood and Underwood

STATE CAPITOLS

THE state capitols of Minnesota, Indiana, Rhode Island and Arkansas show how closely the precedent of the national capitol has been followed. Despite vast differences in skill, beauty, and detail, all four have the same general scheme. The Minnesota capitol (No. 479), perhaps the most lavish of the four, is a masterly example of rather academic American Renaissance, deriving alike from French and Italian sources. The Indiana capitol (No. 480) is full of misunderstood French reminiscences, with detail chaotic and ill applied, and has a dome obviously insufficient to dominate the confusion beneath it. The Rhode Island capitol (No. 481) is made distinctive by the combination of a wall treatment in the wings, evidently inspired by the work of Bulfinch, with a dome studied from that of St. Paul's in London. The corner domed turrets are noteworthy. The Arkansas capitol (No. 482) gains in effectiveness by its simplicity; only the queer circular and semi-circular openings in the attic over the central portion keep it from being an excellent example of restrained classical work.

A MOST monumental Roman character, in coffered vaults, Ionic colonnades, simple masses of broad masonry is shown in the grand staircase and rotunda of the Missouri capitol. The Roman feeling is seen as much in the planning and general arrangement of parts as in the detail.

INTERIORS OF WISCONSIN STATE CAPITOL

THE Wisconsin capitol interior has a rotunda (No.

483   Tracy and Swartwout, architects; photograph by Hugh Stephens

484) which in its blaze of dark rich marbles, its mural decorations, and its large scale is as lavish a piece of eclectic classic as there is in America. Yet there is enough restraint, simplicity and dignity to remove all danger of such richness appearing vulgar.

484   George B. Post and Sons, architects; photograph by
J. W. Gillies

485   George B. Post and Sons, architects; photograph by
J. W. Gillies

The Supreme Court room (No. 485) has a similar dignity and the mural paintings add not only richness of color, but a desirable human note.

Bertram Grosvenor Goodhue, architect; photograph of the architect's rendering

THE NEBRASKA STATE CAPITOL, LINCOLN

A DEPARTURE from the typical, as daring as it is logical and beautiful, is to be found in the Nebraska capitol. Distinguished by a great tower of offices, it is visible for miles across the flat country; it exhibits great classic restraint and simplicity but without historical precedent, and a free and daring use of decorative sculpture — bison at the ends of the walls that flank the entrance steps; Wisdom, Justice, Power, and Mercy on the pylons at the great entrance arch; and the figures of great lawgivers on the buttresses around the Supreme Court windows, all modeled by Lee Lawrie. The whole forms a remarkable combination of architecture and sculpturing, truly American.

487   Bertram Grosvenor Goodhue, architect; photograph
of the architect's rendering

The interiors (Nos. 487 and 488) show the same freedom, richness, logic, and charm. Great vaults richly decorated, and simple bold mass composition below, give a character half Byzantine, half Roman, and yet entirely American and modern.

488   Bertram Grosvenor Goodhue, architect; photograph
of the architect's rendering

489   McKim, Mead and White, architects; photograph by Wurts Brothers

THE GENERAL POST OFFICE, NEW YORK

FEDERAL buildings generally continue the tradition of strict classicism. One of the finest of these is the General Post Office in New York. The long, many-doored public space is perfectly expressed by a colonnade, which in proportion and beauty of detail is the equal of any modern colonnade in the world. Vitality, interest, and decoration are all served by the beautiful and apt inscription on the frieze: "Neither snow nor rain nor heat nor gloom of night stays these couriers from the swift completion of their appointed rounds."

THE UNITED STATES POST OFFICE, WOOSTER, OHIO

THE smaller post offices scattered over the country, designed by the architect of the Treasury Department, are frequently of high architectural merit, and accomplish much in setting an architectural standard for the localities in which they are situated. A building such as No. 490 cannot but have a profound effect upon the architectural taste of those who daily see its dignified simplicity.

490   James A. Wetmore, acting supervising architect

THE PORTLAND, MAINE, CITY HALL

IN town and city halls, although the general tendency at the present time seems to be towards some type of classic, there is much more opportunity for the expression of local styles and tastes. The Portland City Hall (No. 491) is an interesting combination of many forms purely classic with many forms purely Georgian or colonial, all unified by the typical modern spirit of eclecticism. It is an effective and impressive building, although the coldness of its blue-white marble makes it seem a little aloof and remote.

491   Carrére and Hastings, architects, John Calvin Stevens and
       John Howard Stevens, associated

THE TOWN HALL, WESTON, MASSACHUSETTS

This is one of the best examples of a purely "colonial" treatment, with all the grace, the decorative combination of red brick and white stone or wood, and the refined delicacy of scale which characterized the work of the early nineteenth century. Like the Portland example (No. 491), it retains the cupola that was so constant a feature of colonial public building.

THE CITY HALL, PLATTSBURGH, NEW YORK

This example (No. 493) is one of the very few modern buildings inspired directly by the Greek Revival work of the eighteen twenties. Beautifully pro-

492   Bigelow and Wadsworth, architects; photograph by Thomas Ellison

portioned, carefully detailed, with its low dome and Doric portico, it recalls not only the forms of the American Greek Revival, but also its somewhat austerely cold character. To-day, such a style seems rather remote in its grand and aristocratic dignity, a little arrogant, perhaps; modern taste generally prefers the greater warmth and welcome of the colonial.

493   John Russell Pope, architect; photograph by Kenneth Clark

MUNICIPAL GROUP AT SPRINGFIELD, MASSACHUSETTS

Here the civic center of a city consists of an office and court building, an auditorium and a great clock tower. Its rich classic detail, and the double magnificence of its twin Corinthian porticos, are an impressive and dominating decoration for the city square on which they face. Designed thus as frank decorations for the square, there is less need of definite logical expression of function in their design. So the buildings serve a double purpose; practically, they house the city government, and æsthetically they are a civic monument.

494   Pell and Corbett, architects; photograph by Wurts Brothers

495   Hunt and Hunt, architects

THE OLD SLIP POLICE STATION, NEW YORK

In planning this interesting building, the architects turned to the rusticated palaces of Renaissance Florence for a style expressive of strength, solidity and governmental dignity, and achieved by beauty of proportion and careful detail a gracious impressiveness that is distinctive.

PUBLIC BATHS, KANSAS CITY, MISSOURI

Park and recreation buildings demand a lighter, more delicate touch. In their design the forms of the less monumental sort of Italian Renaissance are almost universally dominant. Such buildings as No. 496 reveal how charmingly tile roof, spreading cornice and classic arcade fit into park surroundings, and with their welcoming effect add still more to the beauty of the park as they add to its usefulness.

496   Wight and Wight, architects

497   Arthur Ware, architect

RECREATION PAVILION AND BAND STAND, HOBOKEN, NEW JERSEY

In the Hudson County Park in Hoboken may be seen a richer and more decorative development of a similar idea. With its playful fountain and the lily pool to mirror its rich ornament, it forms a grouping of delightful grace and effectiveness.

THE Q STREET BRIDGE, WASHINGTON

BRIDGES, too frequently merely engineering and utilitarian projects, can by careful design become true works of art. Such is this bridge in Washington. With only the minimum of carefully placed ornament, it nevertheless achieves, by the handling of proportion and mass and well studied use of materials, a forceful dignity like that of much Roman work.

498   Glenn Brown and Bedford Brown IV, architects

499   Carrére and Hastings, architects

THE APPROACH TO MANHATTAN BRIDGE, NEW YORK

BRIDGE terminals offer a magnificent opportunity for architectural embellishment. The oval colonnades and triumphal arch that form the approach to the Manhattan bridge (No. 499) are instinct with the dignity such structures demand. The arch is studied from such French Renaissance arches as the Porte St. Denis at Paris. But to gain its maximum effect, a gateway like this demands broad, open approaches, and a monumental type of street planning which are here sadly lacking.

THE COOK COUNTY COURTHOUSE, CHICAGO

THE tradition of severe classicism is more rigidly followed in courthouses than in any other type of building. In this example, although the building is full nine stories high, the architects have forced the lower three into a basement, and the upper six into one colossal Corinthian order of more than Roman size. Such a design makes the problem of scale almost insoluble; for the great cornice, and the tremendous projecting member that crowns the basement, seem afflicted with absurd gigantism.

500   Holabird and Roche, architects

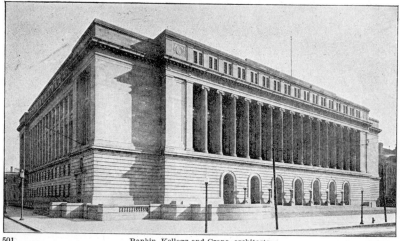

501   Rankin, Kellogg and Crane, architects

THE COUNTY COURTHOUSE AT CINCINNATI

THIS public building gains great dignity by the unbroken wall surfaces of its façade, which throw the Ionic colonnade into vivid relief. An inscription let into the frieze — "The pure and wise and equal administration of the laws forms the first end and blessing of social union" — vitalizes and decorates the somewhat arid dignity of the whole building.

502   Hale and Rogers, architects

THE SHELBY COUNTY COURTHOUSE, MEMPHIS, TENNESSEE

THE courthouse at Memphis is smaller, less austere, more enriched by sculpture, yet equally classic. Its treatment of the Ionic colonnade with its pedimented end motifs is characteristic of the best American classic eclecticism, based perhaps more on Greek detail than anything else, but using Greek inspiration freely, vitally, with no attempt at actual copying.

A LAVISH COURTHOUSE INTERIOR, NEWARK, NEW JERSEY

COURTHOUSE interiors rival bank interiors in the lavishness of their construction and the care in their design. The majesty of finance and the majesty of the law — these two, at least, are adequately housed. The Freeholders Room in the Essex County Courthouse at Newark uses marble walls, mural paintings, and a rich painted beamed ceiling to gain its effect of subdued yet lavish dignity. It is a pity that more of our courts cannot be as impressively and beautifully housed.

503   Cass Gilbert, architect; photograph by Wurts Brothers

504 McKim, Mead and White, architects; photograph by Louis H. Dreyer

PENNSYLVANIA STATION, NEW YORK

RAILROAD station design, combining as it does the most difficult engineering and utilitarian features with the desire for adequate monumental expression, has appealed with especial strength to the American mind. The new terminal building of the Pennsylvania Lines in New York (No. 504) shows how all is united into one great block treated with austere Roman classicism, dominated by the great clerestory windows of the main concourse.

INTERIOR OF MAIN CONCOURSE

THE interior of the main concourse of the Pennsylvania station is one of the truly great productions of American architecture. Despite its use of motifs derived from Roman bath halls, its tremendous size, beautifully expressed by a perfect treatment of scale, its almost Puritan

505 McKim, Mead and White, architects; from a photograph

simplicity of form, its capacity for engulfing crowds, the almost too restrained color of its decorative maps, all form a whole of awe-inspiring grandeur—breath-taking at first sight, and characteristically American.

THE CONCOURSE, GRAND CENTRAL STATION, NEW YORK

HERE are reproduced (Nos. 506 and 507) views of another type of station interior, in which the great blue vault, dotted with stars and lined in dull gold with the figures of the constellations, seems almost an attempt to make it all part of outdoors. Here again careful scale treatment, despite the frivolity and prettiness of some of the carved ornaments, gives tremendous dignity and a sense of magnitude. The simplicity of the great piers and the arched windows is a masterly touch that helps give the impression of power and size.

506   Reed and Stem, architects; Warren and Wetmore, associated

507   Reed and Stem, architects; Warren and Wetmore, associated

MODERN IDEAS IN A RAILROAD STATION

THE waiting-room of the New York Central station at Rochester gains the effect of size and welcome with its swelling tile vault and direct simplicity of form. Although certain details are inspired by Roman work, the whole beauty of this room depends upon pure line and proportion, and the ornament is free and non-stylistic, and the more valuable for its rarity.

508   Claude Fayette Bragdon, architect

509   Bakewell and Brown, architects

THE RAILROAD STATION AT SAN DIEGO, CALIFORNIA

THE Santa Fé station shown in No. 509 is one of the best of the smaller stations, for not only do its fore-court and great arch give an adequate expression of welcome, but also its simple Spanish Renaissance-Mission style embodies the tradition of the locality. It therefore serves admirably to express the railroad station idea, being both gateway and an embodiment of its situation.

A RURAL STATION ON LONG ISLAND

RURAL railroad stations frequently have a picturesque character almost domestic, except for the long roof over the platform. The station at Baldwin, Long Island (No. 510), has the simple mass, picturesque treatment, and rough textures that characterize much of the surrounding house work. Its unostentatious charm and its close style relationship to its locality partly compensate for its lack of functional expression.

510   Frank J. Forster, architect

511   Hubbell and Benes, architects

THE CLEVELAND MUSEUM OF ART — SOUTH FRONT

IT is in museums that the scholarly eclectic classic so popular to-day finds its most logical and its most charm-ing uses. What, for instance, could be simpler, more dignified, more beautiful and more expressive of the museum function than the marble wall surfaces and severe classic detail of the Cleveland Museum of Art?

512   Hubbell and Benes, architects

THE GARDEN COURT, CLEVELAND MUSEUM OF ART

MUSEUM interiors are growing continually more spacious, more simple, more welcoming and human. "Outdoors" is simulated in large courts, where sculpture and large decorative objects are shown in a setting of growing greenery. Such is the garden court (No. 512) of the Cleveland Museum.

513   Green and Wicks, architects; H. W. Wachter, associated

THE TOLEDO MUSEUM OF ART

HERE the architects in No. 513 have used a long colonnade exquisitely detailed to break the formality of its blank walls and produce an impression of welcome and invitation. Landscaping and terraces give an adequate setting. Endowed almost with a dream quality by the beauty of its material and the simplicity of its design, such a building cannot but add much to the richness of the life of the city that enshrines it.

514   McKim, Mead and White, architects; photograph by Wurts Brothers

THE MORGAN LIBRARY, NEW YORK

THE J. Pierpont Morgan Library is as much a museum as a library, and its design is fittingly eclectic, although based principally upon the work of early sixteenth-century Italy. Richness of material and detail and perfection of execution give the whole a position almost unique in American architecture. Before such successful eclecticism, criticisms of style plagiarism — partly deserved — grow faint and seem only captious.

INTERIOR, LIBRARY OF CONGRESS, WASHINGTON

THE Congressional library in Washington, completed 1897, has the honor of being the first modern American building to receive adequate interior treatment (No. 515) by means of paintings, mosaics, and sculpture. The richness of color in ceilings and walls, the lavishness of carving and of veined marbles, had a far reaching effect upon popular taste, despite the overelaborate ostentation and lack of restraint of the library itself.

515 Smithmeyer and Pelz, and Edward Pearce Casey, architects;
photograph by Rau Studios, Inc.

516   Ritchie, Parsons and Taylor, architects

A SMALL–TOWN LIBRARY INTERIOR

THE interiors of the smaller Georgian libraries are frequently rooms of great charm. The Needham, Mass., Public Library (No. 516) has a central delivery room with reading rooms at each end. The vault and the character of the delicate Adam detail — similar to some of McIntire's best Salem work — give the whole its subtle combination of elegance and informality.

THE BOSCAWEN, NEW HAMPSHIRE, LIBRARY

THE smaller public libraries of the country often follow Georgian precedent. In this example a colonial style is daringly modified and modernized. Simple in scheme, it makes no pretensions to being larger than it is; yet marked distinction is given to it by striking mass and delicate detail.

517   Guy Lowell, architect

518   Ellis F. Lawrence, architect

A SMALL LIBRARY IN THE ITALIAN STYLE

But Georgian or colonial are not the only styles used in small libraries. The Albina Branch, Portland Public Library in Portland, Oregon, uses early Italian Renaissance forms with equal skill and attains thereby an equal charm. It is to be remembered that in all of these cases the use of the past styles is seldom archæological, but free, personal, and endlessly modified.

THE BOSTON PUBLIC LIBRARY

Of the larger city libraries, this one, completed 1895, is not only one of the earliest but also one of the most famous, and still one of the best. Inspired by the famous *Néo-Grec* Bibliothèque Ste. Geneviève in Paris, it is much more classic in feeling than the Paris example. Its simplicity, the majesty of its

519   McKim, Mead and White, architects; photograph by Frank Cousins

ranked arched windows, and the beautiful use of inscriptions all give it distinguished charm and true beauty.

520   McKim, Mead and White, architects; © Architectural Book Publishing Co.

DELIVERY ROOM, BOSTON PUBLIC LIBRARY

The Boston Library is as famous for its richly decorated interiors as for its exterior dignity. Puvis de Chavannes, E. A. Abbey, and John S. Sargent have all helped to decorate its walls. The gorgeous color of Abbey's Holy Grail murals above the dark subdued strength of the carved wainscot gives the delivery room a feeling of quiet solemnity and richness.

521   Cass Gilbert, architect; photograph by Kenneth Clark

THE PUBLIC LIBRARY, DETROIT, MICHIGAN

THIS is undoubtedly one of the finest of the more recent public libraries. Its detail is of generally Roman and Renaissance character, and its monumentality and the richness of its ornament, the carving in the frieze, and the polychrome mosaic in the loggia vault, make an ensemble of great beauty. It is a magnificent temple to civic pride and civic education.

522   Cass Gilbert, architect; photograph by Kenneth Clark

THE DELIVERY ROOM

SIMPLE masonry walls with delicately carved medallions and a rich coffered ceiling that give it richness, quietness, dignity, and charm, are the outstanding features of the delivery room of the Detroit Public Library (No. 523).

DETAIL OF CORNER, DETROIT PUBLIC LIBRARY

THIS detail of an end pavilion (No. 522) shows the richness of the carved and modeled detail, carefully located so as to leave the main masses strong and simple.

523   Cass Gilbert, architect; photograph by Kenneth Clark

524   Electus D. Litchfield, architect

ST. PAUL LIBRARY INTERIOR

LIBRARY interiors furnish opportunity for restrained and quiet richness. A certain formality is desirable, but the whole must be kept warm, human, livable. In this doorway (No. 524) of the main reading room, the balance between formal richness and quiet beauty has been surely attained.

A REFERENCE READING ROOM AT INDIANAPOLIS

REFERENCE reading rooms in modern work are usually kept simple. Bookcases below, simple walls and windows above them, and a rich ceiling are the usual elements. In the Indianapolis Public Library (No. 525), a ceiling of almost Pompeian detail gives a quality of lightness and delicacy often difficult to obtain with equal richness in any other style.

525   Zantzinger, Borie and Medary, architects; Paul Cret, associated

526   George W. Kelham, architect; photograph by Gabriel Moulin

THE PUBLIC LIBRARY, SAN FRANCISCO

SOMEWHAT similar in scheme to the Detroit Library (No. 521), although different in detail, and with a similar dignity, is the San Francisco Public Library. The large grilled arched windows have something of the true Roman simplicity and bigness, and the whole is marked by unusual perfection of proportion, to which the statues add an effective human touch.

CHAPTER XVII

MEMORIALS, MONUMENTS AND EXPOSITIONS

AMERICA was fortunate in her earliest monuments, for colonial graveyards are full of slate headstones, with here and there an impressive table tomb, almost all emotionally sincere, beautiful in the lovely design and spacing of the quaint lettering, and despite crude ornamental details, harmonious in shape and proportion. In the first half of the nineteenth century the United States was fortunate, too, in the simple grandeur of that soaring slim obelisk — the Washington monument in Washington — of the Washington column in Baltimore, and of that smaller obelisk that gleams white from the summit of Bunker Hill. In each are the true simplicity, the true dignity and the true unworldliness, that should distinguish a real monument.

But with the coming of Victorianism during and after the Civil War, that good fortune vanished. Crude Gothic ruled the country's cemeteries; tombs were out of scale, harshly outlined, covered with caricatured detail. And sentimentality, like a sticky river, engulfed all, leaving a tradition that persists in rural marble yards to-day. Broken columns, weeping angels — and what angels! — became the fashionable grave monuments; and ill-modeled and worse carved realistic flower-sprays abounded. Polished gray granite with thin, scratchy lettering, and thin, scratchy incised ornament became the favorite material. It was as if the dignity, noble restraint, and sure line of the colonial gravestones or the Washington monument had never been. All the dignity of death and the nobility of memory were swamped in the sticky flood.

Nor did sentimentality confine itself to the graveyard. The end of the Civil War saw hundreds of cities and villages set about the business of erecting a war memorial — and almost without exception the sentimentality of the period gained in them its fullest expression. Moreover, industrialism, with quantity production, stepped in to help complete the sorry tale. Soldiers in stone and soldiers in bronze were followed by soldiers in iron; cast in hundreds from the same mold, or stamped from the same die. And the worst type of realism ruled the making of these molds or dies: softness, formless rotundities, with no sense of modeling, or any appreciation of that first necessity of art — a sense of the material. Carved, stamped, or cast, they were all alike; and frequently, as in much other decorative cast-iron of the time, the iron was sanded and painted to look "just like stone." This was a revelation of a tendency that became so deeply rooted in American art that it still persists; although we no longer sand iron and paint it stone color, we are still content to paint or veneer steel doors to look like wood.

The American Renaissance of the 'eighties and 'nineties produced in memorial architecture, as in all other fields, a revival of classicism. At first it was a mere formal acceptance of new canons, without understanding; it filled cemeteries with miniature classic temples, cold and hard, as inconsequential and inexpressive in their own way as the

219

earlier polished granite blocks in theirs. In fact, many of them possessed more positive sins, for in them ostentation became a virtue, and as much detail as their surfaces would bear was squeezed upon them by the profit-grabbing monument company that was so frequently their designer. As a result parts of the more expensive cemeteries still look like miniature cities inhabited by a swaggering race of pygmies.

We still, alas, have all these monstrosities with us. They were built to endure. And still the broken columns and the draped vases and the polished granite steles and the miniature temples are produced by the thousands in the ubiquitous rural marble yards. But the reaction against all this falsity has begun. Ever since the 'nineties there has been a growing sense of fitness, of emotional sincerity, of freedom from any slavery to archæology in all of the finest monumental work. Statue bases, for instance, have ceased to be tiny crenellated castles; they have become an integral part of the whole, simple, strong, graceful, decorated with emotional aptness. Tombs have become more simple; they are, as a rule, designed with less ostentation and with a growing seriousness.

This emotionalism, that avoids on the one hand the sentimentality of Victorianism, and on the other the cold formality of the era of miniature temples, is deeply founded in the evident purpose of American artists — sculptors and architects both — to think clearly, to feel truly, to face each new artistic problem with an open mind, to strive in each new creation to build or carve or model not what is fashionable, but, as far as conditions and their clients allow, what they truly and personally feel. This tendency marks a triumph of personality over the herd, and it is itself but the expression of a deep national movement towards a better proportioned attitude towards life. This is a movement that is veiled behind all the hurly-burly, the falsities and the crudities of advertising, industrialism, and modern business expansion generally, and that appears with constantly increasing strength in religious controversy and in the development of an American satirical literature. It is peculiarly fitting, therefore, that the two outstanding monuments of this new restraint, this new and deeper emotionalism, should be, one, a memorial of the World War, and the other, the national memorial to him who seems to many the ideal American — Abraham Lincoln.

The Kansas City War Memorial (No. 550) is notable not only on account of the design, by H. Van Buren Magonigle, that, in the competition, was placed first and is now under construction, but also on account of another of the designs submitted (No. 552), that of Bertram Grosvenor Goodhue, of which the immense scale, free style, and compelling emotional power have a true epic character.

The Lincoln Memorial (No. 554), more conservative in character, shows that emotional truth, emotional fitness, is not a matter of mere style. Emotional power in design is more deeply founded than that, in the larger matters of proportion and scale. For although the Lincoln Memorial uses forms once Greek, its perfect colonnade, crowning with gracious dignity its massive base and, within, that mighty statue of the man from the frontier (No. 556), flanked by tablets on which are carved his two most famous speeches, seems, as it shines so whitely above the surrounding green, to be an almost perfect embodiment of the candid integrity and power of Lincoln himself, and of the deep quiet reverence in which his name is held.

There is a class of memorials of a different character whose importance in the development of American architectural taste has been tremendous — the great international expositions — Philadelphia (1876), Chicago (1893), Buffalo (1900), St. Louis (1904), San Diego (1914), San Francisco (1914). In these exposition buildings utility is a second consideration; economy is forgotten. Built for the most part of temporary materials, some purists would deny them the name of architecture entirely; yet in a very real sense they are the surest expressions of American taste in architecture. They are like great myths, the creations of a people's dreams; they are architectural folk lore. And just as dream-made myths may become governing factors in a nation's life, so these dream-created architectural fantasies become guideposts for national taste. To them flocked millions who saw what beauty might be, saw, glowing in sunshine by day, radiant and jeweled by night, what color was and ordered form, and a great conception expressed through the harmony of multitudinous and differing parts. Was it strange that, so impressed, these millions returned to their homes filled with the dream but, mistaking the style, the detail, for the beauty, tried to produce the same beauty by using, however stupidly, similar details?

The Chicago exposition, with its rather cold white monumentality, was the direct result of the new classicism of the American Renaissance, but it was also the cause of a new popular enthusiasm for the classic that became almost a slavery. Buffalo sang with a lighter note, an exuberance of fantastic pseudo-Spanish character, that was similarly the result of an intellectual movement and similarly a cause of its wider popularity. St. Louis, with its extravagant modern French *baroque*, its curved lines, its heavy and ornate classicism, not only expressed but also helped to popularize and propagate that love of ovals and cartouches and all the trappings of some types of French design which characterized the first decade of the present century.

So, more recently, San Diego, with its brilliant Spanish Renaissance, whose simple wall surfaces threw into magnificent prominence its richly jeweled details of doorways and tower, was a result of the modern movement towards a new localism of style, and helped to show the fitness of its style for the traditions and the climate of southern California. But it was at San Francisco, in the greatest exposition of them all, that the dream character was most clearly realized. There, Americans saw for the first time their growing love of color embodied, saw color wedded to architecture, saw their loved classicism blossoming into a new freedom, breaking suddenly into brave and laughing modernistic fantasy, daring to use dramatic contrasts of plain rich-hued wall and magnificent colonnade. There, too, they found everywhere combined with the color and the architecture sculpture that was instinct with imagination and with life. The whole was classic yet free, restrained yet dramatic, majestic and beautiful yet human. It was the deeply-felt dream of modern American architecture.

527   From a photograph by Frank Cousins

GENERAL LOGAN'S TOMB

Tomb and gravestone design followed all the vagaries
of popular taste through the revivals and the senti-
mentalities of "Victorian" taste. The large monuments, too, were equally true to fashion. General
John A. Logan's tomb in the National cemetery at
Arlington (No. 528), dating from 1886, shows well the
mixture of Gothic and Romanesque taste popular at
the time — heavy, severe, impersonal, unimaginative,
but not without a certain stolid dignity.

529   Albert Kelsey, architect; photograph by J. H. McFarland Co.

COLONIAL GRAVESTONES

EARLY colonial gravestones, which are such a
dominating element in the picturesque atmosphere
of many an old churchyard along the Atlantic coast,
have a twofold interest. Their value as physical
source material for the study of colonial history is
unique; unique, too, is the appeal of their intrinsic
charm and frequent quaint beauty. They are often
made of slate, but a red sandstone and a white native
marble are also common. With their curved tops,
frequently adorned with a crude, flat cherub's head,
sometimes with a weeping willow, sometimes with a
more lugubrious skull, they have frequently borders
of Jacobean ornament. But their greatest loveliness
lies in their lettering, which is almost always instinct
with great beauty of spacing, shape, and cutting.
Typical of these is this stone (No. 527) in King's
Chapel Burying Ground in Boston.

528   From a photograph by Soule

THE OLMSTED MEMORIAL,
HARRISBURG, PENNSYLVANIA

THE same eclectic classic influence which has influenced so much modern American public work shows
as well in our modern monuments. But in this field
a classic of mainly Greek inspiration dominates; as
contrasted with the more usual Roman or Renaissance
influence in public and commercial building. The
Olmsted memorial shows that simple, refined forms
of Greek detail are well adapted to a modern
memorial.

THE MILBANK MEMORIAL, WOODLAWN CEMETERY, NEW YORK

THIS memorial is a larger type of more recent construction, and is a perfect example of the dignified use of Greek detail in a modern way. The popularity of Greek forms for monumental use seems to be due to their magnificent combination of a simplicity that gives dignity, and a grace and refinement of detail that removes any trace of heaviness or gloom from their quiet beauty.

530   York and Sawyer, architects; photograph by
John Wallace Gillies

THE MARY BAKER EDDY MEMORIAL, CAMBRIDGE, MASSACHUSETTS

WHILE Greek in its inspiration, the Greek of this memorial (No. 531) is of a kind new and peculiarly interesting, for instead of using merely the conventional acanthus leaf, every particle of the foliated ornament was studied from native New England plants, so that the whole, preserving the virtues of the Greek inspiration, is endowed with a new interest and a new beauty that come from the freshness and intimacy that these well-known forms give.

531   Egerton Swartwout, architect

532   James Gamble Rogers, architect; photograph by John Wallace Gillies

THE HENRY ROGERS MALLORY MEMORIAL

MUCH freer in design is the Mallory memorial at Greenwich, Conn. Here is the skillful piling up of simple masses, principally rectangular, which gives such a dignified and quiet repose, such a satisfactory sense of solidity and power. The contrast of stone and foliage adds to the effect.

THE WAINWRIGHT TOMB, ST. LOUIS, MISSOURI

THIS is another non-stylistic tomb of even more pronounced modernism. Its dome, to be sure, set so simply and strongly upon the cubical base, has a contour that might suggest a Byzantine or even an Arabic prototype, but the ornament, so beautifully placed in strong and simple bands, is of that typical delicate intricacy which Louis H. Sullivan has developed, and which is a distinct contribution to the development of American art.

533   Adler and Sullivan, architects; photograph by *The Western Architect*

THE FARRAGUT MONUMENT, NEW YORK

THIS notable memorial to a famous sailor is to many the most perfect blend of architecture and sculpture America has produced. Although it is distinctly a non-stylistic work, it is flooded with that special dignity, that combination of grace and strength, that is truly classic. The way architectural form and sculptured texture are interpenetrated and the peculiar and gracious appropriateness and perfect placing of the ornament make this monument a masterpiece.

534 McKim, Mead and White, architects; Augustus St. Gaudens, sculptor

THE LINCOLN MONUMENT, LINCOLN, NEBRASKA

THIS imposing monument has blended sculpture and architecture equally well, but in an entirely different way. The simple, thoughtful figure of Lincoln against the perfectly proportioned stele, with its beautifully lettered Gettysburg address, has an effect of tragic and appealing dignity.

535   Henry Bacon, architect; Daniel Chester French, sculptor

THE SOLDIERS' AND SAILORS' MEMORIAL ARCH, HARTFORD, CONNECTICUT

AMERICANS have built triumphal arches, also; most of them temporary, like the Dewey arch of 1899 or the Victory arch of 1918; some permanent. It is an odd fact that the earliest permanent memorial arch, erected in 1885, is not Roman at all, but in that strange *mélange* of Gothic and Romanesque and plain non-stylistic picturesqueness which characterized the taste of its time. Not without a certain fineness of outline, it is in detail strangely awkward, and the band of relief that is its main ornament cuts the whole unpleasantly in two.

536   From a photograph by Soule

THE WASHINGTON MONUMENT, WASHINGTON

BUT there are other monuments in which sculpture plays no part at all. The most famous of these is the Washington monument by Robert Mills, begun 1848, completed 1884 by General T. L. Casey. Its effect lies entirely in the delicate tapering of the great mass of the obelisk — pure geometric form attaining beauty by virtue of its perfect proportion. In the very fact of its total lack of ornament there is a commanding dignity, a mighty strength, eminently fitted for its purpose.

537   Robert Mills, architect; © Detroit Publishing Co.

THE WASHINGTON ARCH, NEW YORK

THE need for economy has prevented imitations in permanent American arches of the lavish carving and ornament which distinguish the triumphal arches of ancient Rome. It is the consequent simplification of every detail that makes the Washington arch in New York the best example. There is no "order"; merely a simple pair of piers supporting the arch, a fine cornice and inscription above.

538   McKim, Mead and White, architects; photograph by Wurts Brothers

539   McKim, Mead and White, architects; J. Massey Rhind, sculptor; photograph by Trinity Court Studio

THE McKINLEY MEMORIAL,
NILES, OHIO

THIS is an example of a monument that is a real building. Its rather cold, careful, refined Greek classicism is full of dignity, its proportions and detail impeccable, but somehow it seems lacking in feeling. This lack may result from the rather questionable appropriateness of the refined and delicate Doric detail in a memorial to such a practical politician as William McKinley.

540 Detail from the McKinley Memorial. McKim, Mead and White, architects; J. Massey Rhind, sculptor; photograph by Trinity Court Studio

541   From the tablet by Paul Manship in the Metropolitan
Museum of Art, New York

MEMORIAL TABLET TO
JOHN PIERPONT MORGAN

THIS tablet, erected in the Metropolitan Museum of Art, is a striking example of that type of memorial which bridges the gap between pure architecture and pure sculpture. With a form strongly architectural, with figures of the greatest beauty, simply placed, and with lettering instinct with freedom and personality, it is a creation of great delicacy, restraint and dignity. In it is revealed a quality characteristic of much sophisticated taste — the self-conscious love of archaic forms — for the influence upon it of archaic Greek sculpture and ornamental detail is obvious.

542   From a print, courtesy of
      the J. L. Mott Iron Works

THE IRON SOLDIER OF THE 1870's

THE end of the Civil War gave birth to a flood of soldiers' monuments throughout the northern states. Unfortunately, the deplorable taste of the time prevented any adequate expression of the sincere emotions they were intended to commemorate. Instead a universal banality is over all; on a pseudo-Gothic base stands a cast-iron, sometimes even a stamped sheet-iron soldier, modeled without art, without vision; in front is a pyramid of cannon balls. The whole is awkward, frequently ill-proportioned, utterly without imagination, and the figures, produced by hundreds from stock patterns, ostentatious, listless, crude.

WORLD WAR MEMORIAL, LANDSDOWNE, PENNSYLVANIA

IN general, the memorials built since the World War are in vastly better taste. This one has no ostentation, no attempt to attain in sheet iron what one would like to have in bronze if funds were adequate, no stock soldier. Instead, a simple shaft, simply crowned, simply inscribed. Ornament is sparingly used and every bit that is used is packed with real meaning. Proportions are carefully studied, and the result is a monument of lasting beauty, eloquent of the restraint of true emotion.

543   Clarence W. Brazer, architect

THE SOLDIERS' AND SAILORS' MONUMENT AT DULUTH, MINNESOTA

ALTHOUGH larger than the Landsdowne memorial, this (No. 544) is characterized by a similar restraint. Simple dignity is its keynote; there is unusual harmony between the architectural members and the impressive and dignified figure. Flagpole bases like this offer a great opportunity for monumental treatment.

545   A. D. F. Hamlin, architect; Hermon A. MacNeil,
      sculptor

A VILLAGE WAR MEMORIAL

THE earlier soldiers' monument at Whitinsville, Mass., shows a similar restraint, a similar simple beauty, in a small village monument. The graceful curves of the triangular base, the three Ionic columns, the crowning eagle and the lovely low relief tablet on the front, all are marked by that delicacy, careful study, and loveliness of line and mass, which make for calm and quiet beauty.

544   Cass Gilbert, architect; Paul Bartlett,
      sculptor

546   C. W. and A. A. Stoughton, architects; E. I. DuBois,
                        associated

PITTSBURGH SOLDIERS' MEMORIAL

THIS memorial takes the form of a great auditorium.
In exterior form, like the Washington Temple of
the Scottish Rite (No. 724), it is inspired by the
famous Greek Mausoleum; but in detail it is wholly
different, for its Doric order is Roman in character,
and its base, influenced by French modern work,
has a heavy monumentality, a coarseness of scale
that is the opposite of Greek refinement. The
colonnade, with the pyramidal stepped roof above,
is, however, markedly impressive.

SOLDIERS' AND SAILORS' MONUMENT, ON RIVERSIDE DRIVE, NEW YORK

IN the design of this monument the site plays an
important part. Set on a rounded bluff overlooking
the Hudson, with a terrace entered directly from
Riverside Drive, it lifts its graceful many-columned
height into the air most effectively as seen either from
above or below. Its beautiful silhouette is a striking
contrast to the squat heaviness of Grant's Tomb
farther up the river. The detail of the monument is
of an eclectic classic type, strongly influenced by
French traditions; its main beauty lies in its conception and its proportion.

547   Palmer and Hornbostel, architects; photograph by
                        Trinity Studio

548   Blackall, Clapp and Whittemore, architects

LOWELL, MASSACHUSETTS, MEMORIAL AUDITORIUM

THE Lowell Auditorium is a more recent example of a memorial amphitheater. Its exterior is extremely
dignified; large, simple, with all the dignity its severe Roman classic forms should give it, and the sense of
integrity which the frank expression of the elliptical auditorium within produces. But one wishes that
economy had not forced the use of buff bricks and cast stone for a building of such monumentality of design
and purpose.

NATIONAL MASONIC MEMORIAL, ALEXANDRIA

In this monument at Alexandria, Virginia, the architects have produced a design unique in many ways. Of marked classical feeling, and with details of both Greek and Roman character, the general idea is utterly new, and in developing it, the novelty of idea has compelled much consistent novelty in the treatment of the classic forms. The varied rhythms in the spacing of the columns in the superposed stages of the building are particularly pleasing in their freshness. It is designs such as this which show the developing freedom in the modern use of past styles.

549   Helmle and Corbett, architects; photograph from the architects' rendering

550   H. Van Buren Magonigle, architect; © by the architect

LIBERTY MEMORIAL, KANSAS CITY

THE climax of modern American memorial design is to be found in two designs submitted in the competition for the Liberty memorial at Kansas City. One is the winning design, by H. Van Buren Magonigle, the other is the design submitted by Bertram G. Goodhue. Magonigle's design uses some forms of classic inspiration, but the controlling idea is not classic, nor Gothic, nor Renaissance; it is American. It is a design of great emotional power, attaining its effect by the boldest uses of plain wall, cubical composition, and a great shaft rising high to be visible for miles around.

THE GREAT SHAFT OF THE MEMORIAL

A PERSPECTIVE view shows how the great shaft springs boldly from the cubical masses below. From its summit is to spring always smoke by day, fire by night. Here is no academic scholarly re-creation of the past; no cold and aloof product of a cloistered mind; but rather an attempt, brave — almost foolhardy — to take the pent-up and

551   H. Van Buren Magonigle, architect; © by the architect

sentimentalized emotion of the whole people, and give to that an expression bold enough to overcome any repression, noble enough to overpower any sentimentality.

552   Bertram Grosvenor Goodhue, architect; photograph from the architect's rendering

THE GOODHUE DESIGN FOR THE LIBERTY MEMORIAL

BERTRAM GOODHUE'S design for the Kansas City memorial, like Magonigle's, uses freely forms of classic inspiration; like his its governing idea is emotional. But it is a less theatrical type of emotionalism that is present; something more reposeful, more serene, and for that reason perhaps all the more powerful, all the more deep. Its great pylon, in which architecture and sculpture are inextricably blent, builds up with magnificent dignity from the surrounding buildings.

THE MEMORIAL FROM THE SIDE

A SIDE elevation shows well how perfectly simple forms are used in Goodhue's design to give the right emotional atmosphere. Great masses of stone with arched windows beautifully placed flank a pilaster decorated wall; buttressed retaining walls terrace up the hillside and give triumphant

553   Bertram Grosvenor Goodhue, architect; photograph from the architect's rendering

accent to the towering side of the pylon. The lack of cornices everywhere, the rounding and softening of edges and corners are most important in giving somber greatness to the whole.

554   Henry Bacon, architect; photograph by Kenneth Clark

THE LINCOLN MEMORIAL, WASHINGTON

BY many considered the most beautiful American memorial building, this monumental shrine, containing the great statue by Daniel Chester French, marks not only the climax of the more conservative tradition of monument design, but also perhaps the climax of classic architecture in America. Before its impressive and austere columned front, words are futile.

A CORNER OF THE LINCOLN MEMORIAL

EXAMINATION of the corner of the Lincoln memorial reveals a little of the endless study and refinement which created its perfection. The columns are not equally spaced; those at the corners are set more closely, in order to give an impression of adequate strength. Greek precedent is not followed slavishly; instead of the ordinary frieze there is the long line of state names and linked wreaths. It is this freedom from direct imitation which gives the whole its magnificent vitality, and adds to its beauty for us. It is an adaptation of a style, and not mere copying that has dictated the forms. This photograph shows amazingly well the way the whole seems to burn against the sky with some light almost its own.

555   Henry Bacon, architect; photograph by Kenneth Clark

THE FIGURE OF LINCOLN WITHIN

IN the interior the austerity of the Doric gives way to the pure grace of the Ionic; and in the middle, on his simple throne, sits Lincoln, calm, reposeful, noble. Queerly enough the old Greek forms from hundreds of years ago seem perfectly in harmony, seem almost perfectly to express the strength and the dignity and the humanity that were Lincoln's. Therein lies part of the reason for the success of the whole.

556   Henry Bacon, architect: Daniel Chester French, sculptor;
photograph by Kenneth Clark

COLUMNS AT THE ENTRANCE, LINCOLN MEMORIAL

LIKE all great buildings, the Lincoln memorial is full of that quality of correct relationship, giving an impression of its true size, which is called *scale*. This view of the entrance shows how the scale of the whole relates to human beings; instead of dwarfing them, as do some large buildings, it is so designed that people only add to its greatness.

557   Henry Bacon, architect; photograph by Kenneth Clark

558   From a photograph showing parts of three of the principal buildings

THE WORLD'S COLUMBIAN EXPOSITION, CHICAGO

IT is impossible to exaggerate the importance of the World's Columbian Exposition in Chicago in 1893. There, for the first time, millions of Americans saw a magnificent extended group in a unified type of architecture; saw the mass effect of simple and monumental classic detail. Although cheap and temporary in material, although the fronts were but decorative screens surrounding vast trussed sheds, which had little real architectural connection with them, although the detail was often overwrought and the ornament banal, nevertheless the ranges of arches, of columns, and pilasters, the vast triumphal entrance arches lining the lagoons were so superior in restraint, in monumentality, in large scale, to anything that had preceded, that popular taste was deeply impressed.

559   Richard M. Hunt, architect; from a photograph

THE CENTRAL BUILDING, CHICAGO EXPOSITION

THE focus of the whole was the great Administration Building. Logically planned to give a great domed central hall, effectively massed into a silhouette of great power, the building had a grandeur of simple line such as most of its visitors had never dreamed. Its detail is, to the modern eye, unconvincing, unduly French, and French of the modern type. Simplicity was not yet attained. But by comparison with any of the monumental work of the 'eighties, this building was a striking masterpiece; an object lesson in the potentialities of classic design.

ENTRANCE OF THE TRANSPORTATION BUILDING

YET one of the finest and certainly the most original of the Chicago Fair buildings was a non-classic building, the Transportation Building. Its great entrance — the Golden Arch — was popularly impressive too; and kept alive before the popular mind that fine free originality in design which all of the late Louis Sullivan's work possesses. In scale the whole is masterly, and the ornament has delicate scintillating loveliness, though the reliefs below are strangely banal. But even the success of this non-stylistic building could not prevent the great wave of country-wide enthusiasm for classic design which followed the Chicago Fair.

560   Adler and Sullivan, architects

561   John Galen Howard, architect; from a photograph

THE BUFFALO PAN-AMERICAN EXPOSITION

IN the exposition at Buffalo (1900), the increased freedom and imaginative quality of its buildings marks an advance over the more academic classic of the Chicago Fair. The climax was the great central "Electric Tower," with its flanking colonnades (No. 561). Owing something to study of the Giralda, in Seville, it has nevertheless a charm of silhouette and an exuberance of detail all its own.

THE LOUISIANA PURCHASE EXPOSITION

AT St. Louis in 1904, the exposition buildings were the culmination of modern French influence in American architecture. This is true both in general conception and in detail. The great sweeping curves of the whole plan, the luxury of the ornament, the love of broken lines, and varied curves, all are typically French features. Yet the result, with all the studied impressiveness that French planning gives, was too big, too obvious, despite its richness too cold, despite its curves lacking in mystery, intimacy, charm.

562   Cass Gilbert, architect

563   Cass Gilbert, architect; photograph by Rau Studios, Inc.

THE FESTIVAL HALL, ST. LOUIS EXPOSITION

AN examination of this building, the center and climax of the whole, with sculpture by Augustus Lukeman, reveals the reason for this failure. It is too ostentatious, too restless. The crowding of luxurious detail blurs

564   Cram, Goodhue and Ferguson, architects; from a photograph

the fineness of the underlying composition; the curving lines of the fountain, the steps, and the planting below, produce only confusion, "brain fag." The whole is "paper architecture"; it would look marvelously well in drawings, but in execution it fails. The American taste has to-day an underlying and controlling love of restraint, simplicity, personality, some hint of mystery or romance, that by its very exuberance this building fails to touch.

CALIFORNIA STATE BUILDING, PANAMA–CALIFORNIA EXPOSITION

As always, the two expositions held in California in 1914 were not only expressions, but also strong inspirations of popular taste, in many ways prophetic of development since. The Panama-California Exposition buildings at San Diego, Cal., took as their controlling idea the Spanish traditions of southern California, and used a style based on the late Spanish Renaissance. By means of the contrast of plain wall and richly massed ornament, of picturesque silhouette, of stucco and colored tile, there was produced a dramatic, fanciful character, full of just that personal charm lacking in St. Louis.

A SPANISH GATEWAY AT THE SAN DIEGO EXPOSITION

A DETAIL of the entrance of the California Building shows perfectly the turgid, bossed, fanciful richness of detail, so brilliantly designed to catch sparkling lights and throw deep shadows. Only the rigid concentration of the ornament makes such richness possible, and produces that effect of dramatic climax which is so breath-takingly effective. It is just this dramatic quality which has become such a marked feature of recent American architecture, and just this free use of Spanish Renaissance precedent that has, since 1914, swept over the architecture of southern California.

565 Cram, Goodhue and Ferguson, architects; from a photograph

566   Bliss and Faville, architects; © Cardinell-Vincent Co.

PANAMA–PACIFIC EXPOSITION, SAN FRANCISCO

IN the exposition buildings at San Francisco, equal dramatic effects were attained by a use of that simplified eclectic classic which is typical of modern America. Byzantine and Roman influences predominate, but are always treated freely — always as inspiration and not as limitation. Color and water reflections were used with a daring never before attempted. The Palace of Education (No. 566) rears plain walls, dome-crowned, and breaks into the rich climax of the great entrance niche with a brave simplicity typical of the whole exposition.

COURT OF THE UNIVERSE, SAN FRANCISCO EXPOSITION

THE American love of romance was satisfied by keeping the outside of the exposition severely simple, and then dividing the interior into a series of courts, each different, and all brilliantly rich. The most monumental was the great Court of the Universe, with its immense Corinthian colonnade, and colossal triumphal arch. Color, freedom of detail, decorative dramatic force, all combined to give a vivid, living effect that shows the advance in classic design since the cold thinness of Chicago or the French exuberance of St. Louis.

567 McKim, Mead and White, architects; © Cardinell-Vincent Co.

CHAPTER XVIII

EDUCATIONAL BUILDINGS

THE development of the architecture of American educational buildings is a symbol of the importance which education holds in American life. America was early distinguished for its colleges; Harvard and William and Mary bear witness to the zeal with which the early colonists started the country on its educational way. Since then the development has been continuous and rapid. The thirty years following the War of Independence saw the founding of innumerable academies and colleges; the opening of the West was soon followed by the growth of the great land-grant state universities, and to-day the eagerness with which the sons and daughters of families only recently Americanized attend public and private high schools and colleges proves that the desire for education is still vital and widespread.

The early development of collegiate architecture is responsible for the strength of its colonial tradition. Curiously, the early builders of the colleges completely deserted the common English quadrangle and cloister, and abandoned the charming collegiate Gothic that was still being built in Oxford well into the eighteenth century. Poverty may have caused this, or some instinctive feeling in Puritan New England that the cloisters and grouped windows of Oxford and Cambridge were "popish" and foreign to their ideals. But whatever the cause, early college buildings were square and severe, rather Georgian in style, usually of brick, and often with the ubiquitous cupola. Sometimes three buildings would face three sides of an open court or campus, as in Harvard; sometimes the whole would be stretched out in a long line, as in King's College, New York.

The colonial style so set remained the usual style well into the nineteenth century. Roman and Greek Revival details are found, but in the majority of cases poverty forced a severe simplicity often of great charm and dignity. Built as late as the architecturally barbarous 1860 period, the Quaker School in New York shows the persistence of the type, and has, despite its date, in its quiet brick walls, its white cornices and its delicate porch, much of the charm of the earlier work.

But there were signs of a coming change. Immediately after the Civil War — a period of educational expansion — Victorian Gothic predominated. It is responsible for most of the horrors which everywhere dot college campuses. Here was a fertile field for pseudo-picturesqueness, chaotic confusion of modern Gothic detail, unschooled love of variety and color, which patterned roofs in red and blue slate, and ringed arches with red and white marble. Picturesqueness and "pleasing informality" too often meant lack of plan either in the single building or in the college group. The resulting chaos seemed to deny the existence of Jefferson's quietly formal University of Virginia.

Modern planning is, however, inspiring comprehensive plans for new institutions and resolving the chaos of existing ones. Several highly specialized style expressions are developing in consequence. Of these, the most important and the most popular is the use of the collegiate Gothic of Tudor and Jacobean England. From Massachusetts to Oregon its monuments are found. Its grouped windows seem admirably adapted to classroom use, just as its formality and intimate scale serve perfectly for dormitories. Moreover, the ideal of English collegiate life is strong in this country; Oxford and Cambridge have been instilled into the essence of English literature, and it is not strange that their architecture should have a profound influence upon the collegiate architecture of the entire English-speaking world.

But the style has its dangers. To be truly effective it must be truly done; to be done truly it must be expensive. Carving, stone-mullioned windows, tracery, vaults and towers are luxuries; to cheapen them is often to lose all of their charm. These forms, moreover, lead all too frequently into mere prettiness. Collegiate Gothic, therefore, has no monopoly of the field. Pure classic or Renaissance forms appear in many examples. Georgian or colonial types seem to have a charm which only truth to tradition can give. But it is perhaps characteristic of the innate conservatism of many of the higher institutions of learning that few attempts, even in the architecturally radical Middle West, have been made to design college buildings with absolute freedom from any historical style idea.

This freedom, on the other hand, characterizes a great deal of our best public school design, and naturally. For the design of a great public high or grammar school is a problem absolutely modern, whereas the collegiate problem is not, and therefore new forms have developed to meet it which make all the best school design creative, modern, whatever the type of ornament used in the decoration. School design, like hotel design, has become highly specialized. The most rigid standards of natural and artificial lighting, of mechanical equipment, to ensure the greatest possible health and comfort for the pupils, are demanded; to satisfy them is the school designer's first task.

This has been true particularly of the larger town and city schools. Rural schools, like all rural buildings in America, until lately have received little architectural attention. Between the district school of our grandparents' day and the typical district school to-day, the differences, if any, are only in the smallest details. Of course there are commendable exceptions; schools built to-day in Delaware show a distinct and encouraging attempt to apply true architectural skill to the problem of the rural school. Contemporary emphasis on the problems of city life has caused this stagnation in rural school building as compared with the colossal advance in town school planning. Scientific school planning, accompanying the enormous recent volume of urban school construction, has sometimes swamped the art of school design. Rigid specialized requirements and universal need of economy tend strongly to the production of forms too often factory-like and mechanical. Light, air, heat, are too frequently embodied in soulless, unstimulating, dead schools. Is this a mark of mechanical ugliness in our entire systematized education, that turns out all pupils depersonalized and stamped with the same die, as it produces devitalized standardized schoolhouses of a common ugliness everywhere?

But the mechanical, factory-like, ugly school is not the rule. More and more beauty is being sought in school design not as a mere expression of local pride, not, as often in days past, as the result of the toleration of the eccentricities of an unfortunately necessary architect, but voluntarily, as a vital part of the growing child's environment, and achieved as a direct result of the increasing breadth of educational idealism. It is these really lovely, human, welcoming schools which form one of America's greatest contributions to the general stream of architecture, because in them is achieved most surely the perfect balance of functional expression, simplicity and efficiency, and pure beauty.

Especially noteworthy in this respect has been the work of the southwestern states, of California in particular, where a one-story plan, with the classrooms around a central court or *patio* has been developed, expressed in various free styles. These schools are doubly interesting, not only because of the true beauty and intimate charm of many of the buildings themselves, but also because in them one can see most clearly style developing as it should develop — new forms created to serve new needs; old forms being changed, subtly, and unconsciously, by their new uses.

A TYPE OF FRAME SCHOOLHOUSE IN THE COUNTRY

This old school for colored children in Christiana, Delaware (No. 568), is typical of the simple frame buildings which still serve as schoolhouses for thousands of country-bred children.

568   From a photograph by the Royal Studio

A 1775 SCHOOLHOUSE IN PHILADELPHIA

The scholastic architecture of America has grown from humble beginnings. A one-room, gabled-roof brick or frame building with every appearance of a small cottage was the early type. The Concord School at Germantown, Philadelphia (No. 569), built in 1775, is a highly developed example for its date, boasting two floors and a belfry cupola. But the domestic character is still strongly marked. Undoubtedly the windows originally had small panes.

569   From a photograph by Rau Studios, Inc.

THE PEIRCE ACADEMY, MIDDLEBORO, MASSACHUSETTS

The early years of the nineteenth century saw a remarkable development of "Academies" throughout the country. Greek Revival forms mark many of them; such, for instance, as the example shown in No. 570. But even at that time it was principally the existence of a cupola which distinguished the Greek porticoed schools from the Greek porticoed houses.

570   From a steel engraving, about 1840, by F. O. Freeman after a drawing by A. C. Warren

A NEW YORK FREE SCHOOL OF 1808

IT was the growth of cities and the necessity for developing schools of many rooms in congested neighborhoods that first produced the elements of a school type. The New York Free School (No. 571), built in 1808, shows this. Using the delicate "colonial" detail of the period, it nevertheless is neither ordinary house nor ordinary public building. It is beginning in its design — window grouping and so on — to express its school function.

571   From an old print in the New York Historical Society

NEW YORK PUBLIC SCHOOLS FIFTY YEARS LATER

NEW YORK Public Schools 37 and 19 show that by the middle of the century (the latter dates from 1859), a definite school type had been evolved. Several stories of windows are paired or otherwise grouped, and, for the time, substantial masonry construction distinguishes them. The details are of the pseudo-Italian type illustrated in Nos. 353 and 378. But there was little understanding of the true science of school planning; the requirements of lighting, ventilation, and sanitation are hardly appreciated at all.

572   Public School 37. From a print in the New York
Historical Society

573   Public School 19. From a photograph by courtesy of the Board of Education, New York

574 From Minard Lafever, *Architectural Instructor*, New York, 1856

THE PACKER COLLEGIATE INSTITUTE, BROOKLYN

MINARD LAFEVER reproduced in 1856 his design for the Packer Collegiate Institute in Brooklyn (No. 574). It is one of the earliest examples of an English Gothic style applied to schools; and despite its Victorian Gothicism, it reveals some of the possibilities that were later to be developed into modern American scholastic and collegiate Gothic.

575   C. B. J. Snyder, architect; photograph by courtesy of the Board of Education, New York

THE MORRIS HIGH SCHOOL, NEW YORK

SCHOLASTIC Gothic as applied to large city schools was developed to its highest point by C. B. J. Snyder, architect for many years of the New York Board of Education. He revolutionized city school design. The Morris High School shows the type of Perpendicular Gothic, much modernized and simplified, which he used. The school function is perfectly expressed by the ranked mullion windows, the type of plan, and the essentially scholastic atmosphere of the detail. Mr. Snyder's contribution to school design was as important in practical matters as in his handling of the style, notably in solving the problems of lighting classrooms on a restricted city lot, of arranging ample corridors and stairs and exits satisfactorily.

576   W. H. Gompert, architect; photograph by courtesy of the Board of Education, New York

A MODERN NEW YORK SCHOOL

THE extremely high building costs after the year 1914 made the problem of the city school increasingly difficult. New York Public School 52 shows how every inch of superfluous ornament has been eliminated, and the whole reduced to almost factory-like bareness. Only the entrance door, a string course or two, and the rather questionable arched heads of the top windows remain of the earlier Gothic type.

THE FACTORY TYPE

THE necessity for floods of light, combined with the necessity for building cheaply, leads inevitably to the factory-like type, of which the school in Britt, Iowa, serves as an example. Economy carried to such degree cannot but starve the growing sense of beauty.

577   G. L. Lockhart, architect; photograph from the *School Board Journal*

578   Garber and Woodward, architects; photograph by Charles H. Longley

DETACHED GROUPING IN SCHOOL PLANNING

OF late there has been a trend away from Gothic towards a Georgian or colonial style in school work. The Withrow High School in Cincinnati shows this style; it shows as well, in its extended and detached grouping, the growing departmentalizing and complexity of modern high school education. The effect of such an environment of spacious beauty — restrained, carefully thought out and full of charm — upon the pupils who enjoy it cannot be overestimated.

579   Garber and Woodward, architects; photograph by Charles H. Longley

AN AUDITORIUM OF SIMPLE DIGNITY

THE auditorium has become, with the growing separation of high schools into different departments, an increasingly important element. As the one place where the school meets together, where commencements, plays, entertainments are held, it is the focus of the school life. THE auditorium of the Withrow High School in Cincinnati has the simplicity, delicacy and dignity that belong to it.

580   George F. Shepard, architect; photograph by Paul J. Weber

A GIRLS' SCHOOL IN THE COLONIAL STYLE

Milton Academy, Milton, Mass., is an example of a "colonial" school in which the style has been closely followed, as befits the ancient traditions of the town, but even here the necessities of the plan have required an un-colonial grouping, very successfully handled. Great ventilator chimneys and a porch of white columns give just the right touch of dignified New England restraint.

A MODERN HIGH SCHOOL LUNCH ROOM

The light and air of the best modern school lunch rooms are a pleasant contrast to the dark, ill-ventilated, smelly basement barracks that too often used to be considered "good enough." There is nothing ostentatious or expensive about this lunch room in the Withrow High School, at Cincinnati (No. 578), but it has a fine atmosphere of light and air and good cheer.

581   Garber and Woodward, architects; photograph by Charles H. Longley

582   Ernest Sibley, architect; photograph by Mattie Edwards Hewitt

MODERN HIGH SCHOOL OF FREER DESIGN

Of a freer type of design, in which the classroom windows are frankly grouped, yet with an air generally Georgian given by dignified portico and cornice and pedimented entrances, is the Leonia High School, in Leonia, N. J. In its frank acceptance of modern conditions, its careful mass composition, and its delicate classic detail, this is an admirable example of modern eclecticism.

A HIGH SCHOOL IN THE GOTHIC MANNER

But there is modern modified, free, eclectic Gothic in school design as well. The Southwestern High School in Detroit is a beautiful example of this. The simply massed brick walls, the simple arched door, the buttress forms that are quite modern in detail, and the light metal ventilating cupola in the roof, all have a flavor not only new, frank, creative, but of true charm as well. Moreover, the large windows are frankly expressive of the school function.

583 Malcolmson, Higginbotham and Palmer, architects; photograph by courtesy of
The Architectural Record

584 William B. Ittner, architect

A JACOBEAN TYPE IN ST. LOUIS

Some of Mr. Ittner's smaller St. Louis schools, in a modernized and eclectic Jacobean, are among the most individual and delightful in this country. This Bryan Mullanphy School is typical. The plan is a perfect school plan, well-lighted, economical; the whole has personality, charm, atmosphere. Such beauty, in a public school, is a national asset.

THE CARL SCHURZ SCHOOL, CHICAGO

There is a continually increasing number of attempts to design schools independent of all historical styles. One of the most successful of these is the Carl Schurz School in Chicago. It is simple and straightforward, and in the rhythm of its repeated motifs there is a distinctly vital effect. But all the entrances seem painfully constricted and uninviting. Except for that, it is an interesting example of the composition of simple wall, pier, window and roof.

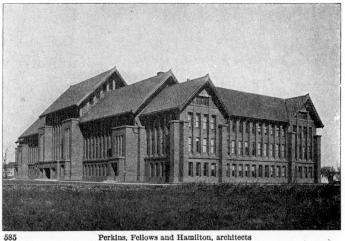

585 Perkins, Fellows and Hamilton, architects

A SCHOOL IN THE "FUTURIST" MANNER

THE Baldwin High School, Birmingham, Mich., is in the futurist or "secession" vein. Again it is the entrances that are at fault, with their border of unmeaning and inappropriate classic detail. The vertical windows with their slim columns, the buttress strips and the plain brick surfaces are exceedingly interesting.

587   Guilbert and Betelle, architects

A ONE–TEACHER RURAL SCHOOL

THE purely rural school has unfortunately received but little architectural attention. Four walls, a gabled roof, a few stock windows, a flag pole, two obvious and objectionable outdoor privies, apparently sufficed for over a century. The state of Delaware has made a great step in advance in having a series of well-planned and beautiful types of one- and two-teacher schools designed for rural districts. The photograph shows the charm of these simple modified "colonial" buildings.

588   F. S. Allen, architect

CONTOURS AND CLOISTERS OF SPANISH MISSION STYLE

THE greatest single advance in schoolhouse design has come from California, with the introduction of the one-story school, the building but one classroom deep, arranged around a *patio*. The High School at National City was the first school of this type done in the Spanish Mission style, whose warm stucco walls, rounded contours, and wide arched cloisters admirably fit the climate and the locality.

589   Allison and Allison, architects; photograph by Frederick W. Martin

GEORGIAN INFLUENCE IN A CALIFORNIAN SCHOOL

THE Grammar School at Glendora has a somewhat similar plan, carried out in a style pleasantly fresh and eclectic, with its delicate Georgian note in the welcoming entrance loggia, its simple stucco arched cloister, and the unusually successful combination of white detail and brick wall with its occasional charming patterns. Such an environment is a continual inspiration to all who come within its bounds.

590   Withey and Davis, architects

AN EARLY BOARDING SCHOOL

THE earlier boarding schools were most frequently merely large houses altered a little if at all. During the Greek Revival period, however, buildings were built specifically for the purpose. Such is the Georgia Female College, with its Doric columns and piers, its wreathed frieze, its attic and typical square cupola — all expressive of the simple, refined, rather austere culture of the day.

THE ANTITHESIS OF THE FACTORY–LIKE SCHOOL

THE Grammar School at Chino, Cal., is a one-story school with Italian detail. Its low central cupola, the contrast of its simple rectangular windows and the rich entrance, and the inviting garden layout with its benches and urns combine to produce an effect of "livability," which is just the reverse of the mechanical harshness of the factory-type school (No. 577).

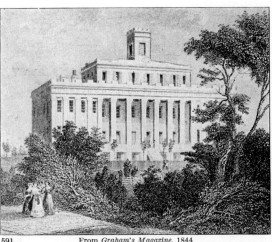

591   From *Graham's Magazine*, 1844

592   Murphy and Dana, architects; photograph by Mattie Edwards Hewitt

THE LOOMIS INSTITUTE, WINDSOR, CONNECTICUT

MODERN boarding schools have been usually in some form of Georgian colonial or Gothic. The Founders' Building — the classroom center — of the Loomis Institute at Windsor, Conn., is in a rather formal type of English Georgian, with various colonial motifs to give it an American flavor. A combined expression of homelikeness, solid, quiet dignity, and refinement has been achieved by this eclectic treatment.

PURITAN SIMPLICITY IN THE LOOMIS CHAPEL

THE Loomis Institute chapel is an attempt to gain something of the cool, quiet delicacy of the New England meeting-house made more simple, more open, and rather more quietly monumental by the use of a lightly paneled elliptical vault swinging from wall to wall. Again the result could only be obtained by the freest and most eclectic use of historical style.

593   Murphy and Dana, architects; photograph by
                Mattie Edwards Hewitt

CHARM FROM A DARING USE OF SCALE

ONE of the most original of Gothic boarding schools is Carson College near Philadelphia. The scale has been kept daringly small, in order to seem intimate and livable to the little girls who live and study there. Endless liberties have been taken with the style; carvings are full of naturalistic field flowers and Mother Goose figures, and figures of children, and the whole is glowing with color. Altogether Carson College, with its grouping of tiny playhouse cottages, its vivid detail, its playful color, is a unique thing — carefully studied, human, charming.

594   Albert Kelsey, architect

PICTURESQUENESS OF PILED GOTHIC

THE Misses Masters' School at Dobbs Ferry, N. Y., is one of several recently built Gothic boarding schools. In these a piled, random picturesqueness, combined with the charm of varied materials carefully used, and simple, domestic details, are frequently the means used to produce the desired effect. Long sloping roof lines, broad wall surfaces of rough stone, grouped windows, a square tower, and a

595   Cram and Ferguson, architects; photograph by Paul J. Weber

little cupola give to this example a character so expressive of its combined school and residence function.

596   From a re-issue, 1739, of the Burgis engraving, 1726, in the King's Collection.
British Museum

HARVARD COLLEGE IN 1726

COLLEGIATE building in America early attained prominence. A view of Harvard in 1726 shows even at that early date three large and monumental buildings, of which one, Massachusetts Hall, at the right, still stands. It is interesting to note that the left hand building, the oldest, has the many gables, grouped windows, grouped chimneys, and Jacobean doorways that are typical of Gothic tradition in America, of which this building was certainly one of the largest and most monumental examples.

COLUMBIA COLLEGE IN 1790

A VIEW of Columbia College in 1790 shows the pre-revolutionary King's College building, with its four pedimented pavilions, its balustraded roof, and the large cupola to give it an official or public stamp. The whole has dignity, scale, and the somewhat heavy, well-proportioned, and monotonous solidity that are the hall-marks of much eighteenth-century English work.

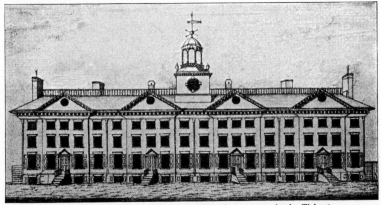

597   From *The New York Magazine*, May, 1790, after an engraving by Tiebout

598   From an engraving, by Fenner, Sears & Co., London, 1832, after a drawing by H. Brown

DARTMOUTH COLLEGE IN 1832

In the Dartmouth College buildings the type of early American collegiate architecture is already well set. A simplicity, often forced by poverty, does not prevent long lines and excellent proportions. In the Dartmouth buildings the delicate detail of the late "colonial" cupola gives grace and distinction to a whole, otherwise rather bleak and undecorated.

GILMAN HALL, JOHNS HOPKINS UNIVERSITY

The late colonial tradition has had an increasing vogue in college as in school design. When Johns Hopkins University moved to Homewood, that famous house near Baltimore (No. 242) set a type that had to be followed. Gilman Hall, the main building of this charming group, has red brick and white trim and variegated

599   Parker, Thomas and Rice, architects

slate roof beautifully and simply combined.   A high tower of colonial character gives the necessary dominance.

600   Flournoy and Flournoy, architects

DOREMUS MEMORIAL GYMNASIUM, WASHINGTON AND LEE UNIVERSITY

Here is evidenced a formal, classic revival quality which is evidently inspired by Jefferson's University of Virginia, though less formality is here given by the use of a brick frieze to give variety to the large-scaled and impressive Doric order.   The enormous size of this gymnasium building, erected in 1915, at Lexington, Va., well expresses the importance that physical education and athletics have assumed even in a small college.

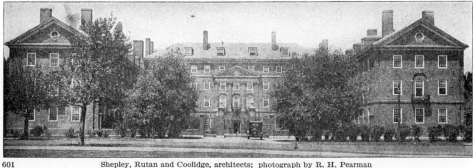

601   Shepley, Rutan and Coolidge, architects; photograph by R. H. Pearman

FRESHMAN DORMITORIES, HARVARD UNIVERSITY

AMONG the finest examples of American Georgian college architecture, these dormitories undoubtedly take a very high, if not the highest, place. This pre-eminence is largely founded upon the admirable restraint of their design. Conforming to the simple dignity of the old Harvard buildings (No. 596), the dormitories depend upon what must always be the mainstay of good architecture — careful proportion and unity — for their effect, and upon the Georgian ornament so sparingly used with perfect consistency throughout.

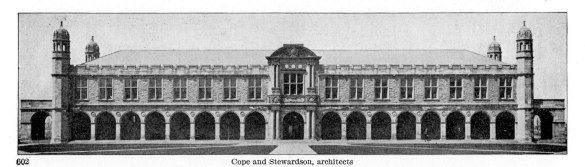

602   Cope and Stewardson, architects

RIDGLEY LIBRARY, WASHINGTON UNIVERSITY, ST. LOUIS

WASHINGTON UNIVERSITY, St. Louis, is an adaptation of an English type which arose when a sophisticated Gothic was merging into a naïve classic, characterized by the charm that all transitional styles possess. The Ridgley Library, with its inviting classic arcade, the naïve charm of its Jacobean entrance motif, the large mullioned windows, and the battlemented roof parapet, has a direct simplicity of form and a human charm of detail that give it genuine beauty.

A GOTHIC CITY SEMINARY

THE more usual type of American Gothic is less subtle, more obviously Gothic, more picturesque. Even on city sites, as here, in the Union Theological Seminary in New York, many gables, much breaking of the surface by vertical lines, many chimneys and pinnacles, are used to break up the natural rectangularity such a site demands. The chapel, with its tower like those of some of the Oxford colleges, is the climax of the group; the most successful part because its forms fit more naturally into Gothic dress.

603   Allen and Collens, architects

604   Doyle and Patterson, architects

COLLEGIATE GOTHIC IN OREGON

THE boys' dormitory of Reed College, Portland, shows how widely examples of collegiate Gothic are scattered over the country — East, West, North, South. It is a brick-gabled building, stone-trimmed, with the several entrances a dormitory requires, and a pleasing informality. Chimneys play, as they should, an important part in the picturesque composition.

THE UNIQUE USE OF GOTHIC AT PRINCETON

THE Princeton Graduate School, with its great memorial tower to Grover Cleveland, is unique among American collegiate Gothic buildings because of its size, the consistency of its finish, and the big simple strength of its conception. The tower, its main exterior feature, is characterized by the skill of the transition from the simple square strength of its base to the lace-like deep shadowed intricacy of its top. It is a fresh version of the usual Oxford type.

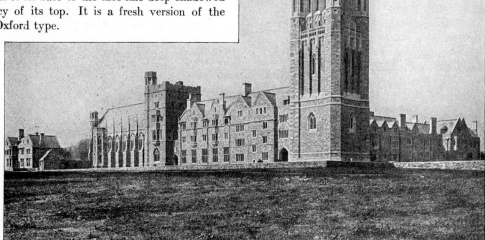

605   Cram and Ferguson, architects; photograph by Paul J. Weber

INTERIOR OF PROCTOR HALL, PRINCETON UNIVERSITY

NEXT to the tower, the most noteworthy feature of the Princeton Graduate School is its Great Hall (No. 606), where the graduate students dine daily in academic dress. The whole hall is in accord with this antique rite; its magnificent trusses, the shadowy open roof, the soft broken color of stained glass windows, and the delicate carving of the oak screen at the end.

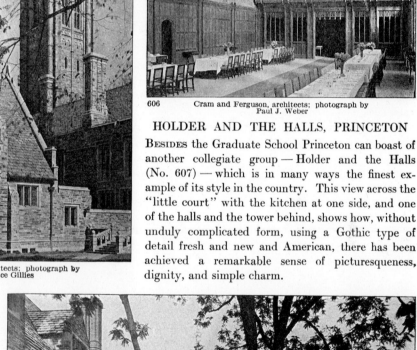

606   Cram and Ferguson, architects; photograph by
Paul J. Weber

607   Day and Klauder, architects; photograph by
John Wallace Gillies

HOLDER AND THE HALLS, PRINCETON

BESIDES the Graduate School Princeton can boast of another collegiate group — Holder and the Halls (No. 607) — which is in many ways the finest example of its style in the country. This view across the "little court" with the kitchen at one side, and one of the halls and the tower behind, shows how, without unduly complicated form, using a Gothic type of detail fresh and new and American, there has been achieved a remarkable sense of picturesqueness, dignity, and simple charm.

THE GREAT QUAD

THE Great Quad in Holder Hall, Princeton, is unusually successful because it is so straightforward. Just the necessary windows and doors a dormitory demands, arched gateways, chimneys; no forcing of strange forms for effect; no torturing of many materials into one to give texture; in short, good architecture.

608   Day and Klauder, architects

609   James Gamble Rogers, architect

THE HARKNESS MEMORIAL TOWER

THE most lavish of the Gothic collegiate groups is undoubtedly the Harkness Tower and dormitories at Yale. The memorial tower (No. 610) is a brilliant departure from the square Oxford variety; it has unusual delicacy, almost softness, of outline, all pulled together and unified by the sweeping vertical lines. It has an intensity of romance that doubtless expresses something of the intensity of modern life — even in a college.

611   James Gamble Rogers, architect

THE WREXHAM TOWER AT YALE UNIVERSITY

ONE of the striking aspects of the Harkness Quadrangle at Yale is the expression, in a multitude of ways throughout the buildings, of the history and traditions of the university running back for more than two hundred years. So Wrexham Tower (No. 609) draws its inspiration from the church at Wrexham, Wales, where Elihu Yale lies buried. In the new tower is set a stone from the old.

610   James Gamble Rogers, architect; photograph by
                    John Wallace Gillies

THE PIERPONT GATEWAY

IN Linonia Court (No. 611) a varied, expressive, and beautiful use is made of various building materials. Bricks taken from the walls of ancient college buildings that once stood upon the site of the quadrangle, stones of various kinds and colors, and tile, are all used so that color, texture, and hardness or softness count for the utmost. Appropriately, the colorful walls reach a climax in the rich hues of a beautiful window that lights a commons room.

CLASSICISM IN A CALIFORNIA UNIVERSITY

VARIOUS types of classic and Renaissance have been used for college buildings. The Benjamin Ide Wheeler Hall of the University of California at Berkeley is a simple, delicately designed piece of academic classicism, dignified, monumental and refined, even if without obvious relationship to California conditions or American traditions.

612   John Galen Howard, architect; photograph by Gabriel Moulin

613   Welles Bosworth, architect; photograph by Maynards

THE MASSACHUSETTS INSTITUTE OF TECHNOLOGY, CAMBRIDGE

THIS magnificent group has a style typically American, although derived eclectically from all sorts of ancient classicism, and despite the dome, mainly Greek. Great delicacy of detail combines with a bold repetition of simple forms to throw into strong relief the Ionic entrance portico and the low dome above. In its scale and its very austerity it is extremely effective. The style, however, does not sufficiently express its function.

THE DORMITORIES AT CAMBRIDGE

THE dormitory group of the Massachusetts Institute of Technology has an additional element of charm in the freedom of its detail. The classic precedent has been treated with something of the playful freedom that Pompeian builders used towards the formal classicism of their day, and the result is a vitality, an imaginative quality that is fresh and inviting.

614   Welles Bosworth, architect; photograph by Paul J. Weber

HAMILTON HALL AT COLUMBIA UNIVERSITY

HAMILTON Hall, at Columbia University in New York, is characteristic of an eclectic Renaissance feeling that is found in much of the best modern classic work. Forced by restricted space to be a building several stories high, Hamilton Hall has, nevertheless, that true restraint, good proportion, delicacy of feeling for detail, which, regardless of style, gives the true academic feeling.

615   McKim, Mead and White, architects; photograph by Wurts Brothers

THE COLUMBIA UNIVERSITY LIBRARY

BY all odds the most imaginative, the most monumental example (No. 616) of all American academic classicism is still the nobly domed, many columned front that crowns the flights of broad and sweeping steps of the Columbia Library. Into its planning was put something of the grand scale of Rome, something of the delicacy of Greece, and yet the combination of those qualities, its directness, its force, are American creations expressive of American culture.

616   McKim, Mead and White, architects; photograph by Wurts Brothers

617   McKim, Mead and White, architects; photograph by A. Tennyson Beals

INTERIOR OF THE COLUMBIA UNIVERSITY LIBRARY

THE main reading room of the Columbia University Library has, in addition to scale and delicacy, another glory all too rare in America, the glory of color. Columns of deep green, gilt capitals, white marble, the deep night blue of the dome, rich dull red and green wall panels, and the russet of old leather doors and screens make a whole that for quiet, subdued and dignified richness is scarce in modern work.

CHAPTER XIX

FACTORIES AND INDUSTRIAL BUILDINGS

THERE is no better example of the sentimentalism that sometimes clouds American thought than the attitude towards efficiency and the factory. We are willing to spend thousands of dollars on purely unnecessary and "inefficient" ornament in the public halls and exteriors of office buildings, but factories may go without — "Oh, it's just a factory; it must be *efficient*." There was a time, when the country was younger and financial competition less strong, when this was not so true: Milbert's view of the Philadelphia waterworks (No. 620) shows a building of considerable dignity and charm. To the early builders of those quiet days, what gave pleasure, what pleased the eye, was not wasted.

But the seeds of architectural dissolution were present even then: Milbert's comment on the somberness of the factories in the Boston suburbs has already been mentioned. The mushroom growth of industry after the Civil War put an end to any attempt at beauty in factories; like cancers the eastern industrial towns spread their ugliness and slums and poverty and squalor, eating out the heart of the lovely countrysides. A factory — then — was merely so many square feet of enclosed ground, built as cheaply as possible; so many running feet of windows, so many spindles or looms or forges. Later, as industries expanded, it was crowding, hit-or-miss additions; it was growing refuse heaps, ash dumps, smoke; it was mill added to mill; gaunt windowed boxes, gaunt furnaces thrust into the air, tall chimneys. Beauty sometimes arose, but it was an accidental beauty, unsought; the beauty of smoke trailing across a flaring sunset, of piled forms seen through grime or fog, of flaring lights from night-fired furnaces, of smoking slag heaps. It was a beauty purely fantastic, often sinister, nightmarish; a beauty to paint or etch, but an unspeakable ugliness and filth to live in. It was not architecture.

From the worst of this, new ideas of efficiency — but it is efficiency that still rules — new ideas of social organization — but still with the largest possible financial return — have rescued us, or are slowly working to rescue us. Even the purely rectangular concrete factories of to-day, boxes that they are, are an improvement over the brick barns of Civil War days. New demands for light and air have forced the development of the metal window; that has helped give some definite expression to the whole. Power houses are susceptible of architectural treatment, dignified and sometimes strikingly beautiful, water tanks suggest towers; grounds are better kept. If the worker's environment is still usually angular, harsh, full of bad proportion, lacking in graciousness or any touch of personality, it is also usually fairly clean.

Certain definite attempts have been made, too, towards an actual architectural solution of the factory problem. A modernized Gothic of rather hard and perhaps purposely expressionistic angularity has been applied to factory design; some modern factories begin to look like true buildings — not mere excrescences (Nos. 626 and 630). A beginning has been made.

Yet, on the whole, the factory problem remains architecturally unsolved. There is yet to come a genius big enough to seize the epic quality of it, to feel the poetry alike of far-flung effort and of each worker's struggle, to take the harsh forms of efficiency and play with them, piling them up, making of them a whole that will inspire, not depress; that will rest, not exhaust; that will continuously satisfy the unconscious need for a surrounding beauty. And there needs to come, too, an industrialist with the vision to realize the value of such an accomplishment, one willing not only to accept, but to pay money for the adding of new beauty to the workaday world.

The warehouse problem is simpler, easier of solution. Wall surfaces have of themselves a certain quiet beauty of restfulness; matters of style do not intrude to distract; warehouse design becomes a mere matter of proportion and the quiet treatment of material. The spacing of openings is the important thing in the composition.

But modern materials have again created new problems. The old tradition of brick warehouse design (No. 622) is overthrown. Reinforced concrete has taken its place. Perhaps because of its simplicity, reinforced concrete has proved a difficult material for American architects to master. It has been tortured into forms for which it was never intended. It has been left as plain, ugly, gray smoothness. Its color is unprepossessing, its texture often stupid. And yet it has unlimited possibilities; some of them are being gradually realized. Among all the many reinforced concrete buildings in America, Cass Gilbert's warehouses for the Army Supply Base in Brooklyn (Nos. 618 and 632) stand out as remarkable. In them there is perfect expression of function, great imaginative beauty in composition, and a true realization of the quality of the material. They suggest what may yet be done with industrial buildings, the very foundation of our civilization.

618   Detail in Court between Warehouses of U. S. Army Supply Base,
         Brooklyn, N. Y.; Cass Gilbert, architect

A CRUDE, BUT PICTURESQUE, NEW YORK STATE MILL OF 1826

THE evident surprise of Milbert at the industrial development of this country at the time of his visit in 1826 is not only shown by various comments in his text, but by several of his drawings. This one (No. 619) shows an early water-power cotton mill on the Black River as a gaunt pile of wooden buildings rough and crude, but distinguished by their picturesque mass.

619   From J. Milbert, *Itinéraire Pittoresque du Fleuve Hudson,* Paris, 1828–29

THE PHILADELPHIA WATERWORKS, 1826

QUITE different in quality is the steam pumping waterworks on the Schuylkill River near Philadelphia. Here Milbert's drawing shows the high gable walls of the typical house of the time, low end wings, and an architectural treatment studied, dignified, simple and charming. Even the tall smoke stacks are given their place in the composition. The unity and culture of Philadelphia life of the time shows even in its industrial buildings.

620   B. H. Latrobe, architect; from J. Milbert, *Itinératre Pittoresque du Fleuve Hudson,* Paris, 1828–29

THE BOX–LIKE FACTORY OF THE RECONSTRUCTION ERA

AN advertisement in 1868 of a factory at Waltham, Mass. (No. 621), shows that the elements of the modern factory are already beginning to appear. Gone are the picturesqueness and the urban charm of Milbert's days — instead there are range upon range of many-windowed sheds with attempts at "architecture" in the style of the period only at important administrative points.

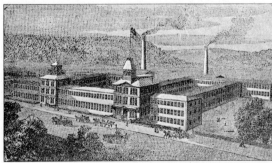

621   From *Frank Leslie's Weekly,* 1868

APPEARANCE OF THE WAREHOUSE IDEA

BUT meanwhile some of the secrets of industrial building were being learned. Simplicity is one; truth to function another. For instance, the Boston Storage Warehouse (No. 622) is a serious attempt — in the vernacular, to be sure, of its time, the 'nineties — to express the warehouse idea in big, strong, rather bleak, and generally well-proportioned forms.

622   Chamberlain and Whidden, architects; photograph by Gramstorff Bros., Inc.

623   C. F. Hoppe, architect; photograph by Wurts Brothers

MODERN INDUSTRIALISM IN CLASSIC DRESS

INDUSTRY means power; and power houses have received more architectural study than other industrial buildings. The Edison Waterside Station No. 2, in New York, is characteristic of the larger coal-burning generating stations of the cities. A great hall, lit with large arched windows, skylight-ventilated, lends itself well to a modernized classic expression.

A POWER PLANT OF TRUE BEAUTY

THE great water-power stations are quite different in character, and offer, with their dams, arches, spillways and the great windows of their generator halls, a magnificent opportunity for functional architectural expression. The power house at McCall Ferry, Pennsylvania, of the Holtwood Power Development (No. 624) is an example of successful treatment.

THE FACTORY REMAINS BOX–LIKE

THE Naumkeag Steam Cotton Company's factory in Salem, Mass., is typical of the great textile mills built of a framework with floors of reinforced concrete and walls filled in with brick and glass. Such factories are a great advance on the earlier sheds and boxes; they are well-lighted and airy, but any beauty they may have is purely accidental; and square, harsh forms almost inevitably result.

624   Trowbridge and Ackerman, architects; from the architects' rendering

625   From a photograph in the Essex Institute

626　　　　　　　　　　　　George C. Nimmons, architect

GOTHIC FORMS IN FACTORY DESIGN

WHERE an attempt is made to give architectural quality to a factory building, the need for large window areas has suggested the use of modified Gothic forms, and the necessity for a high water tank has given reason for a tower. Such a building is the factory of C. P. Kimball & Co., Chicago. In this, a definite attempt has been made to combine functional and structural expression.

A MODERN TYPE OF POWER–HOUSE DESIGN

IN designing factory buildings some designers have considered it more logical, in view of the modernity of the problem, to abandon historical styles entirely. The power house of the Ford Motor Company in Detroit shows the power, airiness and charm that such a treatment can produce.

627　　　　　　　Photograph by Manning Bros.

AN ORIGINAL STYLE APPLIED TO FACTORY DESIGN

How absolute freedom from the trammels of historical precedent has allowed pure form, simplicity and proportion to produce economically a building with a beauty and a very definite flavor or style of its own is shown in the Packard motor car service building in Chicago.

628　　　　　　　　　　　　Albert Kahn, architect

EFFICIENT FORMS MAY ALSO BE BEAUTIFUL

THE problem of the purely commercial factory is more difficult. Except for No. 265, all the factories so far shown have been exceptional; in a way "de luxe." The ordinary plant under contemporary conditions must not only be

629   Frank D. Chase, engineer; photograph by E. W. Bliss Co.

economical, but *most* economical. The profit system cannot afford a penny of expenditure that does not bring return. Therefore absolute unornamented simplicity of structure and form is demanded. All the more honor then to designs like this of the Consolidated Press Co. (now E. W. Bliss Company), Hastings, Michigan, where the boldness of unifying into one enormous window all the necessary light has given an effect truly expressive.

630   George C. Nimmons, architect; photograph by Philip B. Wallace

A WAREHOUSE WITH ARCHITECTURAL EXPRESSION

THE Eastern Store of Sears, Roebuck and Co. in Philadelphia is one of a large type of industrial warehouses that has much in common with the factory. Design for such buildings reduces to a problem of the composition of great rectangular masses, with, at most, richer accents at doors and in a tower.

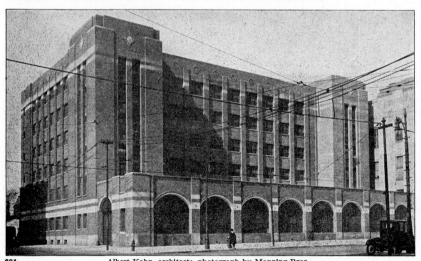

631   Albert Kahn, architect; photograph by Manning Bros.

SIMPLICITY AND ORIGINALITY IN A WAREHOUSE

A STRAIGHT-FORWARD example of design in which purely modern forms furnish the basis of the composition is shown in the warehouse building of the Detroit *Evening News*. Its simple, strong dignity shows that beauty is not dependent on historical precedent; that at least in some industrial buildings freedom from historical precedent may prove helpful.

BEAUTY IN CONCRETE

ONE of the finest of American industrial buildings is the group of warehouses for the Army Supply Base in Brooklyn, designed during the World War (No. 632). Its great craggy walls, its reduplicated vertical lines, its picturesque connecting bridges, form a whole impressive, beautiful, perfectly expressive of function, structure, and the reinforced concrete of which it is built.

632　Cass Gilbert, architect; photograph by John Wallace Gillies

633　Ward and Blohme, architects; photograph by
Gabriel Moulin

DISTINCTION IN A SMALL ADMINISTRATION BUILDING

SMALLER industrial buildings — such as administration buildings of large plants — can often be featured in such a way as to make of them genuine architectural creations. The simple forms allow endlessly varied treatments. The building in San Francisco (No. 633) for the H. N. Cook Belting Co. has large simple arches, delicate Italian shields and a simple roof-tile wall crowning which give it much distinction.

634　Willis Polk and Company, architects; photograph by Gabriel Moulin

A PUBLIC SERVICE STATION MONUMENTALLY TREATED

PUMPING stations, valve stations, and power houses belonging to, or serving, municipalities, are half industrial, half public in character; in view of their public nature they are often given a lavish architectural dress impossible in purely industrial undertakings. The Central Pumping Station of the Spring Valley Water Co. in San Francisco (No. 634) uses blank masonry walls, a decorated doorway, and end motifs to give an impression of dignified monumentality. Fountains in the end motifs serve to lighten an effect which might otherwise be too funereal.

635　Willis Polk and Company, architects; photograph
by Gabriel Moulin

GRACEFUL TREATMENT OF A GAS COMPANY'S STATION

STATION D of the San Francisco Gas and Electric Company has the same use of delicately broken up wall surface, with a rich door and an iron grille across the garden space at the side to give it public character. It is an excellent example of an impression of grace secured by the simplest possible means.

CHAPTER XX

DOMESTIC ARCHITECTURE

THE rapid urbanization of America unfortunately has prevented the development of any truly indigenous rural architecture. The modern American farmhouse is usually a charmless, box-like object designed without careful thought of either use or beauty. Moreover, all the passing building fashions have swept over it in a strange way; distorted exaggerations of carpenters' plan books, interpreted through the vagaries of the village builder, decking it with the wooden Hamburg lace of the fretsaw or the bulbous stock balusters of the machine lathe. It remained for the bungalow books, the stock ready-built houses, and the great mail-order stores of to-day to complete the architectural ruin. The typical farmhouse of America is all that architecture should not be — ill-considered and uncomposed and unpleasing in mass, and covered often with meaningless, ostentatious, machine-made detail that is an unconscious burlesque of the prevailing fashion of its day.

Fortunately, there is the beginning of a reaction against this deplorable condition. The United States Department of Agriculture, the American Institute of Architects through its Small House Service Bureau, and many periodicals are trying to improve rural housing. The recent discussion of the great question of why people migrate to cities — this studied attempt to find a readjustment between the industrial and agricultural bases of modern life — could not but have an architectural effect. Farmhouses, improved in beauty as well as convenience, will appear in increasing numbers as that readjustment is found. The country's loss has been the city's gain. The great development of American domestic architecture is essentially a result of city life; it is essentially a suburban development. A country house is an adjunct to a successful man's city office, so that modern American houses are often country houses, but not rural or peasant-like. They are, on the contrary, among the most highly developed results of sophistication.

This type of American country house had developed along the expected course since the death of the Greek and Gothic Revivals. There was an era of simple square houses, high-ceilinged, large-roomed, often heavy in detail, but with an ample harmony that expressed the dignity of a leisurely social life that has passed away. There were rambling cottages of Victorian Gothic whose tree-embowered picturesqueness is often instinct with a faded charm. There was the era of "quaintness," of the "Queen Anne," when a public, drunk with its new discovery of art, went on an orgy of form and color — the day of spindle work, of scalloped shingles, of tiled fireplaces, of oriental fabrics. There was a period of quiet sanity, a search after the picturesqueness of simple forms, straightforward treatment of materials, direct expression of largeness, welcome, comfort — the era of wide gambrel roofs, weathered shingles, field-stone chimneys, capacious piazzas. And there is to-day the typical modern eclecticism, that seems at first glance to produce merely a chaos — Georgian houses, Italian houses, English houses, the horizontals of the Frank Lloyd Wright type, the awkward bracketed eaves of the "Western bungalow."

Two things give unity to the modern chaos. One is the great development of skillful house planning. The difficulty of obtaining domestic service and the high cost of building have combined to necessitate an efficient plan. Waste of space or motion or material is doubly penalized. The result tends toward compactness, careful localization of service, the abandonment in the average house of all but the most necessary rooms. Back parlors have gone, libraries are going, dining rooms assume less and less importance: the living room — the house-center — grows larger as it absorbs one after another the functions often formerly distributed. The other great factor in house design is the endlessly increasing development in the mechanical equipment in heating, plumbing, electricity. The fireplace as a necessity gave way to the stove, the stove to the radiator, and the fireplace reappears as a luxury. Bathrooms are multiplied; base plugs and lamps and wall brackets are largely displacing the chandelier; kitchens grow smaller, more compact; instead of a second center of life, they are becoming more and more the "engine room" of the house, and are so designed.

Certain æsthetic tendencies also are distinguishable in the modern house. A quieting tonic movement toward simplicity has succeeded the earlier enthusiasm for "styles," chiefly foreign, the beauty of the house being considered in direct proportion to the closeness of the imitation. Later, styles came to be inspirations rather than laws and were chosen not merely by fashion or *a priori* wish but developed from the conditions of the design itself. Traditionalism began to make itself felt; the present love of Georgian and colonial work, so strong in the East, like that of the Spanish colonial in the Southwest, is an expression of the wish to build what really "belongs" — to add to the beauty of a village or landscape by building in harmony with its forms and its history. Similarly, the vogue of the so-called "English" house has its roots deeper than any mere whim; it is, on the contrary, the result of the fact that the requirements of a modern American house often take form most successfully in a plan of "English" type, and because the English house is so simple, frank and charming an expression of its plan and its function.

Another comparatively recent development in American house architecture is the industrial village or garden village or model housing development. Uncontrolled real estate speculation had played havoc with the housing of factory workers in industrial towns. With the World War came sudden industrial expansion which made conditions unendurable. The housing developments put up by the government, by various industrial plants and occasionally by individuals or corporations developed for that purpose have an importance much greater than their own intrinsic merit. They are but a drop in the bucket, a beginning; but they have raised housing standards in localities that most needed it. They have shown that coöperative effort could produce economically houses that were not only well planned, but simply, unostentatiously attractive, and that unity of style and even of type in one locality could produce not monotony, but when carefully laid out, a quiet beauty. Between these beginnings and such great coöperative enterprises as the Hampstead Garden Suburb of Welwyn near London there is still all too great a gulf.

American city house architecture has not had the variety of development that marks the American country house. The plan is too standardized and narrow city lots too limited in their scope. The brownstone fashion yielded to the Victorian Gothic, and that to a Romanesque period when Richardson's forms and Richardson's ornament were horribly caricatured the country over. There followed, with the opening of the twentieth century, a great change in planning; the abandonment of the high stoop, and the development of the typical modern city house plan: a ground floor with entrance, reception room, and, behind, the kitchen, with the main living and dining rooms on the floor above. This change was accompanied by a flood of houses that designers imagined were French, whose bulbous cartouches, heavy garlands, overwrought doors and tortured detail still hold noisy sway on many of our streets. That fashion has passed; the modern house sticks to quieter forms, often of Georgian or quiet Italian inspiration; a new restraint is now the rule which throws the carefully detailed and carefully concentrated ornament into stronger relief.

636   Albro and Lindeberg, architects

A WESTCHESTER COUNTY COUNTRY HOUSE

THE picturesque tradition set for country houses in the last years of the nineteenth century and the early years of the twentieth persists still, though seeking expression in forms more closely related to those of past styles. English country houses of the Gothic and early Renaissance periods furnish an inspiration particularly congenial. This house in Westchester County, N. Y., built for Dr. Gardner, is an excellent example of this influence. Rough stone, stucco and half timber are well used, the forms soft and yet distinct. The curved roof lines, covered with wood shingles, intended to give the softness of thatch, are open to serious criticism as not frankly expressing the true character of the material.

AN ENGLISH ADAPTATION

THE house of Mrs. Lizbeth Ledyard at Stockbridge, Mass., is a simpler and a franker expression of the same general English tradition. Its white painted brick walls, its casement windows, its simple and direct roof forms — no "shingle thatch" here — and the wide bay window give just the touch which the

637   Harrie T. Lindeberg, architect; photograph by John Wallace Gillies

site and the surrounding rolling landscape seem to demand. Good composition, an excellent treatment of the materials used, and an unusual feeling for setting make this house an almost perfect example of its type.

638   Bates and How, architects

A MODERN HOUSE OF ADAPTED ENGLISH TYPE

THE Pratt house at Bronxville, N. Y. (No. 638), is English, too; but of a slightly more artificial and sophisticated type, as befits its locality — a fashionable and carefully developed suburb. Here again the materials are an important part of the effect: rough stucco, and the pleasing contrast between its textured white and the dark of stained half timber and stained clapboards and shingles contribute much to its beauty.

639   Peabody, Wilson and Brown, architects; photograph by Tebbs and Knell, Inc.

THE CHARM OF BROAD SIMPLICITY

THE Barnes house at Manhasset, Long Island, shows how the modern American architect takes the old English ideas of broad roof surface, large chimneys, and informal gabled composition, and carries them still further. The roof surfaces are curved into each other; there is continual variety in heights; chimneys are big and simple, and the brick gables and low wall surfaces surely composed. The whole in its direct and straightforward picturesqueness, in its entire avoidance of fakes or meretricious ornament, and in the way it seems to belong to its wooded site is a model large house.

PHILADELPHIA STONEWORK

AROUND Philadelphia, where there is much easily worked ledge rock, it is the cottage of the Cotswold districts in England (where a similar stone is found) that has furnished the inspiration for much modern work. The McCracken house at Germantown, with its colorful stone walls, its large English chimneys, its attractively grouped windows, and its walled garden suggestive of retired loveliness, is typical of many of the beautiful houses that have been built in that neighborhood. Again it is straightforward simplicity that is the secret of charm.

640   Mellor, Meigs and Howe, architects

HALF–TIMBERING AND ENGLISH GRANDEUR IN AMERICA

THE Lehman house at Tarrytown, N. Y., is inspired by the half-timbered work of Cheshire, England. But again this is not a copy; it is a development. With decorated chimney stacks, varied brick walls, a stone-mullioned hall window, a colorful rough slate roof, and much carved ornament, it is obviously an expensive and lavish design; yet even this lavishness is most

641   John Russell Pope, architect; photograph by John Wallace Gillies

carefully restrained, and the ornament so beautifully designed and so carefully placed that it always seems right, unostentatious, necessary. In its perfect blend of color, material, and composition, it is a true masterpiece of re-creation.

642 John Russell Pope, architect; photograph by John Wallace Gillies

A HARMONIOUS INTERIOR

THE same qualities of contrasting simplicity and schooled and restrained richness characterize the interiors of the Lehman house. The living hall has rough half-timber walls and heavy trusses above, and rich oak Tudor paneling below. A focus of interest is given by the carved stone Jacobean mantel. Such a room makes a pleasing setting for either quiet family life or a large and formal party.

THE CLIMAX OF ENGLISH TRADITION IN AMERICA

"KILLENWORTH" at Glen Cove, Long Island (No. 643), is one of the largest and certainly one of the loveliest of American houses based on English tradition. It makes particularly effective use of stone, slate, water, and the green of growing things.

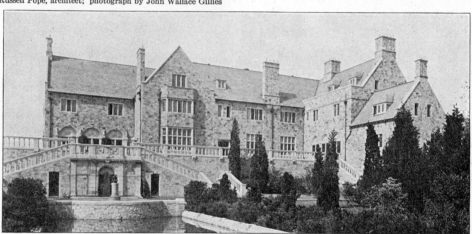

643   Trowbridge and Ackerman, architects

AN ADAPTATION OF FRENCH SOPHISTICATION

FRENCH forms have inspired many modern American country houses. The Goodwin house at Woodbury, Long Island (No. 644), shows how even to a house comparatively small, French Renaissance château forms can give a combination of personality, informality and sophisticated refinement that is typical of much suburban life. Here a high pitched roof, a polygonal

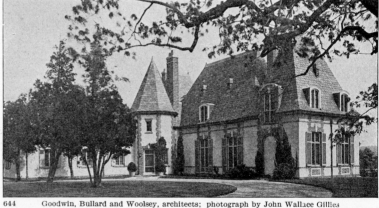

644   Goodwin, Bullard and Woolsey, architects; photograph by John Wallace Gillies

peaked entrance tower, slim French windows, and a pleasing blend and contrast of stucco and brick quoins and window frames give the right atmosphere of cultivated charm.

THE BEAUTY OF SIMPLE COLONIAL

In recent years at least, the most prolific source of inspiration in house design has been the Georgian and colonial of our own country's youth. It has proved to "belong"; its own closeness to us has made it seem at home only in the East, where the origins are found, but throughout the country, except in the Southwest, where the climate is not congenial. The Baum house at Syracuse, N. Y., shows how beautifully a modern adaptation of colonial precedent can suit a small house. Like most modern colonial, this is a free adaptation; it is in no sense archæological.

645 Dwight James Baum, architect; photograph by
John Wallace Gillies

SOUTHERN COLONIAL INFLUENCE IN THE MODERN HOUSE

The Whitall house at Katonah, N. Y. (No. 646), is a development of a southern type of colonial, with great end chimneys, high pitched roof, and small, undecorated dormers. Its dignified restraint, its direct and simple composition are noteworthy, and the charm that is gained, despite its comparatively small size, is remarkable.

646 Polhemus, Mackenzie and Coffin, architects

ANOTHER SOUTHERN COLONIAL ADAPTATION

"Albemarle," the house of Gerard B. Lambert, at Princeton, N. J., is a typical example of a formal type of house with a long two-storied portico inspired by Mount Vernon (No. 174). But, as always in the best modern work, there is no copying; round columns take the place of square piers, the brick texture is made more rough and interesting, and numerous details that belong strictly to earlier and later styles are present. Even in using native colonial precedent, the modern American architect is eclectic; and the unity he achieves is æsthetic rather than historical.

647 Harrie T. Lindeberg, architect; photograph by John Wallace Gillies

THE INSPIRATION OF THE SOUTHERN CLASSIC PERIOD

THE great Doric portico of Villasera resembles the porticos of southern mansions built under the influence of Jefferson; the *cartouche*, or shield-like frame around the pediment window, is English *baroque;* the iron balcony is a piece of free

648   Charles A. Platt, architect; photograph by August Patzig

design; yet all is unified; all welded into one harmonious and delightful whole. This house at Warren, Rhode Island, is a striking example of what might be called creative eclecticism.

649 Howard Van Doren Shaw, architect; photograph by H. Parker Rolfe

MODERNITY AND LIVABLE CHARM

THE garden front of the Willcox house at Radnor, Penn., shows a fresh style, which, despite its affinities with certain English work, is still typically modern and typically American. Here again, as in so much domestic work, the qualities of color and texture of materials — stone, and brick, and touches of wrought iron — contribute much to the total effect. The U-shaped plan, with its raised sheltered terrace and the two loggias at the ends, succeeds admirably in blending the indoors and outdoors into one; in tying house and terrace and garden into one composition.

650   Lewis Colt Albro, architect; Lovett Rile, associate

AN ITALIAN RENAISSANCE HOUSE IN THE MIDDLE WEST

THE Italian Renaissance has been widely drawn upon, in the same eclectic and creative way. The garden front of the Bushnell house at Springfield, O., shows what lovely combinations of arched loggia and simple stucco wall and rich cornice are possible in this style; all vivified with the delicate purity of the early Italian Renaissance detail. More romantic and more tractable than the Georgian, simpler and less sophisticated and more intimate than the French, the Italian Renaissance atmosphere has seemed exceedingly appropriate to much modern use.

IN THE TRADITION OF THE ITALIAN VILLA

THE entrance end of the Rogers house at Southampton, Long Island, shows a picturesque and emotional treatment of Italian Renaissance inspiration. The great expanse of textured stucco wall, the rich classic door, the arched balcony window, the sense of differing levels, the tile roof, and the simply capped chimneys combine to give

651   Walker and Gillette, architects; photograph by John Wallace Gillies

picturesqueness, welcome, and a sense of the romantically mysterious that is instinct with personality.

652 Walker and Gillette, architects; photograph
by John Wallace Gillies

VIVID PERSONALITY IN AN ITALIAN HALL

THE entrance stairway of the Rogers house (No. 652) shows that dramatic simplicity is the note of the interior as well as the exterior. Its simple stuccoed walls and vaulted surfaces, its arched landing window with leaded glass, its brick steps, and its delicate iron handrail bearing pots of growing greenery create a charming sense of invitation.

ITALIAN FARMHOUSE PICTURESQUENESS

THIS modified Italian villa style lends itself with particular fitness to the rambling lines of garages, service wings, and their relation to a house. The service wing of the Duncan house at Columbus, O. (No. 653), with its simple tile roof and upper windows, its wide doors, its charming roofed gateway, and the picturesqueness of its mass composition, has all the charm of many of the smaller Italian villas, and is, moreover, a simple and direct solution of the problem. Its style, as usual, is frankly and freely eclectic.

653   Miller and Reeves, architects

654   Charles A. Platt, architect

HARMONY IN CLASSIC ECLECTICISM

THE modern eclecticism of American classic work is most marked in the designs of Charles A. Platt. It is his peculiar genius to take inspiration from Greece, from Rome, from the Renaissance of Italy, France, England, from our own colonial, and to use these varied inspirations freely, mixing, combining, creating new forms, governed only by the most rigorous æsthetic logic, interested only in producing unity and harmony of atmosphere. This room, in the house of Harold F. McCormick, at Lake Forest, Ill., shows this eclecticism. Basically, perhaps, Italian, it has, nevertheless, details of all sorts — and yet a wonderful harmony of effect.

BRILLIANT POMPEIAN COLOR IN A MODERN COURTYARD

THE Pompeian Court of the home of Harold McCormick (No. 655) shows Platt's work in a more definitely classic design. The entire villa is really as much Roman as Renaissance, and in this beautiful glazed court the Roman influence completely dominates and makes a composition with all the delight of white colonnade, of marble floor, of a central pool and fountain, of walls rich with fanciful form and deep color. Yet here also, it has been, not the little details, but the large spirit of Pompeian work that has controlled the design.

655   Charles A. Platt, architect

656   Pierpont and Walter S. Davis, architects; photograph by
Margaret Craig

DRAMATIC CONTRASTS OF MODERN SPANISH ADAPTATION

WITHIN recent years, starting in southern California, there has been an ever-growing movement toward the use of Spanish Renaissance forms in domestic design. Based originally on the crudely simple and effective Spanish colonial work in California, it has continually broadened, borrowing direct from Spain. The Eltinge house at Los Angeles, Cal. (No. 656), shows the dramatic picturesqueness which such a style, well used, can produce.

MODERN SPANISH AT ITS BEST

THE Dater house at Santa Barbara, Cal., has all the qualities, outside and in, which bring beauty to houses of this type. The free balance of mass — flat roof against pitched tile roof — the clear bright wall surfaces, the openings carefully composed — ornament austerely concentrated, but vividly rich where used — balconies of thin and delicate wrought iron (a true Spanish touch) — have all that careful combination of

657   Bertram Grosvenor Goodhue, architect; photograph by Kenneth Clark

texture, composition and color which produces charm. The patio (No. 658), with its three arches, its Algerian tiles, its contrast of foliage and stucco and the brilliance of the tile work, has a similar dramatic quality.

658   Bertram Grosvenor Goodhue, architect; photograph by Kenneth Clark

CASA FLORES, A RESTORATION

NOR is size or elaboration or great cost necessary for the success of these Spanish-type houses. Absolute and utter simplicity, like this of the Casa Flores, at Pasadena, Cal., can, with its rough walls, its tile roof, its paved courtyard, be made as delightful, as inviting, as beautiful as any richer and more lavish composition. Some of the charm may come from the fact that it is a restoration; age has already touched it, and produced some of that unity with nature which only time can bring.

659   Carleton Monroe Winslow, architect; photograph by Hiller

660   Frank Lloyd Wright, architect

"SECESSIONISM" IN MODERN AMERICA

ONE very important factor in modern American house design is the free modernistic work to be found mostly in the Middle West. Influenced deeply by the flatness of the central plains, it is an architecture of horizontals daringly elaborated and reduplicated. Roofs are flattened, eaves extended, windows ranged into long groups. There is something a little Japanese in the strange charm thus developed, in this house at Highland Park, Ill.

661   Welles Bosworth, architect; photograph
              by Kenneth Clark

AN AMERICAN ITALIAN GARDEN

THE same elements that characterize American country-house design — eclecticism, finish, restraint, refinement — characterize the gardens around them. Colonial, English, French, Italian precedent have furnished the inspiration again and again. The Garden Theater on the estate of Samuel Untermyer at Yonkers, N. Y., shows an eclectic Italian treatment with certain Greek touches, and shows as well how wall and column and ornament and foliage and water are welded into one, as they should be in every good garden.

FARM BUILDINGS OF LATE COLONIAL

FARM groups belonging to large estates have not been architecturally neglected, although the actual "dirt" farmers' farm buildings suffer from that deplorable lack of a true rural architecture that characterizes modern America. All the more pleasing, then, are such groups as this of D. A. Campbell at East Norwich, Long Island, where practical requirements themselves have been allowed to determine the forms, and the whole, by careful composition, and the use of a restrained late colonial style, made into a group of true and simple beauty.

662   James W. O'Connor, architect; photograph by Tebbs Architectural Photograph Co.

FARM BUILDINGS OF FRENCH TYPE

The garage and farm building of E. M. Barnes at Glen Head, Long Island, built in a more picturesque style, borrows markedly from the rural work of northern France. It depends for its effect on picturesque composition, a tower, and outside stairs and arched openings, and on a careful and original treatment of rough brickwork.

ELECTICISM IN A FARM GROUP

In the farm group of C. M. Schwab at Loretto, Penn. (No. 664), there is an influence both from Normandy and England. The lower farmyard, with farmer's cottage, barns and storage sheds on one side, and sheepfold and piggery on the other, is tied together by slate capped walls and wooden gates. Long roofs of variegated slate, rough stucco walls, and the attempt to fit the whole as closely as possible to its hillside site give it the desired country informality.

663   Thomas Harlan Ellett, architect

664   Murphy and Dana, architects; photograph by John Wallace Gillies

A WAR–TIME PROJECT

Because of the congestion in manufacturing centers occasioned by the World War, industrial villages were developed in many parts of the country. Here economy fostered standardization, and that led to unity. The Waterbury housing development, for the United States Department of Labor, uses only two plans, but by reversing, turning, and combining these, and by careful use of inexpensive materials, an effect of unified variety is achieved.

665   Murphy and Dana, architects; photograph by Kenneth Clark

666   Howard Van Doren Shaw, architect

SEASIDE VILLAGE, BRIDGEPORT, CONNECTICUT

THE housing developments at Bridgeport (Nos. 667, 668), started during the World War by the United States Government, and carried on since under private management, are undoubtedly among the most successful as well as the most charming of all such American housing enterprises. With the simplest forms, a strong colonial flavor, and a skillful use of brick, slate, and white trim, there has been produced a whole not only beautiful, but full of an all too rare quality of seeming truly native. Here the institutional quality — the danger of such projects — is absent.

THE CHARM OF A HARMONIOUS TOWN CENTER

THE Market Square group at Lake Forest, Ill. (No. 666), is an example of the civic center developed in a small suburban town. Instead of the usual chaos, the shopper finds the shops centrally and conveniently arranged, in buildings whose charm lies in a mingled English and continental inspiration, freely treated, and in a governing sense of ordered informality and picturesque unity.

667   R. Clipston Sturgis, architect; photograph by courtesy of the Bridgeport Housing Company

668   R. Clipston Sturgis, architect; photograph by courtesy of the Bridgeport Housing Company

669   Electus D. Litchfield and Rogers, architects

A COLONIAL TYPE COMMUNITY BUILDING

NEW shops in the smaller communities usually follow colonial or English inspiration, vitalized by the most delicate treatment of detail. The community building at Watertown, Conn., shows a colonial example, whose red brick, delicate white trim, and bowed show windows fit perfectly into its setting.

HARMONY OF STYLE PRODUCES REPOSE

ONE of the largest and in many respects the finest and most complete of war housing developments was in the village of Yorkship, N. J. By the adaptation of a delicate version of late colonial, appropriate to the locality and the materials available, and skillful simplification and grouping, a series of delightful streets was produced at small cost. This view shows the church and the quiet brick houses along the street that passes it; both church and houses are unified, and the effect is lovely; yet there is no sense of monotony.

670   Electus D. Litchfield and Rogers, architects

INDIVIDUAL VARIETY IN A LARGE HARMONY

THIS detail of one of the rows of houses (No. 671) shows the porch that each house possesses; it shows, too, how charming is the contrast of white detail and red brick and green foliage, and how much more beautiful a well designed row-house of four or six families can be than the all too common rows of disconnected tiny cubes. The effect of such an environment as this of Yorkship on the health, happiness, and sensitiveness of those who live in it is inestimable.

671   Electus D. Litchfield and Rogers, architects

672   Electus D. Litchfield and Rogers, architects

BEAUTY IN A SUBURBAN DEVELOPMENT

PELHAM Parkway Gardens is a successful attempt to make truly satisfying and lovely a development of a rather different sort — the typical, speculative, real estate development. The set-back garages (No. 673) make the backyards as attractive as the front, and the garages themselves, instead of being mere sheds, are distinctive additions to the architectural beauty of the whole.

673   Electus D. Litchfield and Rogers, architects

A DUTCH RENAISSANCE CITY HOUSE

THE French type, although popular and persistent, was not universal. The Flagler house on Park Avenue, New York (No. 675), is a pleasing contrast to the French houses. Not only is the whole quieter, more restrained, better composed, but materials are handled in a simpler and more direct manner.

LAVISH USE OF MODERN FRENCH CLASSIC

AFTER the brownstone period, the *Néo-Grec* period, the Richardson Romanesque period, and such picturesque types as those shown on page 168, there came, with the advent of overwhelming influence from the French School of Fine Arts, a flood of pseudo-French city houses, especially of the wealthier type. Typical is the house of ex-Senator W. A. Clark on Fifth Avenue, New York (No. 674). Louis XIV and Louis XV motifs were principally followed. Coarseness of scale, restless curved lines, ostentatious richness, and particularly the use of the *cartouche*, a richly scrolled curved shield, characterize many of these houses.

CHEERFUL DELICACY OF FRANCIS I

IN designing the residence of W. K. Vanderbilt, Jr., on Fifth Avenue, New York (No. 676), the Francis I style of its immediate neighbor, the W. K. Vanderbilt house (No. 397), was adopted. Of excellent composition and silhouette and with the closest and most pleasing relationship to its older neighbor, this house reveals the advances made in the design and execution of its rich and lovely detail, since the erection of the older house.

PERFECTION OF PROPORTION AND HARMONIOUS RESTRAINT OF DETAIL

THE Kane house in New York (No. 677) is the most perfect modern interpretation of the style of the Roman Renaissance of the early sixteenth century, that has yet been produced. Scale, proportion, and detail are all as nearly final and right as it is humanly possible to make them. The material, too, is distinguished: a limestone full of fossil shells that give a most interesting texture. Despite the simplicity of the whole, its distinction is sure. It is a valuable civic decoration.

677 McKim, Mead and White, architects; © The Architectural Book Publishing Company, New York

A SIMPLE GEORGIAN CITY STREET

GEORGIAN precedent has been found well fitted for city houses as well as country houses. This is particularly true of the smaller types. The houses on Rittenhouse Street, Philadelphia (No. 678), develop the local colonial tradition of Philadelphia in a way peculiarly apt and full of quaint and simple beauty.

678 Stewardson and Page, architects; courtesy of *The Architectural Record*

ECLECTICISM IN THE ADAM MANNER

THE residence of Francis Palmer in New York (No. 679) shows a Georgian style of manifestly Adam derivation applied to a large city house. But the usual eclecticism is at work here; certain notes seem colonial, the roof baluster shapes are Italian and the triangular lintels over the main story windows have a touch of Greek Revival feeling. Yet the fine open spirit of the whole, its grand scale, and the subdued delicacy of the ornament are all typical of the late English Georgian.

679 Delano and Aldrich, architects; photograph by John Wallace Gillies

RENAISSANCE ECLECTICISM

IN the comparatively narrow confines of a crowded city block, the use of pure Italian Renaissance motifs is difficult. In the Pratt house in New York (No. 680) the architect achieves a Renaissance style that is neither purely English nor purely Italian. Though its window treatment, its ironwork, and its scale are English, its general monumentality of conception and the studied purity of its classic detail, slightly *baroque*, are Italian. The effect is unified, dignified, beautiful, and this unified eclecticism is a distinctly American quality.

681   Frederick J. Sterner, architect; photograph by
                          A. B. Bogart

PERSONALITY IN ECLECTICISM

IN this New York City house façade (No. 681) a blend of Italian and Spanish Renaissance elements is used to express quite a different spirit. It has in it something of that true dramatic romance that is usually associated only with larger work in country surroundings. By rigorous suppression of unnecessary detail, by a careful texture treatment of stucco surfaces, by an overhanging tile roof, by graceful ironwork, and by one spot of great richness in the door and the window above it, this romance, this individuality of interest, is achieved.

MODERNISTIC TREATMENT OF A CITY HOUSE

NON-STYLISTIC city houses are not common. Yet this house on Astor Street, Chicago, Ill. (No. 682), has about it no experimental look; it is a definite, simple creation, a study in the use of simple materials frankly expressed, with a daring variety in window spacing that is yet all tied firmly into one. It has the beauty of a carefully proportioned and restrained simplicity, all the more interesting because of its fresh novelty.

680   Charles A. Platt, architect; photograph by
                          Wurts Brothers

682   Pond and Pond, architects

ATMOSPHERE THROUGH CAREFUL
USE OF *BAROQUE*

THE conservatory of the McLean house at Washington, D. C. (No. 683), is elaborate, rich with *baroque* detail, but here the atmosphere, the emotional quality, is the important thing, and detail never an end in itself, never a means to historical ostentation, but used only because of the contribution it makes to the whole. Textures are studied with infinite care, and details perfectly designed, so that the effect is that of the charm, the livability, of an old Italian garden, rather than any harsh newness or "show."

683   John Russell Pope, architect; photograph by
John Wallace Gillies

684   Frederick J. Sterner, architect

THE MODERN ADAM INTERIOR

THE living room of the MacNeill house at New York (No. 684) is a most formal modern interpretation of Adam precedent, with its wall enlivened by the delicate color of reliefs after the manner of Wedgewood porcelains. The rather severe correctness of the period quality is unusual in modern work; but the beauty of the modeled detail in wall and ceiling, studied in the manner of late Greek and Roman reliefs, has a delicacy, a liveliness, seldom found in the old Adam work in England.

THE FREEDOM OF THE MODERN
ECLECTIC COLONIAL

THE living room of the Lathrop Brown house at St. James, Long Island (No. 685), shows the same eclecticism applied to a much simpler and more informal room whose dominant spirit is colonial. With paneling and a corner cupboard of mid-eighteenth-century type are combined, in a truly charming unity, furniture of late Hepplewhite, Sheraton, and Duncan Phyfe styles, a modern upholstered davenport, a Persian rug, and a strictly modernistic — futuristic — wall hanging. Such a room owes its charm to the frankness with which it expresses the personality — the likes and dislikes — of its owner.

685   Peabody, Wilson and Brown, architects; photograph by Tebbs and Knell, Inc.

CHAPTER XXI

CLUBS, APARTMENT HOUSES, AND HOTELS

COMMUNAL living, the inevitable outgrowth of city development, and the ever increasing complexity of mechanical aids to that great modern paradox, "simple living," have resulted necessarily in hotels, clubs, and apartment houses. Increasing land values and the growth of industry which attracts thousands where domestic employment drew hundreds make them a necessity.

Besides being urban, the American population is also a traveling one, traveling for business even more than for pleasure. The westerner going east, the New Yorker going to California, demands greater luxury than when he is at home. This demand, fostered by the widespread advertising of railroads, chambers of commerce and boards of trade, has resulted in the typical American hotel. It is first of all a place of temporary residence. As such, it has tiers on tiers of bedrooms, all, or nearly all, with their own private baths. All the devices of modern mechanics are used to further the traveler's comfort. Electricity, elaborate plumbing, heating plants combine to give him a machine-made luxury. But economy in design is of the utmost importance in hotels, and economy in design means even more efficiency and simplicity of service than it does cheapness of first cost. The result is a building highly specialized, with an enormous and carefully designed mechanical equipment. Hotel kitchens must be planned so as to reduce the number of servants to a minimum. Plumbing must be readily accessible for inspection and repair. Service of all kinds must be carefully centralized, and the whole development is so complex that hotel management has become almost a profession.

But a hotel is much more than a place of temporary or even permanent residence. Developing along more public lines it has become almost a civic monument, a center of communal life. There great dinners are held, balls are given, many political organizations are housed and mass meetings called. There "society," and those who ape it, drink tea, and dance. In the course of this development it has become in a very real sense a town hall, a place in which the whole people feels an instinctive if irrational ownership.

It is this public character that has made necessary the great monumental lobbies, the magnificent ballrooms, the capacious restaurants. This has made the design problem as difficult æsthetically as mechanically, for there is always a double aim to achieve, intimacy and size, formality and charm; the hotel is a public building that must not seem too public, and a personal home that must never be forbidding or eccentric. Twenty years or so ago magnificence was the characteristic of large hotels; a certain ostentation of luxury and wealth, often false and meretricious, through overwrought ornament, heavy gilding, and a lavish use of imitation marbles. Lately there has been an inevitable reaction into quietness and restraint; so much so that to-day many hotels seem effeminate with their stilted delicacies of too small Adam detail. The satisfactory balance is hard to attain.

Apartment houses — tenements — are the result of high land values coupled with the necessity of inexpensive living quarters. And, once the unbridled forces of competition in building, rents, and land speculation are let loose upon that combination, the slum is the inevitable result. Every city has had its slums. Coincident with modern industrial development the slum has grown; a manifest sign of industrialism's one-sided incompleteness as a social force; the open sore that is a symptom of a deep-seated disease.

The slum: congestion continually increasing; dirt; disease; child mortality; despair . . . it is all a commonplace. And yet the slum tenement is a type which covers hundreds of city square miles, which forms the only architectural environment that hundreds of thousands of children know — the slum tenement that turns to the street its overornamented front topped with a rusty tin cornice, and hides away inside its dark rooms, its stinking shafts, its rotting halls, its broken plumbing.

The growth of the slums led to a condition where regulation became necessary as a mere matter of public health and policing. Almost everywhere in the country to-day the design of tenements is rigidly controlled by law. Moreover, with the development of the social conscience, there has been a great deal of thought and of philanthropic or semi-philanthropic effort applied to the subject. Competitions have been held, model tenements of various sorts constructed, and little by little a type of architecture is beginning to develop, founded on the essential elements of tenement house design. These are briefly: air and light in every room; plumbing in every apartment; arrangement of the various units so that the block as a whole shall be as open and airy as possible; rigid economy so that rents may be kept within reach of the worker's wages.

Economy has led to the elimination of waste hall space and the most compact and careful planning; and the realization of the importance of the block design as a whole has shown that only on comparatively large lots can efficient and attractive tenements be constructed. More and more the tendency is away from the construction of tenements by individual owners, toward the development of large units and entire blocks by large corporations.

This fact points out the great difficulty of the whole problem as it is handled in America to-day. With our sublime belief in the potency of individual effort to produce the millennium, we have made it all but impossible for the cities or the states to enter the housing field at all. We sometimes forget that the greatest incentive the usual individual can feel is the obtaining of large financial returns, that unless large returns come from tenements they will not be built at all, and that unless a larger return is obtainable from a tenement hygienic and livable, the unhygienic and unlivable will be built regardless of any "sentimental" protests. Unfortunately, the highest returns of all frequently are derived from the oldest, the most utterly shameless and decrepit buildings, which only the exuberant industrialism of the growing cities keeps filled at all.

We have not yet attained a solution, nor can we, until the cities or the states are given legal power to wipe out slums ruthlessly, and to provide other and better housing in place of that destroyed. Architecturally, we have achieved results that are promising, which show that good urban housing can be built economically. It only remains to see that this good housing *is* built, for its social value is incalculable, and the need for it bitter.

The problem of the design of the so-called "apartment house" — the larger, better-class tenement — is, of course, different and easier. Higher rents allow greater freedom; the elevators and fireproof construction permit expansion upwards. Yet the basic elements — light, air, good mechanical equipment, economy — are the same, and many of the plan forms used are similar. There are more and larger rooms; there is some opportunity for exterior and interior decoration. The attempt to strike a note of domestic and charming intimacy is a violent reaction against the earlier ostentation. Restraint characterizes the best modern apartments — a restraint that leads occasionally into anæmic thinness. Where real architecture has an opportunity, the results are often charming; but the great modern danger lies in the specialization of apartment-house design that has led to monotonous standardization, and in a desire for cheapness, which has put immense quantities of this work into hands incompetent and stupid, with the deplorable results that shout their red and white blatancies even from our finest street corners. And since apartment-house and tenement architecture dominates our city environment, it behooves all who hold an ideal of a beautiful city to make it as true, as dignified, as charming, as the greatest skill and the most inspired imagination can achieve.

The modern hospital problem is similar to that of the hotel. Recently wards have been omitted occasionally, and the buildings frankly called medical hotels. In these large lobbies are unnecessary, but medical and surgical needs create a tremendous complexity of mechanical equipment. Maximum care in planning and orientation is indicated by the necessity for all possible sun and air for each room. In the ward type of hospital this need has resulted in the pavilion plan, with several parallel wings, each housing a ward on every floor with sun porches south and service rooms north. In small cities, with lower land values, the tendency is to separate these pavilions, and a group instead of a single closely organized building is the result.

Clubs are the last class of buildings devoted to communal living. The American country club is a purely native institution, in which American architecture has found a peculiarly congenial opportunity. Long, low, rambling lines lend themselves readily to picturesque groupings; style becomes unimportant, for it is character that counts — a character of intimacy, comfort, welcome, widespreading quiet informality. Whether Georgian or English or purely styleless and picturesque, the success of the best American country clubs is the charm that inevitably comes from the frank expression of these qualities.

The city club is a very different thing. Y. M. C. A. buildings, for instance, and others like them, are part club, part hotel, part settlement house. The requirements of all are similar, and there is no one dominant quality or feature that demands or furnishes opportunity for emphasis of any kind; the result is almost inevitably, therefore, monotonous and lacking in marked character. Other city clubs — more truly clubs in the narrow sense of the term — are, first and foremost, palatial homes, with or without sleeping quarters as the case may be. They must thus have a certain domesticity of feeling; but they often have, besides a formal dignity, a true palatial quality that occasionally is exaggerated into ostentatious arrogance. It is this formality that distinguishes them from mere houses, and that makes them expressive of what they so frequently are — symbols of financial or social or professional success — just as their domestic quality expresses their function as a center of social life — the quiet and luxurious association of men and women of similar tastes, of common interests.

A NEW YORK TENEMENT HOUSE

THE tremendous city growth of the decades immediately succeeding the Civil War — a growth unplanned, unwatched, dependent on the mercies of unscrupulous real estate operators, an immigrant population helpless in a new environment, and the existence throughout the land of a spirit of frenzied "grab" — combined to produce the city slum and the city tenement. In such ramshackle, ill-kempt, crowded, dark and dirty homes in our larger cities thousands of people lived.

TENEMENT LIFE IN NEW YORK

To the congestion and the cheapness and the dirt there was once added the terrible fire-risk of much wooden construction. It was the growth of conditions like this that forced the passage of Tenement House laws.

686 Courtesy of Tenement House Department of the City of New York

THE HALL OF AN OLD TENEMENT

TENEMENT interiors were often worse than exteriors. Not only did thousands of dark unventilated rooms exist — and, in lesser number, still remain — but hallways, left to the tender mercies of a shifting population, a careless janitor, and an absentee landlord, rotted with dampness and dirt, and the public sinks and toilets were broken and filthy. It is difficult to imagine more unsanitary conditions than those revealed by this New York hallway (No. 688). And for quarters in buildings like this the poor and ignorant are charged every penny that owners and agents can extract.

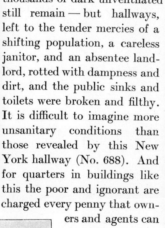

687 Ragpickers Court, Mulberry Street, from *Harper's Weekly*, April 5, 1879

688 Courtesy of Tenement House Department of the City of New York

A "MODEL TENEMENT"

THE creation of a tenement house department in large cities and the increasing stringency of building laws have curbed, at least for new buildings, and somewhat mitigated in old, the worst of these abuses, though conditions in some parts of our cities are still utterly disgraceful. Philanthropic and semi-philanthropic organizations have sought to improve conditions by building carefully planned modern tenements to set a standard, and conditions are improving slowly. The Phipps tenements in New York show how, by the development of waste roof areas, the opening of courts to the street by high arches, the use of large windows, and simple, dignified architectural details, a new atmosphere of welcome, cleanliness, and homelikeness is gained.

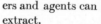

689 Grosvenor Atterbury, architect; photograph by A. B. Bogart

XIII—19

AN OPEN STAIR TENEMENT

THE Vanderbilt model tenements in New York, built originally for tubercular tenants, but later thrown open to anyone, have balconies to allow a certain amount of open-air life, and are carefully planned to give the maximum

690   Henry Atterbury Smith, architect; photograph by Wurts Brothers

number of rooms and families compatible with decency. Its greatest contribution is the "open stair" idea, by which all interior public halls are eliminated, and each apartment opens directly on the outer air.

691 Henry Atterbury Smith, architect; photograph by Wurts Brothers

THE COURT OF A MODEL TENEMENT

THIS view of the court of the Vanderbilt model tenements shows how courts of adjoining tenements are opened to each other by arches, and perfect ventilation secured, whatever the direction of the wind. It shows, too, the open stairs, one in each corner, protected from rain or snow, but open to the air. From each landing, doors lead directly to each apartment. Such an arrangement prevents all possibility of the existence of such conditions as that shown in No. 688, however careless the janitor.

692 Henry J. Hardenbergh, architect; photograph by Wurts Brothers

SPLENDID EXAMPLE OF EARLY APARTMENT DESIGN

THE large, expensive apartment house is quite a different problem. The Dakota Apartments in New York still remains, after twenty-five years, one of the quietest, most homelike, most distinguished in appearance. Its large windows and some of its French detail may seem out of date, and its use of space is less intensive than is required to-day, but its large roof surfaces, its simple dignity of composition, its light and airy court, and its clever blend of picturesqueness and formality have a large and sure serenity that bears witness to skillful designing.

A MODERN APARTMENT

THE typical large New York apartment house of to-day, built under exaggerated building costs, has necessarily developed more and more into a many-windowed box. Often with lavish treatment of the portion near the ground — especially the entrance door — and with a cornice at the top, its many windows form a difficult problem to treat. Small panes help to break up the glass area, arches give richness to the base, and bathroom windows break up the monotony in this Park Avenue apartment (No. 693). But the general result is cubical and uncompromising.

693 Warren and Wetmore, architects; photograph by Wurts Brothers

694   Charles A. Platt, architect

AN ITALIAN APARTMENT

THE Astor Court apartments in New York (No. 694) have a bold, more Italian treatment, with a daringly projecting cornice of copper, richly ornamented. The detail throughout is of the most carefully studied character, particularly successful in its scale, from the rusticated stone of the base to the rich shadows of the cornice, so that the whole forms one of the most dignified, monumental, colorful, and effective apartment houses we have.

A FIFTH AVENUE APARTMENT

THE apartment house at 998 Fifth Avenue, New York (No. 695), reveals that neither money nor pains were spared in its construction. The attempt was made to give the whole the quiet palatial character

695   McKim, Mead and White, architects; photograph
                      by Louis Dreyer

of the best Fifth Avenue private houses, rather than the usual apartment house character. By using limestone for the entire façade, by rich though restrained detail, by an interpretation of Roman palace ideas, and by a composition whose simplicity hides its daring brilliance, the attempt has been brought to success.

696   Marshall and Fox, architects

A TYPICAL CHICAGO APARTMENT

THE North State Street apartment house in Chicago shows the same attempt to emphasize windows and slim vertical piers that appear in some of the Chicago office buildings. Built of terra cotta, this building has the playful detail that seems so appropriate in that material. The bold projecting bay windows, running the full height of the building, are to be observed.

SUBURBAN APARTMENTS

IN the effort to meet the growing building costs of post-war times, a continual simplification of exterior detail has been made. The Garden apartments at Jackson Heights, New York (No. 697), are an example. But no illustration can do justice to the quiet charm of tile copings, variegated brick

697   Andrew J. Thomas, architect; photograph by Wurts Brothers

wall, or even the restfulness to the eye of the regular window spacing. Nor can it show the exceedingly clever planning, by which waste space is eliminated, and every possible inch thrown into useful rooms, or the wide openness that characterizes the whole group.

698   Walker and Gillette, architects; photograph by John Wallace Gillies

COMPOSITION AND TEXTURE GIVE CHARM AND BEAUTY

THE coöperative apartment house on Sixty-seventh Street, New York, shows the same simplification applied to a more lavish and expensive scheme, the same dependence on texture, color, and composition rather than on ornament, and the same originality in planning. Here the "back yard" is mostly on the street, and full advantage is taken of the opportunity of breaking the front, and bringing shadow and variety into the design. Despite simplicity, there is in the entrance and coping and balcony and tiled chimney abundant charm. Buildings such as this grow old gracefully. The contrast between this apartment house and the ordinary one near by is a striking lesson.

699 Richard E. Schmidt, Garden and Martin, architects

A CHICAGO APARTMENT OF GEORGIAN TYPE

THE Lochby Court apartments in Chicago show a similar openness and variety. Although the detail is of early Georgian type, the effect is new, creatively modern. Broad grouped windows convey a fine sense of sun and air. The relation of red brick and white is perhaps a little too spotty, but the charm of the whole, its welcome contrast to the average stupid street front, disarms criticism.

A RAMBLING TYPE

HAMPTON Court at Indianapolis is really more truly a group of separate houses around a court than an apartment; but the existence of communal heating, etc., brings it into the apartment class. A simplified English Tudor style admirably fits the bays and projections of the

700 George MacLucas and Fitton, architects

separate units; and bits of stone and half timber work add interest. The whole open court scheme, with its planting and terraces, is an interesting attempt to use economically and beautifully the awkwardness of narrow, uselessly deep lots that the thoughtlessness of those who laid out our cities and towns has often left us.

701 R. Clipston Sturgis, architect

A WAR–TIME DEVELOPMENT

APARTMENT houses built in Bridgeport, Conn., as part of a war housing development, are examples of a new sort of "model tenement." Carefully planned, so that waste space is eliminated, they have exteriors of absolute simplicity, to which character and charm are given by small paned windows, projecting bays and delicate colonial entrances.

702   Courtesy of R. A. Lancaster, Richmond, Va.

A ROADSIDE TAVERN OF STAGE–COACH DAYS

THE Effingham Tavern, Virginia, is a typical country hotel of the old stage-coach days. Two-storied porches of the extreme and almost attenuated delicacy popular immediately after the beginning of the nineteenth century give an almost official character to a long, low frame building in other respects only an enlarged house.

703   From a lithograph, about 1840, by T. Sanders after a daguerreotype by Adams, courtesy of S. J. Clarke Publishing Co., Chicago

AN EARLY CITY HOTEL, NASHVILLE, TENNESSEE

SIMILARLY, the Nashville Inn (No. 703) is the typical small city hotel of the eighteen twenties and thirties. The porches remain, Greek revival influence shows in the detail, and the long wings with their many chimneys express the function. The stepped gable ends were developed as an easy way to build a gable in brick; they were at one time exceedingly common in western New York, Ohio, and the young West generally.

704   Henry J. Hardenbergh, architect; courtesy of Boomer-Dupont Properties, Inc.

THE WALDORF–ASTORIA, NEW YORK

BETWEEN the Nashville Inn (No. 703) or the Astor House, New York (No. 296), and the modern large city hotel, there is a great gulf, bridged by the forces of congestion, growing luxury, the elevator, and steel construction. The Waldorf-Astoria in New York (No. 704) is an example of the early modern hotel, and its picturesque mass and Flemish Renaissance detail, though already appearing a little out of fashion, still dominate its portion of Fifth Avenue, and its name still retains something of the glamor it once had as a symbol of all that was most luxurious in hotel design.

THE HOTEL PLAZA, NEW YORK

THE Plaza, New York, is a later development of similar style ideas, though expressed in French rather than in Flemish Renaissance detail. In the effort to obtain cheerfulness, the walls are of white brick trimmed with terra cotta — a distinct gain in the modern much-shadowed city. The many windowed wall, the towering roofs, the gracious richness of the detail all have the correct hotel character.

705   Henry J. Hardenbergh, architect; photograph by Wurts Brothers

HOTEL LA SALLE, CHICAGO

It was inevitable that direct French influence should play an important part in hotel design at a time when it was so dominant in other fields as well. The Hotel La Salle, in Chicago (No. 706), is typical of the developed, Americanized version of the strict French tradition. Curved slate mansard, richly decorated dormers, ornamented copper gutters and crestings, and ornamental forms throughout are French, though the height is purely America.

706   Holabird and Roche, architects

707   McKim, Mead and White, architects; photograph by Wurts Brothers

HOTEL PENNSYLVANIA, NEW YORK

Among the large modern city hotels the Hotel Pennsylvania, New York (No. 707), is a most typical example. The division into four wings, whose width is determined by the depth of a room and bath on each side of a corridor, allows practically all the rooms to become outside rooms; interior courts are done away with, and sun and air is brought as much as possible into the center of the building. In exterior composition, this hotel follows the favorite scheme of a monumental basement — here decorated with an Ionic order — a simple brick shaft, and an enriched top, or capital, of four stories.

A CITY HOTEL IN CALIFORNIA

The Hotel Oakland, Oakland, Cal., is built on a U-shaped plan, possible because of the large size of the lot as compared with the necessary number of rooms. Its broad and welcoming court, and the open loggia at the top of the central mass, give it a charm unusual in city hotels. The delicate eclectic Italian detail fits the scheme admirably.

708   Bliss and Faville, architects; photograph by Gabriel Moulin

709   Clinton and Russell, architects; © 1910 Swetland Publishing Co.

THE HOTEL ASTOR BALLROOM

IN the early part of the nineteenth century, hotel public room interiors went through a process of continually increasing richness and complexity. Each hotel tried to outdo the next in luxury—and luxury was reckoned in terms of gilding and broken surfaces. The ballroom of the Hotel Astor, New York, represents the type of room which such a development produced. Despite strangeness and occasional incoherence of detail, the effect is undeniably rich and rather heavily festive.

A MODERN HOTEL IN ST. LOUIS

ONE example of a general type that is rapidly becoming the standard modern city hotel is the Hotel Statler in St. Louis (No. 710). This standardization has resulted largely from the formation of "chain" hotel companies, which build and run hotels in many large cities, and which strive for a distinct similarity, both in plan and detail, in all the hotels under their ownership. A dignified and restrained Italian classic, with occasional Georgian influences, distinguishes the Statler hotels.

710   George B. Post and Sons, architects; Mauran, Russell and
       Crowell, associated. Photograph by Henry Fuermann and Sons

711   George B. Post and Sons, architects; Mauran, Russell and
       Crowell, associated. Photograph by Henry Fuermann and Sons

THE BALLROOM, HOTEL STATLER, ST. LOUIS

WITHIN the last fifteen years there has been a reaction against the overweighted richness that marked the older hotels. Simpler, more classic detail is favored, with ornament carefully restrained. The ballroom of the Hotel Statler in St. Louis (No. 711), with its Corinthian piers, its vaulted ceiling, its simple classic and delicate ornament, is typical of the best newer work, and by its restraint loses neither richness nor festal quality.

712   Warren and Wetmore, architects; photograph by James Suydam

A WESTCHESTER COUNTY COUNTRY CLUB

COUNTRY hotels received all too little architectural attention in the past. But in the wealthier resorts and suburbs there is now growing up a class of carefully built, carefully designed, lavishly appointed hotels to cater to the wealthy. The Westchester-Biltmore Country Club at Rye, N. Y., attempts to combine the functions both of club and hotel, and architecturally to soften its many storied mass into congruity with its country surroundings. Italian detail is used to give an Italian villa air.

A COLORADO HOTEL

MORE successful, because simpler and less forced, is the Broadmoor Hotel at Colorado Springs. Its simple tile roofs, its belvedere, its low flanking wings, and its lake-side terrace, all seem to have just the correct touch of rather sophisticated simplicity.

713   Warren and Wetmore, architects; photograph by L. C. McClure

A LOW AND RAMBLING NEW JERSEY COUNTRY CLUB

A COUNTRY club in an informal type of colonial is the Somerset Hills Country Club at Bernardsville, N. J. Picturesqueness of low and rambling mass, the welcome of large chimneys and capacious porches, and the charm of texture of painted brick, combine to give the delightfully sociable, comfortable, and informal beauty a country club should have.

714   Lord and Hewlett, architects; photograph by John Wallace Gillies

A HOMELIKE COLLEGE FRATERNITY HOUSE

THE Delta Upsilon Fraternity House, Amherst College, Mass., has a livable, quiet simplicity to express its residential function, the dignity of white Ionic pilasters, large chimneys, and an elaborated door to give it club character, and all the charm of a modified colonial detail, simply treated, to bring it in harmony with the old traditions of the college and the atmosphere of the New England town.

715   Putnam and Cox, architects

716   Joseph Evans Sperry, architect

THE BALTIMORE Y. M. C. A.

THE buildings of Young Men's Christian Association and Young Women's Christian Association throughout the country are similar combinations of residential and club buildings, but an extreme rigidity and uniformity of program has produced, frequently, a rather dull and mechanical whole. The Baltimore Young Men's Christian Association building (No. 716), with its free adaptation of Italian motifs, and its attractively varied window spacing, escapes this too common spiritlessness and achieves a dignified and simple formality.

THE ALLERTON HOUSE LOUNGE

THE lounge of the original Allerton House in New York (No. 717) is the center of the club life of this building. Its rich Jacobean wainscoting, its large fireplaces, its inviting furniture, its charm of color and texture, all combine to produce the right atmosphere of solid masculine comfort and informal sociability.

717   Arthur Loomis Harmon, architect

THE UNIVERSITY CLUB, NEW YORK

By the use of a dignified Italian Renaissance without "orders," in the New York University Club (No. 718), an almost perfect balance is achieved between the academic and the personal, without loss of proportion or harmony. In perfection of space composition, dignity of conception, and careful detail, this building is a model, and before its fine façade criticism of its academic style falls silent.

719   Murgatroyd and Ogden, architects; photograph by
Wurts Brothers

718   McKim, Mead and White, architects; photograph
by Wurts Brothers

NEW YORK FRATERNITY CLUBS BUILDING

In New York, Chicago, and some other large cities, there has grown up a class of buildings, typified by the Allerton Houses, which combine small and comparatively inexpensive bedrooms with some of the communal advantages of a club. The New York Fraternity Clubs Building (No. 719), an Allerton House for men, not only has, despite its size, a marked charm of homelike attractiveness, but it is also one of the most daring and successful results of the height-of-buildings regulation. Its picturesque silhouette, its octagonal corner pavilions, its crowning loggia, all make it a contribution to city architecture.

A CHICAGO WOMEN'S CLUB

The Eleanor Club, Chicago, is a similar type of building, in a less congested position, for women. Its solid, comfortable wall surfaces and its restrained Georgian detail serve to mitigate the institutional quality which so frequently spoils the welcome appeal of such buildings. The Eleanor Club is obviously first and foremost a home — dignified, unassuming, simple.

720   Richard E. Schmidt, Garden and Martin, architects

721   McKim, Mead and White, architects; © Architectural
Book Publishing Company

A UNIVERSITY CLUB LIBRARY,
NEW YORK

A skillful blend of the rich splendor of a past style
and an atmosphere of livable personality are achieved
in some of the University Club's interiors, especially
that of the library (No. 721). Here painted, vaulted
ceilings have a restrained richness of color that is the
perfect symbol of that schooled richness of mind a
library ought to represent. If ever the use of the
beauty of Italian Renaissance decoration is justified,
surely it is in an interior of this sort; not only does
the style lend itself to adaptations of a rich and sober
beauty, but also the very nature of the room suggests
a treatment redolent with the flavor of a storied past.

722   McKim, Mead and White, architects

INTERIOR, HARVARD CLUB

The lounge of the Harvard Club in New York
(No. 722) is characterized by atmosphere equally
expressive. In this ample room, with its unusual
height, its walls simply treated with wood wainscot,
stone masonry above, and its dark beamed ceiling,
life seems to flow with a more sociable rhythm, and
the light coming through the high mullioned windows
gives an additional magic.

THE COLONY CLUB, NEW YORK

The former building of the Colony Club (No. 723)
has a colonial façade so full of character that it
sheds a spirit of gracious refinement in contrast to
the usual harsh city rectangularity. Wall texture is
emphasized by laying all the brick with only the
ends exposed, and the white colonnade adds just the
right touch of welcome and delicacy.

723   McKim, Mead and White, architects; photograph by
Wurts Brothers

A MASONIC TEMPLE, WASHINGTON

By far the greatest monument of American Masonry is the Temple of the Scottish Rite at Washington, D. C. (No. 724). Based on the Greek Mausoleum, adapted with perfect grasp of composition and detail, its great square base, its magnificent approach steps, its perfectly proportioned colonnade, and its stepped pyramidal top, form a whole of monumental effect, of true and simple grandeur that is unforgettable.

724   John Russell Pope, architect; photograph by
John Wallace Gillies

725   John Russell Pope, architect; photograph by
John Wallace Gillies

INTERIOR, THE TEMPLE ROOM

The Temple Room of the Scottish Rite Temple (No. 725) has, in addition to the monumental grandeur of Greek form, the richness of polished dark marble, of heavy hangings, of a mosaic floor, of bronze grilles and inset ornament, that give it a magnificence that has in it something more Roman than Greek.

726   Richard E. Schmidt, Garden and Martin, architects

A TYPICAL MODERN HOSPITAL

The Illinois Central Hospital in Chicago, Ill., is typical of the ward type of hospital plan. Bed spacing in the wards determines a regular window spacing; solaria or sun porches are placed at the ends of the wings.

A WELL PLANNED NEW YORK HOSPITAL

THE Fifth Avenue Hospital in New York is one of the first of the hospitals without wards — a sort of medical hotel. Its X-shaped plan is beautifully devised so as to let the sun into the greatest possible number of rooms; and the treatment of the whole, with its creamy stucco walls and its quiet stone trim, is restrained and distinguished.

727   York and Sawyer, architects; photograph by Wurts Brothers

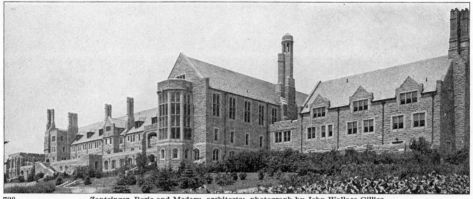

728   Zantzinger, Borie and Medary, architects; photograph by John Wallace Gillies

A "HOME" IN THE COLLEGIATE MANNER

THE "Home" lends itself easily to a somewhat collegiate expression, for its elements — dormitory rooms and central dining and social halls — are similar. Such a collegiate expression has been given to the Grand Lodge Masonic Home at Elizabethtown, Pa. (No. 728). With its gables, its chimneys, its mullioned windows, and the great hall bay, it forms an exceedingly picturesque whole, and avoids the harsh institutional character that so frequently disfigures "Homes" and contradicts their name.

729   Whitehouse and Price, architects

A SETTLEMENT WITHOUT SEMBLANCE OF INSTITUTIONALISM

THE Hutton Settlement at Spokane, Wash., avoids this deadly institutionalism even more successfully. Indeed it is perhaps the most outstanding example in the country of the true welcoming spirit, the true "livability" that such a building should have. It is picturesque, restrained, and gracious.

CHAPTER XXII

THEATERS

AMERICAN theater architecture dates only to the first days of the republic and even then theaters, like the old Boston Haymarket, were scarcely more than glorified barns. But by 1793 such modern motifs as the proscenium arch, boxes, galleries and a richly decorated ceiling had already appeared in New York and Philadelphia. The early type, closely resembling the European theater, lasted long, though its details followed prevailing fashions through Civil War ponderousness, the oppressive and gargantuan luxuriance of the General Grant era, and the painted cupids and discreetly veiled goddesses of the "art" and Queen Anne periods.

Meanwhile, an increasing number of mechanical backstage devices introduced complications, and electricity, replacing gas, necessitated changes. The essential elements, however, remained constant.

The advent of steel framing and a series of tragic fires brought the most important modifications. Rising land values began to restrict the size of lots and it became necessary, commercially, to seat as many people as possible within a constricted area. Consequently the steeply sloping, deep balcony began to replace the horseshoe gallery. The change gave better seating to more people and the introduction of great cantilever trusses and deep girders obviated the necessity of the posts which had been so objectionable. Moreover, the new balcony altered the whole type of the interior.

The older theaters had, in the developed horseshoe plan, an interior full of subtle curves, whose relationship became often the controlling element in the design. Domical ceiling forms seemed a natural result, a logical expression of the curved plan. But the new scheme, essentially an American invention, fitted perfectly well into a rectangular room. It developed width, instead of length. Even when, as is usually the case, the gallery front is curved, that curve can have little relation to the triangular wall shapes made by the sloping gallery, or to the ceiling above. The result has been forms exceedingly difficult to bring into any artistic harmony.

Constriction of space, moreover, has prevented any outstanding stage developments. The average modern stage, lacking storage space and working room, is inadequate for the development of a repertory theater. The sets for one play fill it to overflowing. Nor has the usual theater space for an apron. This universal adjunct to many earlier theaters has become smaller and smaller, necessarily, until it has, for all practical purposes, disappeared.

The theater interior has, therefore, both by reason of the wide deep gallery, and the omission of the apron, become more and more a proscenium arch, featured as a decorative frame for a play, and nothing else. A greater simplicity of wall and ceiling treatment has distinguished the later theaters. Ornament is concentrated on the proscenium arch and its surroundings; side boxes, where they occur, are usually mere decorative adjuncts; treatment of the rest is suppressed.

Additional interest is often given the proscenium arch area, particularly in large theaters, by another factor of recent development, the study of acoustics. This has resulted, first, in the careful choice of interior materials so as to absorb sound and prevent echoes; and second, in the development of certain curved surfaces above and around the stage proscenium which serve almost as sounding boards. These frequently take the form of pendentives at the upper corners of the proscenium arch, and offer admirable spaces for paintings, panelings, or other enrichment, and serve to soften the contrast between the stage and the auditorium. In the smaller, more intimate theaters, however, the rectangular shape is supreme.

Style, in theater design, has kept close to popular fashions. There is a fantastic quality, an imaginative freedom, suitable to a theater, which is both an opportunity and a snare; an opportunity for emotionally significant decoration; a snare for the facile followers of the moment, for clever draftsmen who stretch miles of badly designed acanthus leaves across gilded plaster on wire lath and think they have achieved richness. Indeed, there has been in American theater design an appallingly small number of attempts to express the underlying and controlling nature of the structural forms in any sincere and effective manner. The simplest solutions, in which the auditorium is a mere room, perhaps with paneled walls and a flat ceiling decorated with low relief, while the proscenium arch is featured, seem the best. In them, at least, the theater expresses one of its functions. They are quiet and adequate frames for plays of a certain type.

But the theater is more than a frame for a play; it is also a *Festhalle*, the great place of popular relaxation and enjoyment. Whatever the play, the theater is a place of gladness. The average American, despite critics and dramatists, going to the theater as to a party, craves color, richness, luxury. The best moving-picture theaters have fulfilled this function. Several variations are noteworthy. The proscenium arch is scarcely needed. A static screen, generally small, is, itself, the frame for the action. Nor is there need for close proximity to the stage, and these theaters have become longer, narrower. The proscenium arch, when not suppressed, is elaborated into a rich architectural motif, frame within frame, arches, columns, vaults. An extra stage accommodating an orchestra often precedes the arch proper. The whole is made gorgeous with colored lights and painting. In the "movie house," the American *Festhalle*, richness, luxury, gayety are everywhere; playfulness in style, too; Adam, Roman, Greek. A little pompous archæology — Egyptian, perhaps — anything with a light touch may give the right note, a touch sure, gay but not frivolous.

Not frivolous, lest the infinite influence on future architectural taste be jeopardized. Obviously the taste of millions of weekly movie enthusiasts in a relaxed and suggestible mood will be influenced by tawdriness, frivolity, garish color or by well designed richness, playful gayety, beautiful color and genuinely human humor with perhaps a touch of satire. If the composition shame the slipshod formlessness of the average picture it is supposed to enshrine — as it often does — then some sense of what architecture is, and may be, will develop surely in thousands now ignorant of it.

730   Haymarket Theater, Boston, from the original water-color by Robertson, 1798, in the Boston Public Library

EARLY VIEWS OF THEATER EXTERIORS

Two early views show the development of the typical theater exterior. The first, of the Haymarket Theater in Boston (No. 730) built in 1798, shows a simple, hip-roofed barn, differentiated from the houses beside it only by its height. The second, of the New Theater in Philadelphia (No. 731), shows a step in advance. Distinct architectural dignity appears in the great pediment, and in the wall below, with the central Palladian window, but the entrances are mean and hidden by a rough wooden shed — marquee — and the character of the whole is scarcely different from that of any large public building of the time.

731   New Theater, Chestnut Street, Philadelphia, B. H. Latrobe, architect; from an engraving, 1800, by William Birch & Son

WALNUT STREET THEATER, PHILADELPHIA

WITH the Walnut Street Theater in Philadelphia, all the elements of theater exterior design have been discovered and developed. An accented entrance, wide and spacious, is decorated with Greek Doric columns. Above, a row of large, highly decorated windows under arched heads expresses both the spacious hall within, and helps to give the festal feeling a theater should have.

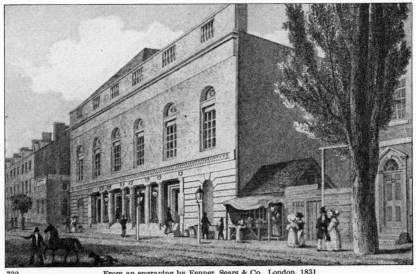

732   From an engraving by Fenner, Sears & Co., London, 1831

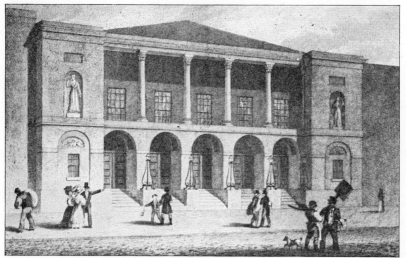

CHESTNUT STREET THEATER, PHILADELPHIA

THE Chestnut Street Theater in Philadelphia carries the functional expression of the theater one step farther. The entrances are arched, enlarged, made more inviting. An open loggia above gives lightness with dignity. End bays have niches with statues; and the origins of the "gay white way" can be seen in the row of lamps that flank the entrances.

733   William Strickland, architect; from an engraving by Fenner, Sears & Co., London, 1831

INTERIOR, CHATHAM THEATER, NEW YORK

THIS drawing of the interior of the Chatham Theater, New York, in 1825 shows the early interior arrangements. It shows, too, how badly arranged horseshoe galleries really are for seeing, as the habitué of Parisian theaters knows — and it shows detail that must have been crude and strange at best. But the richly decorated ceiling and the proscenium arch are elements that long remained universal. It is to be noted that there are no proscenium boxes.

734   From the original drawing by A. J. Davis; in the Emmet Collection of the New York Public Library

735   From *Frank Leslie's Weekly*. Feb. 20, 1868

OLD BOOTH THEATER, NEW YORK

THE typical theater of the 'sixties has lost its functional type. Booth's Theater, in New York, has on its front so much of the characteristic, heavy-handed, pseudo-classic ornament of its time, and it is so villainously capped by its "French" mansard, that composition has been forgotten, and expressiveness and beauty have disappeared. It might be courthouse or town hall or post office or even a private house, so universal had grown the use of the caricatured forms of this Victorian classic — a style even more hopelessly ugly than the Victorian Gothic.

736   Herts and Tallant, architects; photograph by Wurts Brothers

737   Herts and Tallant, architects; photograph by Wurts Brothers

ACADEMY OF MUSIC, BROOKLYN

THE modern theater has returned to its earlier functional expressiveness. In the Brooklyn Academy of Music (No. 736) its simple composition and plain wall give dignity, and the festal quality is gained by the use of much color in the terra cotta trim. The big windows light a spacious upper floor foyer. One regrets that this is a one-fronted building; but the front itself is finely proportioned, dignified, gay.

CONCERT HALL, BROOKLYN ACADEMY OF MUSIC

THE growing spaciousness of theaters and halls has led to ever increasing care of acoustics, resulting in the adoption in large halls of circular, conical, and pendentive forms. These offer remarkable opportunity to the architect; and the interior of the concert hall in the Brooklyn Academy of Music (No. 737) shows how beautifully such forms may be treated.

NEW AMSTERDAM THEATER, NEW YORK

THE abandonment of the horseshoe gallery in favor of the gallery stretching from side to side has made necessary the development of the proscenium boxes. These are often combined with the proscenium arch into one composition. In the New Amsterdam Theater, New York, the curving forms necessary in a large theater are treated in a manner delightfully playful, free, and original.

738   Herts and Tallant, architects

739   Wheelwright and Haven, architects; photograph by Dadmun Co.

THE BOSTON OPERA HOUSE

The Boston Opera House, constructed in heavy English style of brick and stone, is one of those large theaters which attempt to express architecturally not only the entrance and public space in front, but also the high stage behind and the lower storage spaces and dressing rooms which flank it. As in many modern theaters, the marquee is so developed as almost entirely to cut off the entrances below from the composition above them.

CENTURY THEATER, NEW YORK

Among the best of those great theaters, semi-official, which, following the magnificent example of the Paris Opera House, attempt to express outside the threefold division of lobby space, auditorium, and stage, is the Century Theater — once the New Theater — in New York. It follows the tradition of many doors below and fine arched windows above, but it adds a rich Ionic order to decorate them, and breaks up the formality of the whole by the playful forms of the curved stair pavilions at the corners.

740   Carrère and Hastings, architects

741   Carrère and Hastings, architects

THE INTERIOR

The size of the interior of the Century Theater allows a side wall treatment more monumental than is usual. Done in greenish and old ivory tones, with gilt and veined marbles for accent, with dull gold coffered ceiling above, and deep crimson hangings in the arches, this interior has a daring and lavish luxury, a rich gorgeousness of color and form that is festive. It is saved from meretriciousness and restless frivolity by composition conceived with meticulous care, by the congruity of its parts, and by the richness of the materials. Of all American theaters this most nearly approximates the lavish splendor of the European ideal.

A MODERN AUDITORIUM

THE Hill Memorial Hall of the University of Michigan at Ann Arbor, Mich., is a vast auditorium for concerts, lectures and the like, in which acoustic demands dictated the general conical form. This is treated in the frankest, freest, non-stylistic manner with a series of great concentric arches, dotted with lights, so that the greater part of the hall becomes one tremendous frame for the stage. This is a daring and logical idea, but here perhaps unduly heavy in effect.

742   Albert Kahn, architect; Ernest Wilby, associated; photograph by Manning Brothers

743   McKim, Mead and White, architects; © The Architectural Book Publishing Company

MADISON SQUARE GARDEN, NEW YORK

IN the beautiful exterior for Madison Square Garden, no longer standing, exactly the right character was embodied. Comprising a theater, a concert hall, and a great hall for exhibitions or mass meetings, and occupying an entire block, the design presented great difficulties. In the building proper was revealed a more than ordinary skill in the use of terra cotta. The tower, modeled somewhat on the Seville Giralda, ranked with the world's loveliest towers.

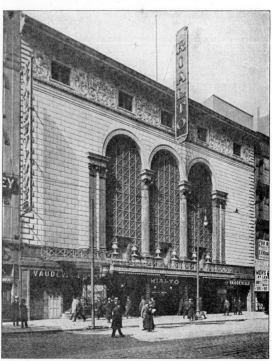

THE RIALTO THEATER, CHICAGO

THE façades of smaller theaters have developed several typical schemes. The Rialto Theater in Chicago (No. 744) shows one type, with a principal motif, usually arcaded, a decorative frieze, and wide entrance doors under a spreading marquee. Here the inspiration has been the Italian Renaissance and the material, terra cotta, has been treated with a fitting gayety, though one might criticize the tiny scale of the wall "stones."

744   Marshall and Fox, architects

THE BOOTH THEATER, NEW YORK

THE front of the Booth Theater, New York, is of an entirely different type. The main feature is a wall treated gaily in polychrome stucco, with three great doorways in rich arched frames of terra cotta. Here all is lightness, gayety, radiant color; fit expression for a place of light amusement. Buildings like this make one wonder that rich color has not been more widely used to diversify the necessarily flat fronts of many city buildings.

745   Herts and Robertson, architects

INTERIOR, THE MOROSCO THEATER, NEW YORK

THE change from horseshoe to straight galleries has both simplified and complicated the problem of theater design. It has given more wall space; at the same time it produces all sorts of the most awkward angles and shapes where galleries meet the side wall. The Morosco Theater in New York (No. 746) is an example of a satisfactory solution. Proscenium boxes are merged into the wall design, and treated with Corinthian columns and high hangings; other walls are simply paneled. The detail is all of a simple and delicate eclectic classic, rich, yet restrained.

746   Herbert J. Krapp, architect; photograph by White Studio

747   Adler and Sullivan, architects; courtesy of *The Western Architect*

McVICKER'S THEATER, CHICAGO

THE free Néo-Byzantine ornament has a rich texture, a grace of line, and a lace-like delicacy that seem particularly appropriate to theater design. In the old McVicker's Theater in Chicago (No. 747) line after line of it decorates the wall above the boxes. The tapered octagonal columns seem awkward and ungracious, but except for them the whole composition sparkles with a delicate gayety.

THE MUSIC BOX THEATER, NEW YORK

AMONG the most beautiful of modern theaters is the Music Box Theater in New York (No. 748). It is in a modernized Adam style, and borrows much from our own native tradition in its quiet wall and roof surfaces and its delicately proportioned loggia. (Compare No. 733.) Proportion, detail, atmosphere make its façade a true ornament to the city, and prove that gayety is quite compatible with repose and dignity.

748   C. Howard Crane, architect; photograph by
John Wallace Gillies

INTERIOR, MUSIC BOX THEATER

THE interior of the Music Box Theater has the same qualities of lightness, delicacy, good proportion, and restraint that distinguish the exterior. It is all extremely sophisticated work — as sophisticated as the name of the theater — but no sophistication can kill beauty founded on such true design.

749   C. Howard Crane, architect; photograph by
John Wallace Gillies

INTERIOR, CONCERT HALL, KILBOURN HALL

IN the Eastman Theater and School of Music at Rochester, N. Y., there is a concert hall, Kilbourn Hall (No. 750), which is perfectly planned. Its beamed and coffered Italian ceiling, its paneled wainscot, with quiet stone and hanging fabrics above, its painted frieze, and its simple, straightforward proscenium arch make a perfect environment for the music — quiet, restful, simple, rich.

750   Gordon and Kaelber, architects; McKim, Mead and White,
associated; photograph by Louis H. Dreyer

751   Gordon and Kaelber, architects; McKim, Mead and White, associated; photograph by Eastman Kodak Co.

MAIN AUDITORIUM, EASTMAN THEATER AND SCHOOL OF MUSIC, ROCHESTER, N. Y.

THE side walls of the great auditorium and theater in the Eastman Theater and School of Music (No. 751) are distinguished not only by a rich and monumental architectural treatment of eclectic Renaissance type, but also by two exceptionally fine mural decorations by Ezra Winter and Barry Faulkner. These can be criticized as breaking the wall surface too utterly; but in a theater this theoretical fault becomes a virtue; it tends to lighten the dead weight of a large wall area and to bring outdoors into the auditorium.

752   C. Howard Crane, architect; photograph by The Heiser Company

ALLEN THEATER, CLEVELAND

THE "movies" have worked great changes in theater design. Since it is not distance from the screen, but the angle of the spectator's view that is important, theaters have grown longer, narrower, and galleries have been shifted farther back. At once, more wall surface is available for architectural treatment. The Allen Theater at Cleveland (No. 752) shows what brilliant advantage can be taken of this. Here it is filled with three enormous arched windows. That the windows are false, and electric-lighted behind, would be reprehensible in a more serious building, but is quite within the theater psychology.

753   Thomas Lamb, architect; photograph by Tebbs Architectural
Photo Co.

THE CAPITOL THEATER, NEW YORK

IN the enormous Capitol Theater, in New York (No. 753), the great size has permitted an unusually monumental treatment over the boxes at the sides of the proscenium. Gorgeous dull gold glints from the Corinthian order under the play of colored lights; there seems just the right balance of rich textiles, fluted columns, paneled vault. It is quite possible that the careful and beautiful detail of the best "movie" theaters, such as the Capitol, the Allen Theater, and especially the Eastman Theater, may do much toward the education of the American people to higher standards of architectural taste.

754   General View of Interior. Meyer and Holler, architects

GRAUMAN'S THEATER, HOLLYWOOD, CALIFORNIA

755 Approach to Theater, showing Fore-Court and Shops.
Meyer and Holler, architects

IT is natural that southern California, the center of the motion picture industry, should have some of the most interesting "movie" theaters. Such a building should have the most imaginative, the most untrammeled design. In Grauman's Theater in Hollywood, an interesting experiment of playful, romantic treatment of an adapted Egyptian style was tried. One can imagine its producing just that feeling of rather wondering romantic curiosity that makes the most congenial atmosphere for a moving-picture entertainment.

GRAUMAN'S METROPOLITAN THEATER, LOS ANGELES

BUT the strangest, newest, most imaginative of all is Grauman's Metropolitan Theater at Los Angeles, Cal. (No. 756). It is American eclecticism developed to an extreme degree; Greek, Roman, Persian, Art Nouveau and Cubist elements are fused into an unbelievable unity. The proscenium arch, with its strange concrete detail, the jagged cubist beam soffits below, the pseudo-Greek column in the corner, are contrary to all the rules, yet they are expressive of a true personality, a weird and strange beauty.

756 William Lee Woollett, architect; photograph by Kopee

757   William Lee Woollett, architect

A CORNER OF THE LOBBY

THE lobby of Grauman's Metropolitan Theater is kept more simple. Plain wall surface, polygonal piers, deep concrete girders above set the note, and relief is given by the rich mezzanine rail, the queerly profiled stair parapet, and the symbolic beast that crowns it — "aspiration" — conceived as a combination of upward looking deer and earthy snail.

THE MEZZANINE FOYER OF THE METROPOLITAN

THE mezzanine foyer of Grauman's Metropolitan Theater (No. 757) shows strange primitive Ionic capitals, Greek guttæ in the architrave above, Greek frets, and the great girders that carry the steps of the gallery all exposed and covered with modernistic all-over patterns. It is all immensely rich, a little mad.

758   William Lee Woollett, architect

759   Carrère and Hastings, architects; photograph by the U. S. Army Air Service

THE ARLINGTON AMPHITHEATER

THE most ambitious and monumental of American outdoor amphitheaters is the theater memorial in Arlington Cemetery, Va. Its sweeping oval colonnade has immense dignity, and the pedimented memorial building that gives it accent is an admirable example of quiet, dignified and monumental classic design.

CHAPTER XXIII

THE CHURCH

FROM the colonial meetinghouse of New England and the Anglican church of Virginia a twofold ecclesiastical tradition has developed. The cool, open, public quality of the meetinghouse and the quiet, intimate character of the Virginia church coalesced, almost, in the beautiful Wren type of the later eighteenth century, but the coincident growth of Protestantism and Roman Catholicism, together with the Gothic Revival, has split wide the breach again.

Confusion marks the development of church architecture after 1840. The Oxford movement and its enthusiasm for ritual resulted in the accentuation, even in America, of its architectural expression, the Gothic Revival, and of the gulf between "Catholic" and "dissenting" sects. Among the latter the Gothic Revival coincided with a great development of preaching which brought the pulpit itself to the climax of its importance about the middle of the century. Church organizations, which multiplied directly as the increase of sects and denominations, demanded a new type of church building. Small wonder that two forms persisted! Miracle, rather, that absolute chaos was avoided!

The typical mid-century preaching church, usually a vast auditorium, sometimes on an amphitheater plan, always centered about the pulpit, like the first Broadway Tabernacle in New York (No. 303). From behind rose choir stalls and organ pipes, while below and in front was the communion table. This type of chancel persisted for decades, whatever the variations of the nave. In contrast to this form and to many similar colonial and early republican edifices, the Gothic Revival, returning to the earlier system, suppressed the pulpit — moving it to one side — deepened the chancel and emphasized the "east end" with the altar rather than the pulpit as a climax.

English Gothic established itself so firmly as almost to be an official style and the more closely the American church imitated that of a fourteenth-century English parish the more beautiful it was considered. In New York, Trinity Church (No. 761) and Grace Church (No. 762), surpassing all their contemporaries in exquisiteness of design and execution, indisputably established the English Gothic as a model. This style became so popular that it was soon unconsciously burlesqued, mistreated, badly handled, made ostentatiously absurd. For the unavoidable expense of successful Gothic opened the door to a multitude of falsities and imitations in foolish materials; cheap wooden tracery, cast-iron masquerading as stone, pseudo-Gothic carving, and planning that was caricature or worse.

Meanwhile the Roman Catholic church, which had succumbed at first to the English Gothic Revival, and had later grown to feel the inconsistency of its use by the Roman Catholic and Protestant churches at the same time, was feeling around for a style of its own. During a dreary period of chaotic experimentation Italian Gothic, various types of Romanesque and many Renaissance styles were tried, often without sufficient historical knowledge or any sense of planning.

To all the churches, Catholic and Protestant alike, the Romanesque of Richardson came as a great liberating force. The Gothic had, on the one hand, degenerated into the ridiculous caricatures of "carpenter Gothic"; and on the other, despite the brilliant attempts of such great architects as C. C. Haight or Peter B. Wight to infuse into it vitality and personality, had become codified, standardized, dead. Richardson's greatest work, Trinity Church in Boston, was epoch-making, because it united to bigness of conception and honesty of execution an interior that was warm and throbbing with rich color and vitality. So the shackles of the Gothic Revival were broken and a new fashion was set that produced all over the country a great number of Romanesque churches, all with brilliantly polychromed interiors, varying from excellent examples of the style to the most bizarre, crude and stupid imitations.

The idea of the "social conscience," the broadening of the whole conception of religious morality to include the entire social organism, played an influential part in the late nineteenth-century development of church architecture. The idea of the right relationship of the individual to his social environment had a double result. It produced the "institutional church" and a highly developed parish house with a gymnasium, club rooms, lecture rooms. The church also was regarded as belonging to the people, and this, paradoxically, made the most dissenting sects study anew the æsthetics and practical questions of church design. Excepting the Methodists and occasionally the Baptists and the Christian Scientists, the denominations soon abandoned the preaching church, for a church belonging to the people reaches beyond any mere sermon into the realms of deep, simple, religious emotions, of mystery, quiet, awe that lead to worship. The traditional forms of Romanesque, Basilican or Gothic, the chancels and arrangements originally associated with the Episcopal church alone have been used more and more in an effort to inspire these emotions and the clear, too bright atmosphere of the preaching church frequently has been abandoned.

There are, however, a few special types of modern church which have kept themselves aloof from this trend. First of all there is the Christian Science church — auditorium pure and simple, light, airy, absolutely open (No. 789). Circular and polygonal types have come to be favored especially, and the style is almost invariably a rather cold and magnificent classic. There is also a special Methodist type, for the Methodists cling with great tenacity to their traditional preaching-church type. It is developed in many ways — cross-shaped, circular, octagonal, fan-shaped. The church is usually closely organized and combined with Sunday School room and parish house into one composition; the whole is always open and light, but frequently bizarre and queer, and almost always rather cold in detail. Of course there exists a special Synagogue type. Although classic styles are occasionally used, more often the detail is of a Moorish or Arabic type, sanctioned by age-old tradition, and used in conjunction with forms often of great and daring originality. The plan is usually simple, and often approaches a square.

But whatever the type or the style, there seems at the present time to be a marked trend toward a carefully considered and restrained emotionalism in our church architecture. Not only does this characteristic mark the best Romanesque and Gothic and Renaissance work, but it also saves from coldness the best modern colonial churches. In all the styles, too, there is a growing disregard of historical precedent. Eclecticism is dominant; modern American Gothic is neither French nor English nor Italian nor early nor flamboyant. It is governed by emotional consistency alone. Little by little, the terrific amount of false construction that marred much recent church work is beginning to give way to a greater simplicity; ostentation is no longer considered a virtue. Structural honesty, free style treatment, a warm and human emotionalism of effect — these are the dominant ideals behind the best types of American churches to-day.

A TYPICAL EARLY NINETEENTH–
CENTURY CHURCH

AFTER the fading of pure late colonial tradition in the second and third decades of the nineteenth century, church design fell into chaos. The Greek Revival never exerted the complete sway in church design that it did in other types of architecture. The Dutch Reformed church in Hackensack, New Jersey, built in 1726, but enlarged in the nineteenth century, is, in its present form, typical of church design in this period. Its pointed windows and crude Gothic tracery may date from the original building, but whereas in the eighteenth century such forms are rare; in the nineteenth they became well-nigh universal.

760   From a photograph by John A. Wilson

TRINITY CHURCH, A VITAL INFLUENCE ON CHURCH DESIGN

THE Gothic Revival found full expression in some American churches at an early date. The most noteworthy is undoubtedly the lovely English Gothic of Trinity Church in New York (No. 761), dating from the 'forties, and designed by an English architect whose work in America had a vital influence on the development of American taste. The interior of Trinity has not only beauty of composition, sureness and correctness of form, but also a richness and charm of Gothic detail then unknown in this country. The interior is still distinguished by a quiet emotional atmosphere.

761   R. M. Upjohn, architect; photograph by Wurts Brothers

GRACE CHURCH, NEW YORK

GRACE Church in New York (No. 762) is another of the masterpieces of this early American Gothic Revival. Its exterior, like Trinity, based on English Gothic precedent, is full of grace, delicacy, rich loveliness. But it is beginning to show the modern American eclecticism; its spire is more German than English. So strong is the composition, and so sure the detail and so perfect the execution, that not even its present commercial surroundings, not even the change of taste toward a freer and less academic style, can kill the soaring lace-like beauty of the whole.

762   James Renwick, architect; photograph by Wurts Brothers

763   Cram, Goodhue and Ferguson, architects

INTERIOR, THE FIRST BAPTIST CHURCH, PITTSBURGH

THE interior of the church (No. 764) in its sincere treatment of the materials of which it is composed, in the imagination which has so perfectly combined elements from historical Gothic styles with elements new and original, and in the beauty of the composition which leads so brilliantly up to the chancel, is typical of those qualities which made the earlier churches of these architects epoch-making buildings.

765   Charles T. Matthews, architect; photograph by
                    Wurts Brothers

A MODERN GOTHIC CHURCH

THE history of modern Gothic church design is largely the history of the work and influence of one firm — Cram, Goodhue and Ferguson (later dissolved into two firms, Bertram G. Goodhue, and Cram and Ferguson). Their work, from the first, is distinguished by daring eclecticism and great originality. The First Baptist Church in Pittsburgh, Pa. (No. 763), is a characteristic example of their earlier work. Tracery and details of English perpendicular type are combined with a daring use of rectangular lines, and of segmental rather than complete arches, and the whole given a silhouette more French, with its tall *flèche* (spire), than English.

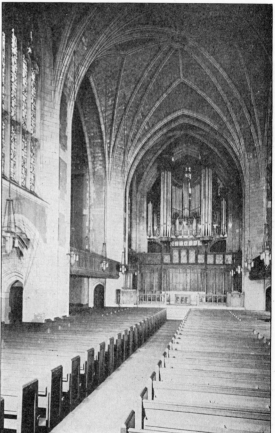

764   Cram, Goodhue and Ferguson, architects

AN ADAPTATION OF FRENCH GOTHIC

THE Lady Chapel of St. Patrick's Cathedral in New York (No. 765) is one of the surest and loveliest of the more academic modern adaptations of developed French Gothic. There is in buttress, pinnacle, *flèche* and tracery that peculiarly satisfying grace and lightness that characterize French work of the middle of the thirteenth century.

A FREE GOTHIC CHANCEL

In the chancel of the Chapel of the Intercession in New York (No. 766), one sees the developed quality of this free kind of Gothic. The occasional harshness and awkwardnesses of the earlier work are gone; instead there is the beautiful open timber-trussed ceiling, striking in its color, height, and airiness. Restrained simplicity in detail bursts into flowered richness at just the right points, so that the whole is full of a deep-textured solemnity, a truly reverent religious atmosphere too frequently missing in American churches.

767 Cram, Goodhue and Ferguson, architects; photograph by Kenneth Clark

THE REREDOS OF ST. THOMAS'

The interior (No. 768), with its beautiful reredos added later by Bertram G. Goodhue, is more severe than much of their other work, more coldly perfect both in form and color, yet perhaps by that very severity impressively grand. The influence of the late French flamboyant work shows in the treatment of the nave arches; but there is nothing academic or historical about it; all is newly blended, creative, and even its coldness is vividly alive. It is the coldness of the aristocrat, not that of the dead.

766 Bertram Grosvenor Goodhue, architect; photograph by Kenneth Clark

ST. THOMAS' CHURCH, NEW YORK

Typical of eclecticism of style, and of poetic imagination and schooled richness, is the exterior of St. Thomas' Church, New York (No. 767). There is French influence in doorway and rose window and the general picturesqueness of the whole, English influence in all sorts of details; and both brought into a perfect artistic harmony; both used only because they were natural forms to express the desired emotional atmosphere. The design owes much of its effectiveness to the contrasts of severe plainness juxtaposed with lace-like richness.

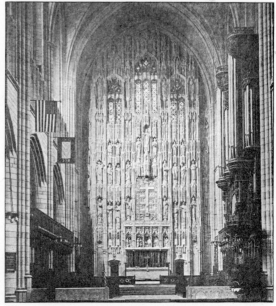

768 Bertram Grosvenor Goodhue, architect; photograph by Kenneth Clark

769   Zantzinger, Borie and Medary, architects; photograph
by John Wallace Gillies

MODERN GOTHIC AT ITS BEST

In many ways the finest of these modern Gothic large city church interiors is that of St. Vincent Ferrer in New York (No. 770). In it there seems to be the perfect balance between freedom and academic style. Its proportions are so beautiful, the materials in its structure so well used and expressed, that its effect is profoundly satisfying.

WASHINGTON MEMORIAL CHAPEL, VALLEY FORGE, PENNSYLVANIA

The Washington Memorial Chapel at Valley Forge, Pa. (No. 769), is of a Gothic more academically correct, and yet more full, too, of warmth and intimacy. Its rich pinnacled choir stalls are particularly noteworthy. The contrast of stone arches with the dark timbered roof does much to give this interior its distinction; and it is touches of this sort that make the whole a creative work despite its closeness to precedent. Proportion, contrast, color, richness rightly applied are effective in any style.

770   Bertram Grosvenor Goodhue, architect; photograph
by Kenneth Clark

THE CATHEDRAL OF ST. JOHN THE DIVINE, NEW YORK

Taking a place among the greatest of European cathedrals in vastness, the Cathedral of St. John the Divine in New York is bound to be, when completed, an impressive monument of American ecclesiastical architecture. The exterior shows a close following of precedent. The design for the flanks of the nave, with its mighty buttresses, is beautifully free and modern and yet true to the essence of the Gothic spirit.

771   Cram and Ferguson, architects; photograph from the architects' rendering

THE NAVE OF THE CATHEDRAL

THE proposed nave interior of the Cathedral of St. John the Divine is more daring, more brilliant and even more successful. The soaring verticality of its piers shows an American architect attempting, and successfully, to gain an effect of tremendous height that the builders of Beauvais attempted, and failed in achieving. The romance of perspective, the effect of varied and differing views, yet all ordered and unified, the tall arches and shadowed heights of the vaulting, form a whole that is simple, beautiful, overwhelming.

772   Cram and Ferguson, architects; photograph from the architects' rendering

773   Rossiter and Muller, architects

AMERICAN GOTHIC IN A SMALL CHURCH

AMERICAN Gothic has made equal progress in the design of the smaller country churches. Between the design of such a "carpenter Gothic" church as that shown in No. 313 and St. Michael's Church at Litchfield, Conn. (No. 773), a great way has been traveled. In St. Michael's there is the sureness of mass composition that one expects to-day; and there is also a delightful contrast of rough stone and rich decoration, and tracery of late "decorated" character. The whole is distinguished by true poetry of design.

THE ELLINGWOOD CHAPEL AT NAHANT

NOR is great cost necessary to beauty any more than great size. This chapel at Nahant, Massachusetts, shows how great is the charm that can be produced by the simplest means. Here there is no expensive tracery (and cheap wooden tracery is an abomination) or any rich carving, only rough stone walls, a slate roof, and a few small windows. Yet the effect is finer, more beautiful, than that of many a church that cost two or three times as much. One can create inexpensively, never without composition.

774   Cram and Ferguson, architects; photograph by Paul J. Weber

775   Cram, Goodhue and Ferguson, architects; photograph
by Kenneth Clark

AN INTERIOR OF LOVELY SIMPLICITY

THE interior of St. George's Church at Richmond, Philadelphia (No. 776), shows an expression of the same truths. Color, texture, strong simplicity of form well composed create the effect of quiet and sure poetry which this simple interior possesses.

777   Cram and Ferguson, architects; photograph by Paul J. Weber

A MODERN CHURCH INTERIOR

THE dramatic character of much modern church design is well illustrated by this interior of St. Mark's Church at Mt. Kisco, N. Y. (No. 775). The dark shadows of the simple timber roof make a striking contrast with the richness of the delicate rood screen; intricacy of fine-scaled ornament on the screen gives a sense of richness and mystery to the climax — the chancel — behind.

776   Walter H. Thomas, architect; photograph by
Philip B. Wallace

AN IMPRESSIVELY SIMPLE
COMPOSITION

THE interior of All Saints' Church, Peterborough, N. H. (No. 777), is another remarkable example of impressiveness simply gained. By the use of simple forms, whose primitive character is the result not of affectation, like much modern primitive art, but of a direct use of the materials available, by beautiful composition, and by a careful use of the colors and textures of different materials, there is produced just that charm which the American traveler seeks in old churches abroad, and so seldom finds at home.

MADISON SQUARE PRESBYTERIAN CHURCH, NEW YORK

BUT American church architecture is by no means limited to the Gothic which seems to be traditional in Episcopal churches. The so-called "dissenting" sects and the Roman Catholics have made frequent use of the Renaissance. The old Madison Square Presbyterian Church in New York (no longer standing) showed the enormous possibilities of domed design. Its use of polychromed terra cotta was remarkable, and its pedimented portico one of the most perfect in proportion and detail in America. Influenced in part by northern Italian Renaissance, it was nevertheless instinct with fresh form and lovely composition.

778   McKim, Mead and White, architects; photograph by
Louis H. Dreyer

MADISON SQUARE PRESBYTERIAN CHURCH — INTERIOR

THE interior of the Madison Square Presbyterian Church was almost Byzantine in its simple forms and richly decorated surfaces. The all-enclosing dome, with its ring of windows, made a perfect frame for the Presbyterian service. Yet all was so handled, so decorated, so softened into rich quietness of atmosphere, that there was none of that strident obviousness frequently found in Protestant churches, and yet no sacrifice of use was made. It was a church planned for its purpose — preaching.

779   McKim, Mead and White, architects; photograph by
Louis H. Dreyer

THE DOMED CHAPEL OF AN INDIANA CONVENT

THE Immaculate Conception Convent and Chapel at Ferdinand, Ind. (No. 780), raises its domed mass most impressively above its terraced hilltop, and reveals the value of the domed silhouette in giving character to a city sky line. The chapel itself is in that mixture of Romanesque and Renaissance styles which characterizes many churches of Milan and its environs. Particularly noticeable is the effective use of brick which this style permits.

780   Victor J. Klutho, architect; photograph by Eugene Taylor

781   Henry D. Dagit, architect; photograph by Tebbs Architectural Photo Co.

A NEW AND ORIGINAL ADAPTATION OF BYZANTINE

THE interior of the Church of St. Francis de Sales in Philadelphia is Byzantine in its great dome and its carved details, but in its use of rich terra cotta moldings, its insets of colored tile, its brick laid in striking patterns, and its round windows, there is a fresh note, based, to be sure, on some Byzantine ideas, but used in a way new and original.

THE CHAPEL AT COLUMBIA UNIVERSITY

THE Chapel of St. Paul, at Columbia University, New York (No. 782), is in many ways the most altogether successful of American domical churches. The beautifully proportioned entrance portico, the graceful swell of the dome, the careful treatment of the richness of inset limestone, and the frank treatment of the brickwork with here and there patterns and insets of shells, all make a building not only beautiful in composition, but full of intimate quaintness, of details subtle and lovable. This chapel, moreover, is as unique in its structural as in its æsthetic qualities, for it is entirely a masonry structure.

782 Howells and Stokes, architects; photograph by A. Tennyson Beals

783 Howells and Stokes, architects; photograph by A. Tennyson Beals

THE STRIKING TREATMENT OF THE INTERIOR

THE interior of St. Paul's at Columbia University is an even more striking creation, because so freshly original, with structure and materials so frankly expressed. Moreover, the brick, the terra cotta arches with their sculptured evangelists, the tile vaults, the dull gleam of bronze gallery fronts, the rich brown of inlaid walnut choir furniture and organ front, make a harmony of color unusually subdued, quiet, yet rich, a harmony to which the glowing blues and reds of La Farge's stained glass apse windows give just the necessary climax.

THE ROMAN BASILICA INFLUENCE

ROMAN basilica types have influenced many modern American churches. St. Gregory's Roman Catholic Church in Brooklyn has the type of façade, with portico and tall campanile, found on certain Roman early Christian basilicas. Here again, however, American eclecticism is at work; the niches and pilasters of the upper part of the front have a Renaissance flavor and the rose window is Romanesque. Yet it is all unified; the same spirit pervades every detail of the whole, and the result is a church beautiful and impressive.

784   Helmle and Corbett, architects

THE INTERIOR OF ST. GREGORY'S

THE interior (No. 785) with its arcades, its clerestory windows, its rich early Christian *baldachino* (canopy), is closer to precedent. The long range of arcades and the successive painted trusses of the roof lead the eye surely and inevitably to the richness of marbles, of mosaic, of richly colored paintings, which make the chancel an adequate climax.

785   Helmle and Corbett, architects

A CHAPEL OF SPANISH RENAISSANCE

THE Pauline Roman Catholic Chapel at Broadmoor, Colorado Springs, Colo. (No. 786), has a basilican plan, but uses another type of inspiration, more suited to the locality — the simple yet dramatic forms of the Spanish Renaissance as developed in the American colonies. Quiet stucco walls, and the picturesque asymmetry of the front with its campanile, form a striking foil for the rich *baroque* doorway.

786   MacLaren and Hetherington, architects; photograph by The Photo Craft Shop

AN EFFECTIVE INTERIOR

THE interior of the Pauline Roman Catholic Chapel at Broadmoor demonstrates that expense and richness are no more necessary to an effective classic interior than they are to an effective interior in Gothic. The well designed composite column capitals are the only ornament used; otherwise there is only the broad surface of stucco. No moldings break the strong curve of the arches. Yet careful proportion, direct simplicity in roof and walls give an impression of dignity, of reverence, that many churches much more elaborate totally lack.

787   MacLaren and Hetherington, architects; photograph by The Photo Craft Shop

788   Shepley, Rutan and Coolidge, architects; photograph by Paul J. Weber

THE CHRISTIAN SCIENCE TYPE

THE Second Church of Christ, Scientist, at Roxbury, Mass., has, by cutting every inch of ornament save the cornice cresting, and by a frank domical expression of the great auditorium within, produced an exterior of marked originality, to which good proportion gives an added and controlling beauty, and simplicity an added power.

THE SIMPLICITY OF THE INTERIOR

The interior has a similar originality and power. The vault is kept simple; the rostrum given importance by railing, reading desk, and organ. Pews and a rostrum railing of almost colonial type add an intimacy and grace too frequently lacking in the similar open interiors that are so frequently found in Christian Science churches.

789   Shepley, Rutan and Coolidge, architects; photograph by Paul J. Weber

790   Myron Hunt, architect

AN ADAPTATION OF SPANISH MISSION DETAIL

THE First Congregational Church at Riverside, Calif., is a brilliant adaptation of Spanish mission detail to the problem of Congregational church design. The simple stucco wall surfaces and the welcoming arches of the arcade well express the character of the church, and the richness of the *baroque* spire and the transept windows, beautifully detailed, add the requisite religious character.

791   Harry W. Jones, architect; photograph by C. J. Hibbard

CHAPEL IN LAKEWOOD CEMETERY, MINNEAPOLIS

THE chapel in Lakewood Cemetery at Minneapolis, Minn., is, in general form, purely Byzantine. But in detail there is a strong admixture of modernist, *art noveau*, influences decidedly French. Again the dome asserts its importance; the rise and sweep of its swelling form, over the ranked windows around its base, is the secret of its impressiveness.

792   Harry W. Jones, architect; photograph by C. J. Hibbard

SOMBER SPLENDOR OF THE INTERIOR

IN the interior of the Lakewood Cemetery chapel, the great fault of its exterior, its lack of he'ght, is still further evident. One feels painfully the need of more pier under the great arches; one feels stunted, crushed. But aside from this, the combination of simple surface with rich surface ornament of marble and mosaic, culminating in the loveliness of the crown of angels around the dome, makes an effect of somber Byzantine splendor seldom attained in this country.

793   Louis H. Sullivan, architect

A METHODIST CHURCH OF ANTITRADITIONAL FORM

METHODIST churches have sought strange forms. Their structures until recently have expressed that reaction against an outworn and comfortable form-alism which character:zed the movement that created Methodism. St. Paul's Methodist Episcopal Church at Cedar Rapids, Iowa (No. 793), is as consistently antitraditional in detail as in form, and expresses in its severe rectangularity of window forms, the blockiness of its tower, the uncompromising squareness of the doors, something of that rigidity of puritanism that is the Methodist pride.

794   Cram and Ferguson, architects

A LARGER CHURCH IN MODERN COLONIAL

THE Montclair Presbyterian Church (No. 795) is a larger church of a similar colonial type. Its graceful spire is particularly charming, and the simplicity of the brick walls makes its richness all the more appealing.

796   Eckel and Boschen, architects; photograph by
The Pollock-Gilbert Co.

A MODERN ADAPTATION OF COLONIAL

IT is only natural and right that the beautiful types of colonial church developed in the latter part of the eighteenth and early in the nineteenth centuries should exert a strong influence on modern American churches. One of the most interestingly original of modern adaptations of colonial church forms is the Second Unitarian church in Boston (No. 794). A front of distinctly English feeling is combined with a parish house wing as distinctly American in its gambrel roof, and the two portions are merged together by a high tower whose rich steeple forms the climax of the whole.

795   Carrère and Hastings, architects; photograph by
Mattie Edwards Hewitt

COLONIAL INFLUENCE IN A CHURCH INTERIOR

THE interior of the First Presbyterian church at St. Joseph, Mo. (No. 796), is, in the main, closely inspired by colonial precedent, and gains, thereby, an effect of sure and quiet serenity. But the rather stiff platform, the choir gallery behind, and the all-over decoration of the chancel walls seem hardly in keeping with the gracious dignity of the rest; plaster vault gracefully curved, white columns, pews white and scroll ended, and rich organ front.

THE MODERN MOORISH SYNAGOGUE

THE unusual and successful design of the Temple
Emanu-el in New York (No. 380) early fixed a
tradition — due perhaps to Spanish or Portuguese
influence, and found in other countries besides
America — of some type of modernized Moorish
for synagogue design. Developed recently in ways
extremely free, it has at other times produced buildings of almost purely Mohammedan type, whose
appropriateness is open to serious question. Such is
the Temple Irem at Wilkes-Barre, Pa. (No. 797),
which seems strangely exotic.

797   Olds and Puckey, architects, © J. Horgan, Jr.

'798   Walter S. Schneider, architect; Henry B. Herts, associated;
photograph by Wurts Brothers

A MORE AMERICANIZED FORM OF
MOORISH

MUCH more American, much more modern, much
more real in its beauty, is the interesting Temple
B'nai Jeshurun in New York (No. 798). Its bold
sweep of warm yellow stone is simple and most effective; and in the treatment of the doorway, set within
its rich tall niche, there is just enough of the Moorish
spirit to give the typical synagogue expression. All
the ornament is of the most modern character.

A MODERN
SYNAGOGUE
INTERIOR

IN the interior of the
Temple B'nai Jeshurun
there is the same mod-
ernistic treatment of
details, with a Moorish
touch; the same con-
centrated richness, the
same refusal to be bound
to any style, and a
resultant effect of re-
strained power.

799   Walter S. Schneider, architect; Henry B. Herts, associated; photograph by Wurts Brothers

AN ALTAR OF SPANISH RENAISSANCE

THE High Altar of the Carmelite convent at Santa Clara, Cal. (No. 801), uses the richness of the late Spanish Renaissance, with twisted columns and broken pediments and rich surface ornament and figure sculpture, to achieve the desired result of dramatic climax. This is added to by the beautifully simple height of the whole, the picturesque lighting, and the treatment of the ornament which gives many mysterious glints of delicate light in the shadowed spaces.

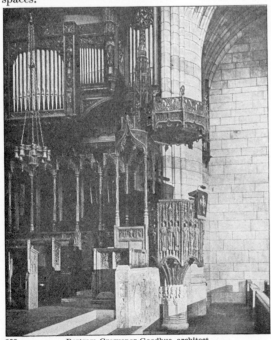

A CHANCEL RICH IN FORM AND COLOR

PERHAPS the greatest development in modern church design has been in the furnishing and the decorative details of the chancel. After a period of cold restraint — reaction against the often garish color of some church interiors influenced by Tiffany work and the work of Richardson — there has been a recent return to richness in form and color, due to the growing realization of the chancel as the focus of the church. The chancel of the chapel of St. Bartholomew's Church, New York (No. 800), shows how beautifully the richness of mural decorations in color contrasts with the simplicity of rough plaster walls.

A BEAUTIFUL CHANCEL DESIGN

IN the carving of modernized Gothic detail for choir stalls, pulpits, organ fronts and the like, results have been produced that seem almost final. The pulpit, choir stalls, and organ front of the chancel of St. Thomas' Church, New York (No. 802), show how the extreme delicacy of scale, combined with great intricacy of form, based on various late Gothic precedents, but developed to a point that no late Gothic example ever reached, produces a scintillation of light and shade, a mysterious richness of effect, to which the austere strength of the stone church is an excellent foil.

CHAPTER XXIV

THE FUTURE OF AMERICAN ARCHITECTURE

AT first sight, the attempt to prophesy with regard to the future of American architecture may seem both futile and dangerous. There are so many unforeseen developments that may occur in the American life of the future, and architecture is so completely based on, and therefore sensitive to, the entire character of our civilization that any forecast must be of the most tentative sort. There exist, however, certain important tendencies which have been increasing notably within recent years, but which are nevertheless manifestly incomplete. Their fruition in the future can therefore be considered at least probable.

The first of these tendencies is the growth of stylistic freedom. The day of the "revival," the imitation, of archæological forms, is gone. History is no longer conceived as a series of fixed patterns, a magic lantern show rather than a moving picture, and any sentimentalizing of the past is more and more foreign to the practical sense of the average man. Another reason for the growth of style freedom is the fact that more and more American architects are becoming aware of the comparative unimportance of the entire question of style correctness. Artistic consistency is never ruled by dates, and emotional power in architecture can never be achieved until the larger matters of plan and composition have entirely absorbed and re-formed the details of architectural expression like moldings, columns, and ornamental forms which make "style." It is precisely these larger matters of planning and composition which are most profoundly affected by new materials, new technical processes, and new social conditions. As soon, then, as plan and composition, so deeply responsive to the changing mechanizing of modern life, begin to control detail as completely as they should, style changes are inevitable, and true style freedom will arrive. Already the tendency toward this attitude is evidenced in all the best modern work.

This style freedom will not mean the necessary abandonment of all the forms the past has given us. It will mean freedom from slavery to "secessionism" just as it means freedom from Gothic or classic. It will mean an attitude in the light of which all the modern discussion of styles, all the cries of the style-rebels and the creeds of the style-conservatives, will appear childish and futile. Forms which men have loved through the centuries will not pass away at the threat of a theory, nor will reverence for them prevent the creation of new forms. The questions that will be asked of the details of a building in the future are not, is it correct, is it old, is it new, but rather, is it a natural, inevitable result of its place, its function, and its material; and above all, is it beautiful, does it speak deeply to the emotions as all great art must?

Another marked present-day tendency whose further development may be confidently expected is a growing love of the dramatic in building composition. We are growing away from that love of uniform all-over richness that characterized the days, say, of the cast-iron store fronts; more and more our buildings, particularly the smaller, less formal buildings, are designed with a growing sense of the value of the dramatic climax. Plain wall — a simple texture of pleasant materials — leads up to a sudden contrast of rich doorway or a bit of intricate ironwork; restraint is balanced against concentrated and climactic exuberance. The fact that economy in building is increasingly necessary has undoubtedly influenced this development profoundly; it is a striking example of the way economic conditions may affect æsthetic ideals. But there is more than mere economy in this movement; it is based on a growing keenness and subtlety in popular taste. This growing love of the dramatic climax in architecture has by no means reached its fullness; the future is sure to see its further development, which will add charm to our country houses, restfulness and yet excitement to our cities, dramatic and emotional power to the beauty of all our buildings.

Another present-day trait, strangely mixed with good and evil, is our growing love of varied materials, varied textures and colors. To-day as never before, brick and stone and stucco and wood and marble are boldly used, played with, balanced against each other. Harmonious variety in texture has been achieved with a growing sureness and beauty. Yet this same love of varied materials, together with some uncritical sentimentalization of the past, has given rise to the greatest American architectural sin — our love of imitations, falsities, clever "fakes." At a time when there is a variety of possible building materials never before obtainable, when sheet metal and drawn metal and wood fiber and rubber and an enormous number of different kinds of brick and stone and plaster, and a thousand other products of mechanical invention and chemical research have been put to use as building materials, each new material crying aloud, it would seem, for a new treatment suitable to it, each new invention a new opportunity for the artist — it is a strange fact that our love for texture and materials has forced us to make of all this newness merely fraudulent imitations of the old. So rubber is marbleized, wood fiber-boards are nailed on a wall in stone ashlar patterns, and there is "stone" cast in molds, "stone" baked in ovens, "stone" put on with a trowel, and we even sometimes torture the loveliness of wood shingles into the exaggerated curves of a futile imitation of thatch! So deeply is this habit ingrained in us that one is shocked to discover, in a building almost universally acclaimed as one of the most prophetic of modern buildings, interior steel doors elaborately painted with a careful imitation wood finish.

Let us hope the future will change all this; that our architects will realize and meet the challenge of the new materials, and devise for them forms and colors that make them an architectural asset instead of a liability. There is reason to hope, at least, that all this flooding river of imitations itself has its source in a love for material and texture that, rightly used and rightly disciplined, would inevitably, and eventually will, end it.

Somewhat allied to this love of materials is a growing tendency toward the development of local styles. Modernity has stretched its great ruthless form over the whole country; at one time it seemed as though only a drab uniformity would result. Three facts have combined to prevent this. One was that vague combination of pure traditionalism, the type of the landscape, and the accumulated appearance of a locality that one can only call "spirit of place." Another was the fact that despite the development of cheap transport and the centralization of industries there are places where certain building materials are bound to be cheaper and more available than others. The third is the all important fact of differences of local climate.

The first of these three facts has resulted in the development of modern colonial work along the Atlantic coast, and, to a less extent, in the development of the wide-spreading horizontal lines in the bungalows of the Middle West. In the East, there are villages and certain parts of old cities where the years have placed their stamp so unmistakably that it would seem a crime, not only against tradition, but also against all the laws of æsthetic harmony, to build in any way that did not harmonize with the marked colonial atmosphere of the place. Archæological correctness is neither necessary nor desirable, but the magic of such localities — rare enough in America — can only be preserved and will be, more and more, as the public grows more sensitive, by keeping all new buildings in character with the old, by using some sort of modernized colonial forms.

The second factor, that of materials locally available, is strikingly illustrated by the stone houses of the suburbs of Philadelphia and parts of New Jersey. Here there is an abundance of stone of pleasing color that splits readily into convenient sizes and shapes, and builds into walls of great beauty. The result has been one of the few areas of truly native stone architecture that gives a remarkable charm of harmony and of textured color to the whole region. Such convenient local materials often give a distinct and subtle individuality to places that are at first sight much alike.

The third factor, that of climate, is responsible for what is easily the most obvious of the local styles of America — the stucco, tiled-roof houses of southern California and the states immediately east of it. Traditionalism, the "spirit of place," took part in this development as well; the two together rendered it inevitable, and the result has been an architecture so true to its climate and its landscape, so sensitive to the double tradition of Indian pueblo and Spanish *conquistador*, that it forms one of the most vital modern developments that American architecture has undergone.

But by all standards the most hopeful tendency in American architecture to-day, whose further development will produce its greatest triumphs, is a growing sense of form. This, after all, is the dominant thing in all great architecture. And its expressions in the great body of modern American architecture were, until recently, fitful, evanescent, confined to monumental buildings, and even there conditional and circumscribed. Our cities were becoming mere rows of stupid boxes; all the architect could do was to dress them in prettinesses of detail. Then came the zoning law into many of our cities, with its restrictions on height, its requirements for setbacks. Adopted purely as a practical measure, it proved a magic wand to set American city architecture free from its nightmare of eternal cubism. Suddenly a latent form sense and imagination developed; buildings became interesting in outline and silhouette as well as in detail. Romance was born; piled masses soared into the sky that seemed to do something. No longer was the high building apparently built by the mile and cut off to order, but it was composed, break on break, buttress on buttress; it began and it ended. City building ceased being rather drab prose, however polished: the possibility of poetry entered in.

This encouraging development of the form sense is not limited to large city buildings. Its effects are already evidenced, for example, in the Kansas City memorial (No. 550) and the Nebraska capitol (No. 486). Eventually it will affect every slightest production of American architecture, for a people who have made the towered Shelton (No. 829) their own will not forever endure the architectural stupidity of the average home, the inexcusable dullness of the blocks of two-family matchbox houses, or the square barrenness of thousands of ugly farmhouses, or the overdecorated absurdities of the tenements and apartments, in which, all together, the great majority of Americans are now forced to live.

803   Delano and Aldrich, architects; photograph by John Wallace Gillies

A MODERN EXAMPLE OF COLONIAL RE–CREATION

THE Knickerbocker Club in New York is typical of the feeling for historical style which is sure to characterize much of the coming American architecture. It is recognizably colonial or Georgian of the later period, but nevertheless there is not a single detail which gives the impression of its being a mere copy. It is a creative variation on the late colonial theme; with the refinement that is the mark of the style emphasized.

FREE USE OF STYLE IN A CITY HOUSE

EQUALLY free and modern in its interpretation of a historic style is the house of Mrs. Alice McLean in New York (No. 804), which uses details of an Italian *baroque* style in a way simple, effective, and admirably adapted to their purpose — the quiet decoration of a city street. More and more American architecture will make use of such free adaptations and re-creations of style types.

804   DeSuarez and Hatton, architects; photograph by Mattie Edwards Hewitt

805   Edward C. Dean, and William Lawrence Bottomley, architects; photograph by John Wallace Gillies

A CITY GARDEN IN THE NEW MANNER

THE garden façade of the Turtle Bay Gardens in New York (No. 805) is even freer in its treatment of historical precedent. With window frames of Venetian type, it combines a loggia whose proportions are modern. Charm and a certain dramatic contrast of rich and simple have dictated the design in every part; historical considerations are secondary. Another view is shown in No. 818.

NEW TENDENCIES IN A DINING ROOM

THE dining room of Timberline at Bryn Mawr, Pa., is recognizable as basically Italian in inspiration. Its use of wood paneling, however, is a new and modern touch, and the whole, with its rich painted frieze, its beamed ceiling glowing with color, its stone mantel, and its Italian furniture, is typical of the newer style of American architecture, that, starting with some given emotional spirit, gives to it an expression that is not bound by historical accuracy of details.

806   Charles A. Platt, architect

807   Frank Lloyd Wright, architect

HORIZONTAL ACCENTUATION IN A MODERN RESIDENCE

AMONG the chief exponents of the free type of design, Frank Lloyd Wright takes an important place. This view of a portion of his own house (No. 807) reveals the deep and quiet beauty that long, low, horizontal lines may give, and an emotional quality all the more real because its forms are themselves newly created.

HARMONY FROM A REVIVIFIED GREEK BASIS

THAT a perfect harmony may be produced by the combination of these two main style trends — eclecticism and style adaptation, and pure nonstylistic creation — is shown by this building for the Academy of Sciences in Washington (No. 808). The basic inspiration is Greek, but every particle of ornament has been revivified, recreated, filled with a vital symbolism, and sculpture of remarkably successful architectural type makes it all alive and interesting.

808   Bertram Grosvenor Goodhue, architect; photograph of the architect's rendering

A HOUSE OF NONSTYLISTIC DESIGN

THE house of Miss E. R. Hooker in New Haven is typical of another trend that is bound to influence profoundly future architecture in America: the trend toward free, nonstylistic design, as opposed to historical or even eclectic design. All the beauty of this house is due to its proportion and its material — the careful relationship of all its parts.

809   Delano and Aldrich, architects; photograph by Kenneth Clark

811   Bertram Grosvenor Goodhue, architect; photograph
of the architect's rendering

810   Bertram Grosvenor Goodhue, architect; photograph
of the architect's rendering

THE NEW AMERICAN GOTHIC

THESE designs for the University Chapel of Chicago University show that the same merging of new ideas with Gothic feeling is possible, and can produce a whole of great beauty and originality. Great piled masses of masonry, touches of sculpture, all in the least stylistic manner, add to, rather than detract from, the Gothic feeling of rich tracery. It is Gothic, obviously, but a Gothic which is purely modern, purely American, looking forward into the future.

THE CHARM OF SIMPLE CONTRAST

The growing love of the dramatic element in American architecture can be well seen in this music room door from Shallow Brook Farm at Mt. Kisco, N. Y. (No. 812). Simple stucco surfaces and the dark green of tall cedars frame a door whose richness of carving and wrought iron is the dramatic climax of the whole.

812   Benjamin Wistar Morris, architect

813 Bertram Grosvenor Goodhue, architect; photograph
by Kenneth Clark

DRAMATIC EFFECT IN A DOORWAY

Even greater dramatic climaxes are possible in the Spanish Renaissance style so popular in southern California. The doorway of the house for Herbert Coppell at Pasadena (No. 813) shows how effectively and dramatically the imaginative exuberance of the Spanish *baroque* doorway is framed by the broad expanse of simple unbroken stucco walls.

AN UNCONVENTIONAL INTERIOR

Dramatic effects can be produced as powerfully in interiors as outdoors. Indeed, the opportunities for dramatic interior design are unlimited, for American rooms are usually more conservative than exteriors, and in the future imagination and emotional quality must more and more enter into them. The conversation room in the house of Waldron Gillespie at Montecito, Cal. (No. 814), with its broad divans, its pool and fountain, gives some indication of the original charm that may arise.

814   Cram, Goodhue and Ferguson, architects

815   Reginald D. Johnson, architect

THE DRAMATIC NOTE IN A MODERN GARDEN

In a large garden the opportunities for such dramatic effect are enormous. In this terraced garden and loggia for J. P. Jefferson, in Montecito, Cal. (No. 815), the most was made of the opportunity. Here water, greens of all kinds from differing plants, urns, the shadowed loggia arches, and the inviting stairway give a sense of romance, of the mysterious beyond, that is exceedingly dramatic. This is architecture and gardening that together have an infinite power for suggestion, for liberating the beholder's imagination.

816   Arthur Loomis Harmon, architect

AN EFFECTIVE CONTRAST OF MATERIALS

Stucco is one of the materials coming into wider use whose treatment to-day evidences that joy in the possibilities of materials that is marked for still further development in the future. The house of H. W. Bell at Ardsley, N. Y. (No. 816), has a rough textured stucco wall made all the more effective by its contrast with brick arch and window sills.

SIMPLE TREATMENT OF AN ESTATE COTTAGE

The superintendent's cottage on the estate of Major Clarence Fahnestock at Cold Spring, N. Y. (No. 817), shows not only this love of texture and color, of stucco and stone balanced against each other, but also the

817   Lewis Colt Albro and Lovett Rile, architects

romance and charm that can be produced by the simplest means. In such sincere simplicity lies much hope for the future.

ROMANCE AND CONTRAST IN A CITY GARDEN

THE end of the gardens of Turtle Bay Gardens in New York displays a high degree of dramatic and personal charm where one might least expect it — in a city back yard. As always, contrast is fundamental to it: contrast of stone path and green growing things, of stucco and iron rail, of plain surfaces and accents of rich sculpture.

818   Edward C. Dean and William Lawrence Bottomley, architects

819   Edward C. Dean, architect; photograph by Kenneth Clark

ORIGINALITY IN USE OF MATERIALS

THE court of the Cosmopolitan Club in New York (No. 819) owes the greater part of its distinction to its original and sincere use of materials. The brickwork, with its lines of narrow tiles, the flagged pavement with grass in the joints, the water spout, the little touches of richness in lantern and fountain all help the general effect. In the future, as here, simplicity will create true charm.

A HOUSE IN A TRUE LOCAL STYLE

THIS residence in Germantown, Philadelphia (No. 820), shows stonework of a smooth texture, and a more finished and sophisticated style. Yet the use of the stone in forms that are natural to it yields inevitably a house in the true local style. A development of such local styles is a hopeful factor in American design.

820   Mellor, Meigs and Howe, architects; photograph by Philip B. Wallace

McIlvain and Roberts, architects

FRANK TREATMENT OF LEDGE STONE

In the house of Noah Swayne II of Ardmore, Pa., it is the frank treatment of ledge stone and shingles, combined with the charm of simple form, that is prophetic of the treatment of such materials in the architecture of the future. This love of the qualities of materials is typical of modern American design.

A HOUSE OF THE STRATIFIED STONEWORK OF PENNSYLVANIA

The garden front of the house of Robert T. McCracken, in Germantown, Philadelphia (No. 822), shows the charm of the stratified masonry of this Pennsylvania stone, and shows how it can furnish the keynote for the whole design. The terra cotta urns on the garden wall, and the painted door merely accentuate the charm of texture and color of the stonework itself, for every detail has been designed to harmonize with the dominant material.

NEWER DEVELOPMENT OF LOCAL STYLE

The local school of Pennsylvania stonework bears witness to the growing demand that a building must fit its environment so closely as to make the development of local styles necessary. Awbury, also in Germantown, Philadelphia (No. 823), shows how the characteristics of the local stone have fixed the character of the design and given distinction to the whole composition. Such a building seems to belong to its environment; it becomes as real a part of the landscape as the great trees that surround it.

822   Mellor, Meigs and Howe, architects

Edmund B. Gilchrist, architect

A MUSEUM OF PUEBLO INSPIRATION

In the Southwest other influences and other materials have developed a local style. The New Mexico Art Museum at Santa Fé, N. M., is a bold adaptation of forms developed from Indian pueblo sources by Spanish missionaries; and the beautiful way these forms harmonize with the land-

824   Rapp Brothers and Hendrickson, architects; photograph supplied by the Museum of
New Mexico, Santa Fé

scape and the climate shows the value of designing in the spirit and tradition of a special locality.

825   Mead and Requa, architects

FAITHFUL ADAPTATION OF PRIMITIVE TRADITION

The beach cottage of Wheeler J. Bailey at La Jolla, Cal., is another modern expression of the same tradition. Here in ladder and beams perhaps too consciously the crudity of primitive precedent has been reproduced. Such closeness to precedent, however questionably artificial, bears witness to the strength of local tradition; and sensitiveness toward site and tradition is at the very basis of all true local styles.

A NEW VARIATION OF SPANISH TYPES

Even more typical of the local style of southern California, founded on Spanish Renaissance and Spanish mission types, is the residence of W. T. Jefferson at Pasadena, Cal. Here tile roofs, rough stucco walls, and a rich *baroque* door are used in a way that is in no sense a copy of any past work, but fresh and dramatic and original, and yet in the most harmonious accord with the climate and the traditions of its site — in other words, in a neces-sarily local style.

826   Marston, Van Pelt and Maybury, architects; photograph by Hiller

A DESIGN BASED PRIMARILY ON FUNCTION

THE growing sense of form in modern American architecture, which is, for the future, its most important characteristic, is shown in so many modern buildings that choice of examples is difficult. The Edward Smith School at Syracuse,

827   James A. Randall, architect

N. Y., is an outstanding example because the interesting forms which constitute its greatest beauty are directly and inevitably and frankly developed from the conditions of the problem — a one-story school — whose functions are so surely expressed. Style plays a secondary rôle in such a design.

828   Louis C. Mullgardt, architect; photograph by Gabriel Moulin

CAREFUL DETAILS WHICH FORM AN EFFECTIVE WHOLE

THE beauty of the Court of The Ages (No. 828) at the Panama-Pacific Exposition in San Francisco expresses both the modern trend of style and the growing mastery of form. Here every form and least shape adds to the vivid and vital gayety the expression of which was the emotional purpose of the design. The beauty and the power and the freshness are the result of form composition; the style is effective not primarily because of its newness, but because each detail is perfectly fitted to the form and purpose of the whole.

A MODERN TYPE OF RESIDENTIAL HOTEL

THE Shelton in New York (No. 829) sums up in itself a remarkable number of those trends whose development will be the making of the American architecture of the future. There is style freedom in the detail of Néo-Byzantine character; there is interesting material treatment in the brick walls, and there is romance in roof gardens, and in grotesques. But above all else it is form sense, form composition which makes the soaring masses of this tower so vivid, so exciting, so prophetic. With such a sense of form as the dominating background, the city of the future will be vital, romantic, imaginative, beautiful.

829   Arthur Loomis Harmon, architect; photograph by Sigurd Fischer

BUILDING HEIGHT RESTRICTIONS EVOKE A FORM SENSE

THIS group of three drawings shows admirably how the height restrictions of New York lead inevitably to the development of a sense of form. The first (No. 830) is the maximum amount of building allowed by the law in a city block, developed from the law itself, with but slight regard for architectural tendencies. The second (No. 831) shows the same building after courts have been cut down through it to allow the lighting of its great areas. The third (No. 832) shows the same form with the sloping planes replaced by setbacks occurring at two-story intervals. Already, with such slight modifications from the maximum allowed by the law, the powerful form composition of the whole is beginning to be evident. Here the question of style is secondary; the effect is an effect entirely of form composition, that results inevitably from the restrictions of city building. It is interesting to note in these drawings that the frank treatment of legal and practical demands leads without effort to forms that have not only architectural quality, but even a strange beauty of their own. They thus alike reveal the task and the triumph of architecture: to create from, and with, practical necessities a beauty that is an inspiration.

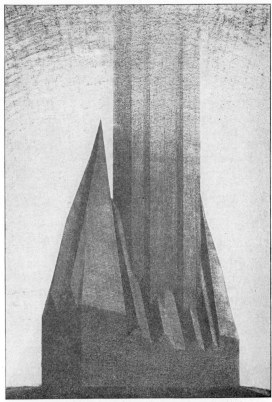

830 From a study by Hugh Ferriss; photograph by Wurts Brothers

831 From a study by Hugh Ferriss; photograph by Wurts Brothers

832 From a study by Hugh Ferriss; photograph by Wurts Brothers

6. Original engraving appears in the German edition of de Bry. View of Jamestown is the first that is known. For a discussion of the Jamestown view see Volume I, page 189.

9. Engraving is after an original drawing in the British Museum by John White, who went to Virginia first in 1585.

10. Sketch of Indian habitations is by Samuel de Champlain, who in 1604–07 explored, surveyed and charted the coast of New England. The site of Plymouth he named Port Louis.

11. House demolished in 1921. For a technical description with elevations and floor plans see *Old Houses of Connecticut*, New Haven, 1923, Bertha Chadwick Trowbridge, editor.

15. View is conjectural.

16. Walls were completed in 1615, the roof in 1623, the towers not until 1791.

28. The standing figure in the foreground is that of the late A. F. A. Bandelier (1840–1914), the archæologist.

40. For a technical description of this house with elevations and floor plans, see *Old Houses of Connecticut*, New Haven, 1923, Bertha Chadwick Trowbridge, editor.

55. The earliest view of the Province House appears on the Burgis view of Boston, 1723. Building was used by the state until 1796.

67. House stood until 1867. See Volume I, *Notes on the Pictures*, No. 536.

68. Artist, a Frenchman, visited the United States about 1825. Drawings of scenes faithful and reliable. See 222, 294, 425.

74. House received its name from the tradition that it was occupied and fortified by Nathaniel Bacon in the Virginia rebellion of 1676.

151. Drawing done by an English officer during the Revolution. It has internal evidence of having been done by the same hand that drew the picture of the field of Bunker Hill, reproduced in Volume VI.

160–161. Accurate view by English miniaturist who settled in Philadelphia in 1794; engraved a series of plates of views around Philadelphia and of country seats in the United States.

164. The Hall as photographed has been changed very considerably since 1776.

212. Bartlett was an Englishman who made four visits to America between 1836 and 1852. Illustrations appear in *American Scenery*, 1840, and in *Canadian Scenery*, 1842.

221. Connecticut legislature held its last session here in March, 1878; building then altered for municipal purposes; famous spiral staircase, the work of Asher Benjamin, was removed.

222. See 68.

224. Artist, an Englishman, was an amateur who painted landscapes and made copies.

225. Artist a good scene painter who came from London in 1792; the edifice was originally intended as a residence for President Washington, who never occupied it. It became the Governor's House and was subsequently used for a customhouse from 1799 to 1815, when it was taken down.

226. Wall, born in Dublin, came to New York in 1818; painted landscapes and pictures of Hudson River scenery in oil and color.

236–237. Howe sketched many views of places on the spot, traveled through New York, New Jersey, Virginia, Ohio and other states, making drawings that later appeared as wood engravings in his various *Historical Collections*.

238. Scenes in Meyer's *Universorum*, according to prospectus for this work, are by artists who "explored the most romantic regions of this country." Engravings signed "Drawn after nature."

239. Drawing by English naval officer who traveled through Atlantic coast states and Ohio and Mississippi valleys, in 1827 and 1828.

252. See 160, 161.

253–255. Engravings originally appeared in *The History and Topography of the United States*, London, 1830–32, edited by John Howard Hinton, A.M. See also 268, 270, 282, 300, 302, 314, 315.

291–292. See 236.

294. See 68.

303. Artist a well-known painter of historical subjects, associate of the National Academy, 1847.

304. See 238.

321. Work is similar to Meyer's *Universorum* (see 238) and published under the same imprint.

322. See 236.

337. Artist painted life in the Mississippi valley, engravings after his originals having a popular vogue.

339. Location of the scene of the sketch is Wolf's Point at the fork of the Chicago River. George Davis was a schoolmaster in 1834, and city clerk in 1837.

345–347–348. See 238.

346. Artist descended the Mississippi River, making sketches *en route* which were afterwards published as lithographs, printed at Düsseldorf.

INDEX

Titles of books under author are in italics; titles of illustrations under architect or other producer are in quotation marks.